The Complete Guide to
GREENHOUSES & GARDEN PROJECTS

• Greenhouses • Cold Frames • Compost Bins • Trellises
• Planting Beds • Potting Benches & More

Creative Publishing
international

MINNEAPOLIS, MINNESOTA
www.creativepub.com

Creative Publishing international

Copyright © 2011
Creative Publishing international, Inc.
400 First Avenue North, Suite 300
Minneapolis, Minnesota 55401
1-800-328-0590
www.creativepub.com

Printed in China

10 9 8 7 6 5 4 3 2 1

Library of Congress Cataloging-in-Publication Data

The Complete Guide To Greenhouses and Garden Projects :
Greenhouses, Cold Frames, Compost Bins, Garden Carts, Planter
Beds, Potting Benches and More.
    pages cm. -- (The Complete Guide)
  At head of title: Black & Decker.
  Includes index.
  Summary: "Includes plans and step-by-step instructions for
building several greenhouses and other garden projects. Projects
suitable to homes and landscapes in urban, suburban and rural
settings"--Provided by publisher.
  ISBN-13: 978-1-58923-599-1 (soft cover)
  ISBN-10: 1-58923-599-1 (soft cover)
  1. Greenhouses--Design and construction--Amateurs' manuals. 2.
Garden structures--Design and construction--Amateurs' manuals. I.
Black & Decker Corporation (Towson, Md.) II. Title. III. Series.

SB416.C64 2011
690'.8924--dc22

2010042930

The Complete Guide to Greenhouses & Garden Projects
Created by: The Editors of Creative Publishing international, Inc., in cooperation with Black & Decker.
Black & Decker® is a trademark of The Black & Decker Corporation and is used under license.

President/CEO: Ken Fund

Home Improvement Group

Publisher: Bryan Trandem
Managing Editor: Tracy Stanley
Senior Editor: Mark Johanson

Creative Director: Michele Lanci-Altomare
Art Direction/Design: Brad Springer, Jon Simpson, James Kegley

Lead Photographer: Joel Schnell
Set Builder: James Parmeter
Production Managers: Laura Hokkanen, Linda Halls

Page Layout Artist: Danielle Smith
Tech Editor: Chris Marshall
Photographer: Richard Fleischman
Shop Help: Charles Boldt
Proofreader: Ingrid Sundstrom Lundegaard

Author: Philip Schmidt
Contributing Writers: Pat Price, Nora Richter Greer
Illustrations: Robert Leana II, Michael Prendergast

NOTICE TO READERS

For safety, use caution, care, and good judgment when following the procedures described in this book. The publisher and Black & Decker cannot assume responsibility for any damage to property or injury to persons as a result of misuse of the information provided.

The techniques shown in this book are general techniques for various applications. In some instances, additional techniques not shown in this book may be required. Always follow manufacturers' instructions included with products, since deviating from the directions may void warranties. The projects in this book vary widely as to skill levels required: some may not be appropriate for all do-it-yourselfers, and some may require professional help.

Consult your local building department for information on building permits, codes, and other laws as they apply to your project.

Contents

The Complete Guide to Greenhouses & Garden Projects

Contents (Cont.)

Introduction

You hold this book in your hands because you're someone who likes to work and play in the dirt. Or at least you like the thought of it, and you're looking for inspiration to help you get out there. In either case, you've come to the right place. Like a garden itself, this book is filled with diverse bounty. It is a compendium of information, advice, projects, and nitty-gritty details to help you satisfy your passion to grow things.

If you're already an avid gardener and are thinking about taking your hobby to the next level, the Greenhouses chapter is the place to start. Surely you've dreamt of bending the rules of nature just a bit, starting spring a little earlier, extending summer into October, or maybe creating a tropical paradise in the dead of winter. Even the simplest of greenhouse structures can expand the possibilities of what and when you can grow, and they make it much more fun and comfortable to garden in (what used to be called) the off season.

Today's greenhouses are widely available in a variety of styles and sizes to fit just about any budget. And you always have the option of building your own custom house or assembling one from a kit. Projects for building the most popular types of hobby greenhouses are included here, along with answers to the essential greenhouse questions, like what type of structure is right for your needs, where and how to build it, what materials to use, and how to maintain it.

While many attractive greenhouses are available for sale in kit form, most would only blend in with your home style if you happen to live in a drive-thru restaurant. If you'd like to have the advantages of a fully functioning greenhouse but you want to maintain the architectural style of your house, then you'll want to follow along the custom Victorian greenhouse project. There, you'll find a complete, start-to-finish demonstration of a custom lean-to greenhouse with Victorian styling to match the Queen Anne house to which it is attached. Even the door and the windows are made from scratch using ordinary building materials.

And no matter what type of gardening you do, the Garden Projects chapter is bound to have something you can really use: planting beds, a compost bin, trellises, potting benches...you name it. Best of all, every design uses simple, inexpensive raw materials that you work with your hands into something that's much more than the sum of its parts. Sounds a lot like gardening, doesn't it?

Greenhouses

Enter a greenhouse and you've crossed the threshold of an extraordinary place. You're greeted by a profusion of flowers and the rich textures of foliage. Sweet fragrances mix with the earthy smell of soil. Diffused light shines through the misty air. In the silence, you can almost hear the plants growing. Traffic rumbles by unnoticed, and the distractions of the "real" world seem miles away.

Once the province of the wealthy, greenhouse gardening is now practiced by almost two million American homeowners, according to the American Horticultural Society. You'll find greenhouses on city rooftops and tucked into suburban gardens. No two are identical, even if they're constructed from the same kit; the contents of a greenhouse make it unique. Some house vegetables (tomatoes and cucumbers), some shelter tropicals (schffleras and dieffenbachias), and some are home to flats of germinating begonias. A select few protect rare orchids and plants imported from exotic tropical locales. But they all serve a common purpose: a place where gardeners can lose themselves among green and growing things.

In this chapter:

- Choosing a Greenhouse
- Where to Site Your Greenhouse
- Greenhouse Styles
- Greenhouse Elements
- Custom Victorian Greenhouse
- DIY Gabled Greenhouse
- Freestanding Kit Greenhouse
- PVC Hoophouse
- Shed-style Greenhouse

Choosing a Greenhouse

Greenhouses can take many forms, from simple, three-season A-frame structures to elaborate buildings the size of a small backyard. They can be custom designed or built from a kit, freestanding or attached, framed in metal or wood, glazed with plastic or glass. Spend a little time researching online greenhouse suppliers and you'll discover almost unlimited options. Although it's important to choose a design that appeals to you and complements your house and yard, you'll need to consider many other factors when making a decision. Answering the following questions will help you determine the type, style, and size of greenhouse that suits your needs.

How Will the Greenhouse be Used?

What do you plan to grow in your greenhouse? Are you mostly interested in extending the growing season—seeding flats of bedding plants early in the spring and protecting them from frost in the fall? Or do you want to grow flowers and tropical plants year-round?

Your intentions will determine whether you need a heated greenhouse. Unheated greenhouses, which depend solely on solar heat, are used primarily to advance or extend the growing season of hardy and half-hardy plants and vegetables. Although an unheated greenhouse offers some frost protection, it is useful only during spring, summer, and fall, unless you live in a warm climate.

A heated greenhouse is far more versatile and allows you to grow a greater variety of plants. By installing equipment for heating, ventilation, shading, and watering, you can provide the perfect environment for tender plants that would never survive freezing weather.

How you plan to use the greenhouse will also determine its size, type, and location. If you only want to harden off seedlings or extend the growing season for lettuce plants and geraniums, a small, unheated structure covered with polyvinyl chloride (PVC) sheeting or even a cold frame—a glass- or plastic-topped box on the ground—might be all you need. If your intentions are more serious, consider a larger, more permanent building. A three-season greenhouse can be placed anywhere on your property and might even be dismantled in the winter, whereas year-round use calls for a location near the house, where utilities are convenient and you don't have to trek a long way in inclement weather.

The Cost Question ▶

The cost of a basic freestanding greenhouse can range from the very economical (plastic sheeting and PVC hoop frame) to the surprisingly expensive (custom-designed and built). It all depends on your tastes and aspirations, and on your budget. The following real-life samples will give you a sense of the cost variations (remember, though, that prices can vary widely, depending on features and accessories you choose to include):

- A 5-ft. × 5-ft. pop-up mini greenhouse from one mail order source sold for $165.
- A small, 6-ft. × 8-ft. greenhouse with rigid polycarbonate panels sold for $795.
- A more spacious 8-ft. × 17-ft. rigid panel kit with motorized windows sold for $4,970.
- The most elaborate polycarbonate kit greenhouses we found, available by mail order, sold for $7,900 for an 11-ft. × 24-ft. structure.
- For a custom-designed and built greenhouse of the same size (11-ft. × 24-ft.), one homeowner recently spent $23,000—a price that could have been much higher for a greenhouse designed with ornamental metalwork or stone foundations.
- A 20-ft. × 30-ft. hoop kit using plastic sheeting and PVC tubing was recently available for $1,600.
- A full-featured lean-to greenhouse kit, 10-ft. × 10-ft. in size, sold for $5,724.

The ideal greenhouse has flexibility, combining some built-in features (like the shelves in this greenhouse) with ample open spaces so you can adjust the way the structure is used as your needs and interests change.

Attached to the exterior wall of the house, this lean-to style greenhouse has all the features for complete growing success: running water (A); electrical service (B); a heated plant-propagation table (C); a heater (D) for maintaining temperatures on cold nights; ventilating windows (E) and sunshades (F) for reducing temperatures on hot days; drip irrigation system (G) for maintaining potted plants; a full-length potting bench (H) with storage space beneath; paved flooring (I) to retain solar heat.

Do I Want a Lean-to or a Freestanding Greenhouse?

Greenhouse styles are divided into two main groups: attached lean-tos and freestanding. Lean-tos are attached to the house, the garage or an outbuilding, usually on a south-facing wall. An attached greenhouse has the advantage of gaining heat from the house. It's also conveniently close to plumbing, heating, and electrical services, which are required to operate a heated greenhouse.

On the downside, lean-tos can be restricted by the home's design: They should be built from materials that complement the existing structure, and a low-slung roofline or limited exterior wall space can make them difficult to gracefully incorporate. Siting can be tricky if the only available wall faces an undesirable direction. In cold climates, they must be protected from heavy snow sliding from the house roof. Lean-tos are typically smaller than freestanding greenhouses and can be subject to overheating if they aren't vented properly.

A freestanding greenhouse can be sited anywhere on the property and is not restricted by the home's design. It can be as large or as small as the yard permits. Because all four sides are glazed, it receives maximum exposure to sunlight. However, a freestanding structure is more expensive to build and heat, and depending on its size, it may require a concrete foundation. Utilities must be brought in, and it is not as convenient to access as a lean-to. Because it is more exposed to the elements, it can require sturdier framing and glazing to withstand winds.

Heated Greenhouse Environments ▸

Heated greenhouses can be classified by three temperature categories: cool, warm, and hot. Each of these environments supports different plants and gardening activities.

COOL MINIMUM NIGHTTIME TEMPERATURE: 45°F (7°C)

In a cool environment, you can start seeds and propagate cuttings early in the year so they will be ready for planting in garden beds at the beginning of summer. Unless your climate is mild, however, you'll probably need a propagator to provide a little extra warmth for starting seeds. Vegetables and hardy and half-hardy plants do well in this type of greenhouse. Although the temperature in a cool greenhouse is suitable for protecting frost-tender plants, their growth during winter is minimal.

WARM MINIMUM NIGHTTIME TEMPERATURE: 55°F (13°C)

A warm greenhouse is suitable for propagating plants, raising seedlings, and growing a wide range of plants, including flowers, fruits, houseplants, and vegetables, even during the coldest months. You can sow tomato seeds in January and harvest the ripe fruits in June. Though this type of greenhouse provides a highly desirable environment for plants, heating it can be extremely costly, especially if you live in an area with long, cold winters.

HOT MINIMUM NIGHTTIME TEMPERATURE: 65°F (18°C)

Only a few serious gardeners will invest in a hot greenhouse because it is prohibitively expensive to heat. This type of environment is ideal for growing exotic tropical plants, such as orchids, bromeliads, and ferns.

How Big Should the Greenhouse Be?

Some experts recommend buying the largest greenhouse you can afford, but this isn't always the best advice. You don't want to invest in a large greenhouse only to discover that you're not up to the work it involves.

Of course, buying a greenhouse that is too small can lead to frustration if your plant collection outgrows the space. It is also much more difficult to control the temperature. One compromise is to buy a greenhouse that's one size larger than you originally planned, or better yet, to invest in an expandable structure. Many models are available as modules that allow additions as your enthusiasm grows.

When choosing a greenhouse, take into account the size of your property. How much space will the structure consume? Most of the expense comes from operating the greenhouse, especially during winter. The larger the structure, the more expensive it is to heat.

Be sure the greenhouse has enough room for you to work. Allow space for benches, shelves, tools, pots, watering cans, soil, hoses, sinks, and a pathway through the plants. If you want benches on both sides, choose a greenhouse that is at least 8 ft. wide by 10 ft. long. Give yourself enough headroom, and allow extra height if you are growing tall plants or plan to hang baskets.

How Much Can I Afford to Spend on a Greenhouse?

Your budget will influence the type of structure you choose. A simple hoop greenhouse with a plastic cover is inexpensive and easy to build. If you're handy with tools, you can save money by buying a kit, but if the greenhouse is large, requires a concrete foundation, or is built from scratch, you may need to hire a contractor, which will add to the cost.

Location is important: If you live in a windy area, you'll need a sturdy structure. Buying a cheaply made greenhouse will not save you money if it fails to protect your plants or blows away in a storm. And cutting costs by using inefficient glazing will backfire because you'll wind up paying more for heating.

How Much Time am I Prepared to Invest in a Greenhouse?

You may have big dreams, but do you have the commitment to match? Maintaining a successful greenhouse requires work. It's not hard labor, but your plants depend on you for survival. Although technology offers many timesavers, such as automated watering and ventilation systems, there's no point in owning a greenhouse if you don't have time to spend there. Carefully assess your time and energy before you build.

Unique Appeal ▶

Some greenhouses and sheds are valued because they are clean and efficient. Some pay back purely in seedlings and produce. But others have a more intangible quality, perhaps even a treasured lineage that we cherish.

Today, almost nothing remains of Century Farm, located on a dirt road in the bluff country of Hay Creek Township of southeastern Minnesota, near the Wisconsin border. Century Farm was a small family dairy farm that vanished like so many when larger farm co-ops began to absorb little Midwestern family businesses in the 1970s and 1980s. When the farm was built in 1890, the lumber used to build the corn cribs and chicken coops, the dairy barn and pig shed was hauled by sled from Wisconsin forests across the frozen surface of the Mississippi River. The logs were milled by a saw mill put together on site; and a hundred years later, you could still see the rough marks of the huge circular saw blades that cut the planks.

Century Farm has now vanished, but the limestone foundation stones and weathered wooden planks that were part of the original farm buildings continue to live on as the walls of a dozen different garden sheds in suburban backyards across Goodhue County. For when the barns came down on Century Farm, the family reclaimed the lumber and offered it to friends for use in fences and garden structures, as a kind of living memento of a gentler time.

A compact greenhouse is just the right scale for this small, enclosed backyard.

Where to Site Your Greenhouse

When the first orangeries were built, heat was thought to be the most important element for successfully growing plants indoors. Most orangeries had solid roofs and walls with large windows. Once designers realized that light was more important than heat for plant growth, they began to build greenhouses from glass.

All plants need at least six (and preferably 12) hours of light a day year-round, so when choosing a site for a greenhouse, you need to consider a number of variables. Be sure that it is clear of shadows cast by trees, hedges, fences, your house, and other buildings. Don't forget that the shade cast by obstacles changes throughout the year. Take note of the sun's position at various times of the year: A site that receives full sun in the spring and summer can be shaded by nearby trees when the sun is low in winter. Winter shadows

are longer than those cast by the high summer sun, and during winter, sunlight is particularly important for keeping the greenhouse warm. If you are not familiar with the year-round sunlight patterns on your property, you may have to do a little geometry to figure out where shadows will fall. Your latitude will also have a bearing on the amount of sunlight available; greenhouses at northern latitudes receive fewer hours of winter sunlight than those located farther south. You may have to supplement natural light with interior lighting.

To gain the most sun exposure, the greenhouse should be oriented so that its ridge runs east to west (see illustration, below), with the long sides facing north and south. A slightly southwest or southeast exposure is also acceptable, but avoid a northern exposure if you're planning an attached greenhouse; only shade-lovers will grow there.

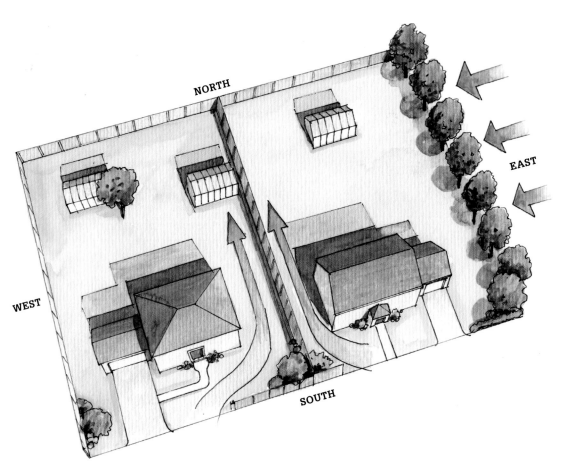

The ideal greenhouse location is well away from trees but protected from prevailing winds, usually by another structure, a fence, or a wall.

Siting Factors

Several factors influence the decision of where to build your greenhouse. Some pertain to your property, some to the structure, and some to your tastes.

CLIMATE, SHELTER, & SOIL STABILITY

Your local climate and geography have an impact on the location of your greenhouse. Choose a site that is sheltered from high winds and far enough away from trees that roots and falling branches are not a threat. (Try to position the greenhouse away from areas in which children play, too.) If you live in a windy area, consider planting a hedge or building a fence to provide a windbreak, but be careful that it doesn't cast shade on the greenhouse. Avoid low-lying areas, which are prone to trapping cold, humid air.

The site should be level and the soil stable, with good drainage. This is especially important if heavy rains are common in your climate. You might need to hire a contractor to grade your site.

ACCESS

Try to locate your greenhouse as close to the house as possible. Connecting to utilities will be easier, and you'll be glad when you're carrying bags of soil and supplies from the car. Furthermore, a shorter walk will make checking on plants less of a chore when the weather turns ugly.

AESTHETICS

Although you want to ensure that plants have the perfect growing environment, don't ignore aesthetics: The greenhouse should look good in your yard. Ask yourself whether you want it to be a focal point—to draw the eye and make a statement—or to blend in with the garden. Either way, try to suit the design and the materials to your home. Keep space in mind, too, if you think you might eventually expand the greenhouse.

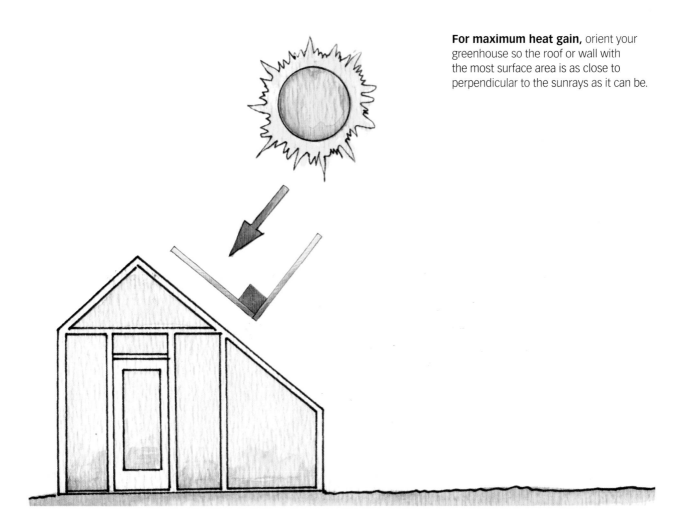

For maximum heat gain, orient your greenhouse so the roof or wall with the most surface area is as close to perpendicular to the sunrays as it can be.

Greenhouse Styles

When choosing a greenhouse, consider the benefits and disadvantages of each style. Some offer better use of space, some better light transmission; others offer better heat retention, and some are more stable in strong winds. Keep in mind how you plan to use the greenhouse—its size and shape will have an impact on the interior environment.

TRADITIONAL SPAN

A Ventilating roof windows
B High gable peak provides headroom
C 45-degree roof angle encourages runoff
D Solid kneewalls block wind, provide impact protection and allow insulation

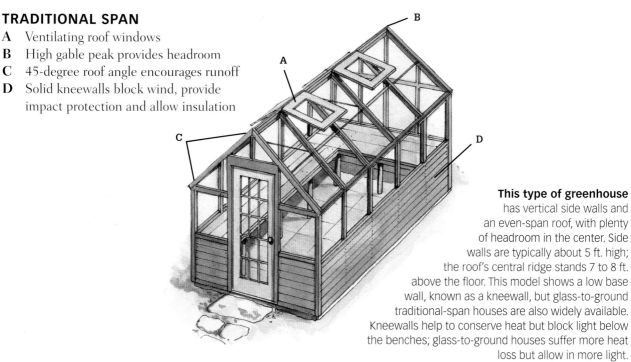

This type of greenhouse has vertical side walls and an even-span roof, with plenty of headroom in the center. Side walls are typically about 5 ft. high; the roof's central ridge stands 7 to 8 ft. above the floor. This model shows a low base wall, known as a kneewall, but glass-to-ground traditional-span houses are also widely available. Kneewalls help to conserve heat but block light below the benches; glass-to-ground houses suffer more heat loss but allow in more light.

LEAN-TO

A Adjoining house provides structure and heat
B Aluminum frame is lightweight but sturdy
C Roof vents can be set to open and close automatically
D Well sealed door prevents drafts and heat loss

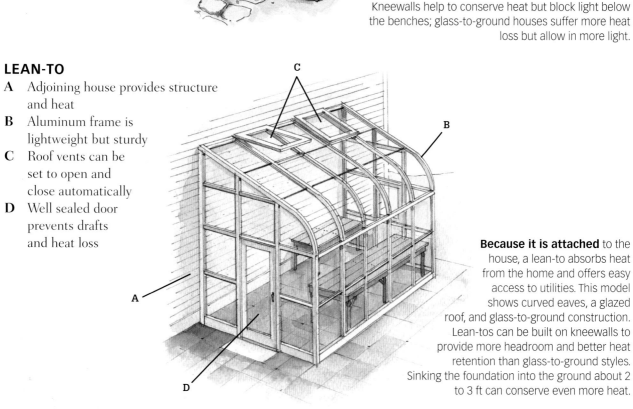

Because it is attached to the house, a lean-to absorbs heat from the home and offers easy access to utilities. This model shows curved eaves, a glazed roof, and glass-to-ground construction. Lean-tos can be built on kneewalls to provide more headroom and better heat retention than glass-to-ground styles. Sinking the foundation into the ground about 2 to 3 ft can conserve even more heat.

THREE-QUARTER SPAN

A Adjoining house provides shelter
B Half-lite door insulates but allows some light in
C Operating side vent
D Gable creates headroom

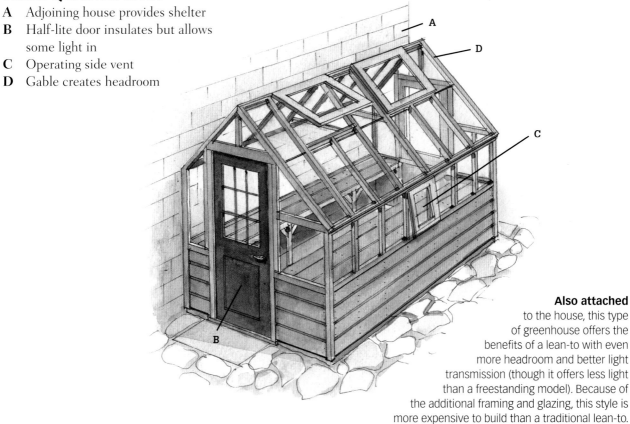

Also attached
to the house, this type of greenhouse offers the benefits of a lean-to with even more headroom and better light transmission (though it offers less light than a freestanding model). Because of the additional framing and glazing, this style is more expensive to build than a traditional lean-to.

DUTCH LIGHT

A Tapered sidewalls encourage condensation to run off
B Lower side vent encourages airflow
C Tile floor retains heat
D Roof angle minimizes light reflection

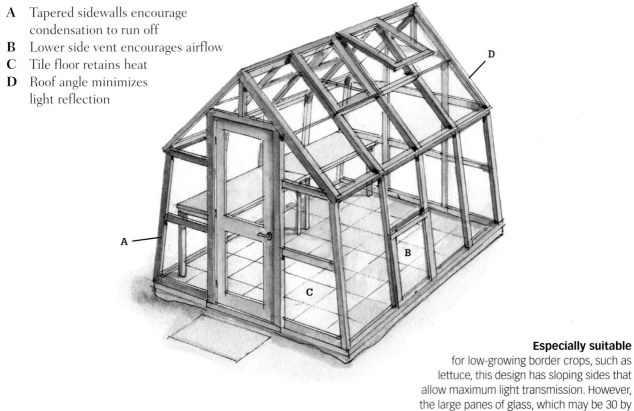

Especially suitable
for low-growing border crops, such as lettuce, this design has sloping sides that allow maximum light transmission. However, the large panes of glass, which may be 30 by 59 in., are expensive to replace.

MANSARD

A   Full-width door frame
B   Sliding doors can be adjusted
     for ventilation
C   Lower side vents encourage airflow
D   Stepped angles ensure direct light
     penetration any time
     of day or year

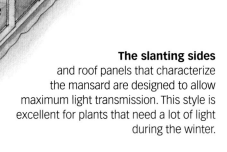

The slanting sides
and roof panels that characterize
the mansard are designed to allow
maximum light transmission. This style is
excellent for plants that need a lot of light
during the winter.

MINI-GREENHOUSE

A   Brick wall retains heat
B   Upper shelf does not block airflow
C   Full-depth lower shelf creates
     hot spot below
D   Full-lite storm door

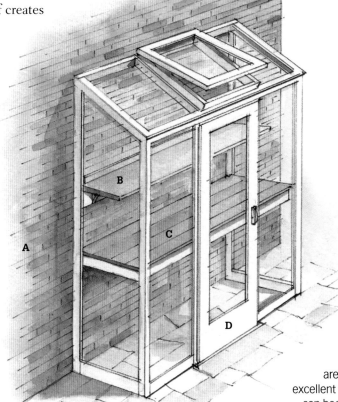

A relatively
inexpensive option
that requires little
space, this greenhouse
is typically made of
aluminum framing and
can be placed against a
house, a garage or even
a fence, preferably facing
southeast or southwest,
to receive maximum light
exposure. Space and access
are limited, however; and without
excellent ventilation, a mini-greenhouse
can become dangerously overheated.
Because the temperature inside is difficult to
control, it is not recommended for winter use.

DOME

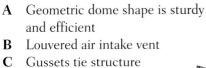

A Geometric dome shape is sturdy and efficient
B Louvered air intake vent
C Gussets tie structure together
D Articulated door is visually interesting (but tricky to make)

This style is stable and more wind-resistant than traditional greenhouses, and its multi-angled glass panes provide excellent light transmission. Because of its low profile and stability, it works well in exposed locations. However, it is expensive to build and has limited headroom, and plants placed near the edges may be difficult to reach.

POLYGONAL

A Triangular roof windows meet in hub
B Finial has Victorian appeal
C Built-in benches good for planters or for seating
D Lower wall panels have board-and-batten styling

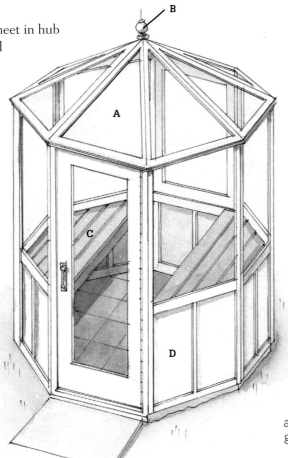

Though it provides an interesting focal point, this type of greenhouse is decorative rather than practical. Polygonal and octagonal greenhouses are typically expensive to build, and space inside is limited.

ALPINE HOUSE

A Banks of venting windows at both sides of peak

B Adjustable louvers for air intake

C Cedar siding on kneewall has rustic appeal

D Fixed roof windows lend stability

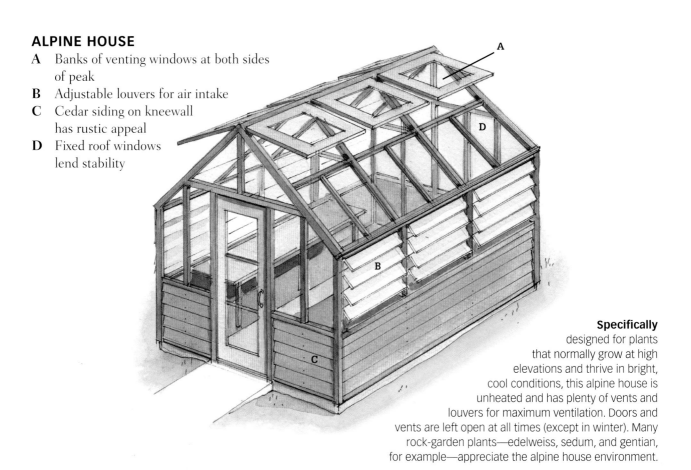

Specifically designed for plants that normally grow at high elevations and thrive in bright, cool conditions, this alpine house is unheated and has plenty of vents and louvers for maximum ventilation. Doors and vents are left open at all times (except in winter). Many rock-garden plants—edelweiss, sedum, and gentian, for example—appreciate the alpine house environment.

HOOPHOUSE

A Bendable PVC tubes provide structure

B 4-mil plastic sheeting is very inexpensive glazing option

C Roll-up door

D Lightweight base makes hoophouse easy to move

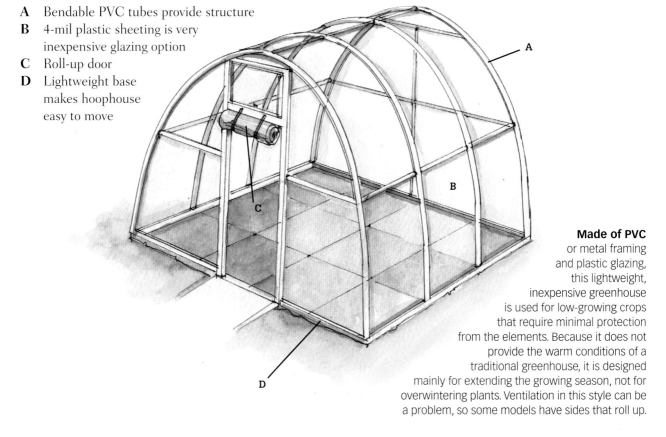

Made of PVC or metal framing and plastic glazing, this lightweight, inexpensive greenhouse is used for low-growing crops that require minimal protection from the elements. Because it does not provide the warm conditions of a traditional greenhouse, it is designed mainly for extending the growing season, not for overwintering plants. Ventilation in this style can be a problem, so some models have sides that roll up.

CONSERVATION GREENHOUSE

A High peak for good headroom
B Louvered wall vents
C Sturdy aluminum framing
D Broad roof surface for maximum heat collection

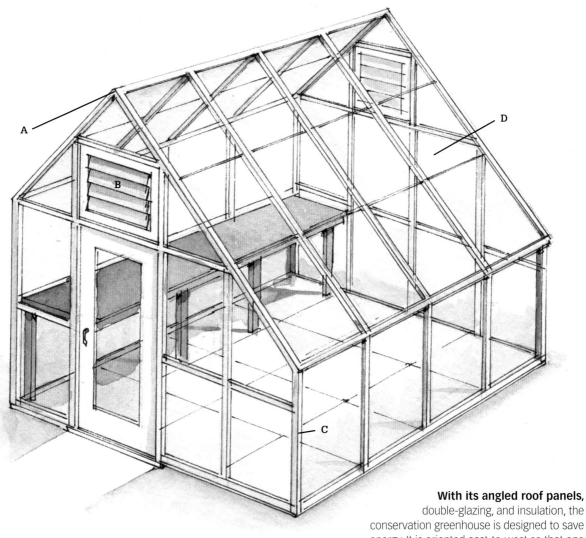

With its angled roof panels, double-glazing, and insulation, the conservation greenhouse is designed to save energy. It is oriented east-to-west so that one long wall faces south, and the angled roof panels capture maximum light (and therefore heat) during the winter. To gain maximum heat absorption for the growing space, the house should be twice as long as it is wide. Placing the greenhouse against a dark-colored back wall helps to conserve heat—the wall will radiate heat back into the greenhouse at night.

Free Greenhouse Design Software ▸

The United States Department of Agriculture (USDA) has developed a computer software program called Virtual Grower that you can use to create your own custom greenhouse design. It helps you make decisions about roof and sidewall materials, operating temperatures, and other variables. It even has a calculator for estimating heating costs. The software can be downloaded free of charge: www.ars.usda.gov/services/software/download.htm?softwareid=108.

Easy-to-Build Greenhouses

Some greenhouse designs are so simple that construction requires only a weekend or two. The foundation can be an anchored wooden frame or, for a more permanent structure, a concrete base.

HOOPHOUSE

Economical and versatile, a hoop-style greenhouse (also called a hoophouse or a quonset house) is constructed of PVC or metal pipes that are bent into an inverted U shape, attached to a base and connected at the top by a ridgepole. A hoophouse is usually covered with plastic sheeting. A door can be set at one end, and there may be an exhaust fan or flap vent that can be rolled up for ventilation. Because the hoop greenhouse is lightweight, it is not a good choice in areas with strong winds. (For instructions on building a hoophouse, see pages 86 to 91.)

A-FRAME GREENHOUSE

An A-frame greenhouse is small and lightweight and can be made of wood or PVC. A series of A-frames is attached to a wood base and covered with plastic sheeting or rigid plastic panels, such as polycarbonate or fiberglass. Because of the steep pitch of the roof, this type of greenhouse easily sheds rain, snow, and leaves and provides more headroom than a hoop greenhouse. It can also be portable. (For instructions on building an A-frame greenhouse, see pages 72 to 77.)

A hoophouse is a simple greenhouse made by wrapping clear plastic over a series of U-shape frames. See page 86.

An A-frame greenhouse is easy to design and build yourself with just some wood and sheet plastic. See page 72.

Greenhouse Kits

No matter what kind of greenhouse you have in mind, chances are you can find a kit to match your vision. Dozens of companies offer kits in diverse styles, sizes, materials, and prices. Some offer door options—sliding versus swinging doors, for example, with and without locks and screens. Some offer glazing combinations, such as polycarbonate roof panels with glass walls. And some even offer extension kits for certain models, so you can add onto your greenhouse as your space requirements grow.

Kit basics usually include framing, glazing panels, vents (though usually not enough—it's a good idea to buy extras), and hardware. A good kit will come predrilled and precut, so you only need a few tools to assemble it. Kits do not include the foundation, benches, or accessories.

Be sure the kit you choose comes with clear, comprehensive instructions and a customer-service number for assistance. Also ensure that it complies with your local building codes and planning regulations. Depending on the company, shipping may be included in the price. Because kits are heavy, shipping can be expensive; be sure to figure it and the cost of the foundation, benches, all necessary accessories, and the installation of utilities into your budget. (For more information about constructing a greenhouse kit, see pages 78 to 85.)

This kit greenhouse has an aluminum frame and polycarbonate panels. It features sliding doors and a roof vent. With nearly 200 square feet of floor space, it was a good bargain at around $800. See page 78.

Cold Frames

An inexpensive foray into greenhouse gardening, a cold frame is practical for starting early plants and hardening off seedlings. It is basically a box set on the ground and topped with glass or plastic. Although mechanized models with thermostatically controlled atmospheres and sashes that automatically open and close are available, you can easily build a basic cold frame—or several, in a range of sizes (see Projects, page 112). Just be sure to make the back side of the frame about twice the height of the front so that the glazing can be slanted on top. Also ensure that the frame is tall enough to accommodate the ultimate height of the plants growing inside. The frame can be made of brick, plastic, or wood, and it should be built to keep drafts out and the soil in. Most important, the soil inside must be fertile, well tilled, and free of weeds.

If the frame is permanently sited, position it to receive maximum light during winter and spring and to offer protection from wind. An ideal spot is against the wall of a greenhouse or another structure. Ventilation is important; more plants in a cold frame die from heat and drought than from cold. A bright March day can heat a cold frame to 100° F (38° C), so be sure to monitor the temperature inside, and prop up or remove the cover when necessary. On cold nights, especially when frost is predicted, cover the box with burlap, old quilts, or fallen leaves for insulation.

Hotbeds ▸

Similar in construction to cold frames (but not as common), hotbeds have been around since Roman times. Emperor Tiberius directed his gardeners to grow cucumbers in dung-filled carts that were wheeled outside during the day and brought into a rudimentary "greenhouse" at night so that he had a supply of the vegetables year-round. This type of garden incorporates horse or chicken manure, which releases heat as it decomposes. The manure is set within the bed frame below ground level and is then topped with a layer of soil. (If you prefer, you can forgo the manure and lay heating cables between soil layers.) To prevent overheating, ventilate a hotbed as you would a cold frame.

Geraniums peek out from this well-used cold frame. The plants gain precious warmth from the brick wall, which absorbs solar heat during the day and releases it during the night.

Sunrooms

A greenhouse can certainly satisfy the desire to grow a profusion of plants year-round, but it's not everyone's cup of tea. Even the most avid gardener will agree that operating and maintaining a greenhouse requires a major commitment—in a greenhouse, the plants depend solely on you for their well-being. The sunroom, on the other hand, allows you to surround yourself with flowers and plants in a sunny, light-filled room that is designed primarily for your comfort.

Like the greenhouse, the sunroom's roots are found in the orangeries and conservatories built on the grand estates of Europe. In the 19th-century conservatory, fashionable women gathered under the glass in exotic, palm-filled surroundings for tea. The 21st-century garden room invites us to do the same, in a comfortable interior environment from which we can appreciate the outdoors year-round. Large windows and doors open onto the terrace or garden. A high roof, which might be all glass, lets in abundant natural light. Decorative architectural features announce that this place is different from the rest of the house—separate, but in harmony. Like the conservatories of old, sunrooms can be used for growing plants and flowers indoors, but they are just as often used as sitting rooms, from which to admire the plantings outside the windows.

The sunroom can be a grand conservatory—an ornamented, plant-filled glass palace attached to an equally grand home. Or it can be a modest room containing little more than a few potted plants and a comfortable reading chair. Grand or modest, the sunroom is neither wholly of the house nor of the garden; it is a link between the two, a place in which you can feel a part of the garden but with all of the comforts of home.

Like greenhouses, sunrooms can be as simple or as elaborate as your budget and style will allow. This sunroom blends beautifully with the house.

Greenhouse Elements

Once you've chosen the perfect greenhouse for your property and needs, there are still many decisions to be made before you're ready to begin construction. Does it need a foundation? What type of frame and walls are best? How will you heat it or cool it? And what do you put in it? The systems you will need to operate a successful greenhouse vary with the type of greenhouse you've chosen.

Of course, once you've sorted out what you need, you will actually have to build your greenhouse. If you know your way around a tool box, and the greenhouse is relatively simple in design, you might want to consider building it yourself. But, unless you're a qualified electrician or plumber, you will probably have to hire professional help for some aspects of the construction.

Don't forget to call your municipal planning department to find out what regulations might apply in your area and whether you'll need a building permit for your greenhouse. Planning regulations and building codes regulate electrical and plumbing installation, construction (the size and strength of the frame or materials), footings and foundations, setbacks, and allowed square footage. The height of your greenhouse, in relation to existing structures, might also fall under code requirement, as can fire resistance.

A greenhouse is composed of several major systems that perform important functions. When planning your greenhouse, you'll need to make choices about each system, which include the foundation, floor, frame, glazing, ventilation, watering, heat, storage, and more.

Foundations

As with a house or any outbuilding, a greenhouse needs a proper foundation to support the walls and the overall weight of the structure. Without it, movement in the underlying soil—due to settling, erosion, or frost heave—can damage the greenhouse framing, affecting door and window operation and possibly cracking the glazing. A foundation also keeps the bottom of the greenhouse framing members off of the ground, to prevent premature rot or corrosion.

If you're building a greenhouse from a kit, the manufacturer can recommend appropriate foundation options. And for any greenhouse project, consult your city's building department: foundations for greenhouses and other outbuildings may fall under the local building code, and you might need a permit for the project.

Most greenhouse foundations are one of four basic types: earth anchors, landscape timbers, concrete footings or piers, and concrete slabs. Many kit greenhouses can be installed over a compacted gravel base or atop a prefab metal foundation base (often offered as an optional accessory). Traditional greenhouses often were built atop short kneewalls made of brick or mortared stone. This is still an option today, but the added work and expense makes it uncommon among hobby greenhouses.

Kneewalls ▸

Kneewalls are low walls to which a greenhouse frame can be attached. They can raise a greenhouse to maximize headroom and can help to retain heat. However, they also eliminate growing space behind the walls and below the benches. If you only plan to grow potted plants on the benches, this may not be a problem—you can use the area underneath the benches for storage.

Kneewalls can be built with concrete blocks on a concrete footing, but a more attractive option is to use stone or brick and mortar. To help integrate the greenhouse with your home, build the kneewall from materials that complement the exterior of the house.

Earth anchors, or anchor stakes, are often used to tie down very lightweight greenhouses and crop covers to prevent them from blowing away. A typical anchor is a long metal rod with a screw-like auger end that is driven into the ground. An eye at the top end is used for securing a cable or other type of tether attached to the greenhouse.

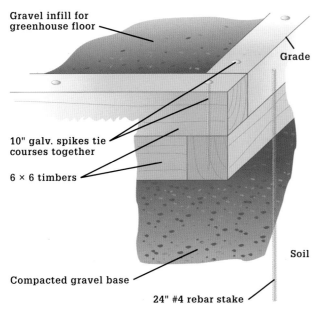

Gravel infill for greenhouse floor

Grade

10" galv. spikes tie courses together

6 × 6 timbers

Soil

Compacted gravel base

24" #4 rebar stake

Timber foundations are simple frames made with 4 × 4, 6 × 6 or larger landscape timbers. The timber frame is laid over a leveled and compacted gravel base (which can also double as the floor or floor subbase for the greenhouse interior) and pinned to the ground with rebar stakes. One level, or course, of timbers is suitable for very small houses, while two courses is recommended for larger structures.

A concrete footing can provide a structural base for a kit foundation or a masonry kneewall. Standard footings are continuous and run along the perimeter of the structure. They must extend below the frost line (the depth to which the ground can freeze in winter; varies by climate) to prevent frost heave and should be at least twice as wide as the foundation walls they support. Any foundation wall built atop the footing should extend at least 6" above grade level.

Pier footings are structural concrete columns poured in tube forms set below the frost line—the same foundation used to support deck posts. Pier foundations are appropriate for some kit and custom greenhouses and are often used on large commercial hoop-style houses. Anchor bolts embedded in the wet concrete provide fastening points for the greenhouse base or wall members.

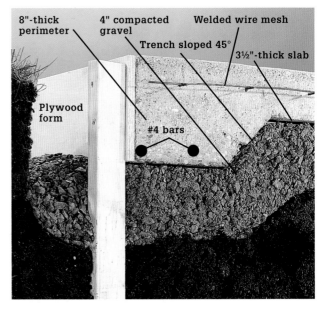

8"-thick perimeter

4" compacted gravel

Welded wire mesh

Trench sloped 45°

3½"-thick slab

Plywood form

#4 bars

Concrete slabs make great foundations and a nice, cleanable floor surface but are overkill for most hobby greenhouses. In some areas, it may be permissible to use a "floating" footing that combines a floor slab with a deep footing edge (shown here). Otherwise, slabs must be poured inside of a perimeter frost footing, as with garage or basement construction. To prevent water from pooling inside the greenhouse, concrete slabs must slope toward a central floor drain—a job for a concrete pro, not to mention a plumber to install the drain and underground piping.

Floors

Even if your greenhouse is small or temporary, a dirt floor is a bad idea. Watering of plants and even condensation will quickly lead to a muddy mess that invites weeds, disease, and pests. There are plenty of inexpensive options for greenhouse floors, all of which are easy to install yourself. In general, any water-permeable surface that works for a patio or walkway will make a good floor for a greenhouse.

For long-term stability, improved drainage, and a level floor surface, it's highly recommended to start any greenhouse floor with a 4 to 6" subbase of compacted gravel. Cover the subbase with commercial-quality landscape fabric (not plastic; the fabric must be water-permeable) to inhibit weed growth and to separate the gravel base from the upper layers. From there, the simplest floors can be made with any type of suitable gravel, such as pea gravel or trap rock.

Brick and concrete patio pavers are other great options and offer a more finished look and feel over gravel floors. Pavers are laid over a 1 to 2" layer of sand and should be surrounded by a border (foundation timbers or patio edging will suffice) to keep them from drifting. Once the pavers are set, you can sweep sand over the surface to fill the cracks and lock the units in place. Another floor option—flagstone—is installed in much the same way. You can save money on a paver or stone floor by using pavers or stones only in the walking areas and covering the spaces under benches and other non-traffic areas with gravel.

A poured concrete floor is stable and washable, and requires no routine maintenance.

Concrete pavers set in sand offer a longlasting, stable floorcovering that breathes and allows for good drainage.

Pea gravel

Crushed stone

Pathway gravel is the easiest and cheapest flooring to install. Pea gravel, trap rock, and some river stones are good for both drainage and cleanliness. Highly compactible materials, such as decomposed granite, remain solid and level underfoot but leave a lot of grit on your shoes (if that's a concern). In any case, choose a material that's comfortable to walk on; loose or large gravel or stones can be unstable or laborious for travel.

Framing Materials

FRAMING MATERIALS

Although wood and aluminum are the most popular greenhouse framing materials, other products, such as steel and PVC, are available. Each type has advantages and disadvantages, so choose the one that best suits your purposes. For example, if you plan to hang baskets or put up shelves, or if your area gets a lot of snow, you'll need to choose a sturdy material to accommodate the extra weight.

WOOD

Advantages: Often the first choice for custom greenhouses, wood framing is attractive, does not transfer heat as readily as aluminum, and has fewer condensation problems. It is also sturdy and, if you use cedar or redwood, rot-resistant and fragrant. You can easily fasten shelves, hooks, and other items to a wood frame. Western red cedar and redwood are recommended, but you can also use pressure-treated wood.

Disadvantages: Wood framing requires regular maintenance, and because it is bulkier than aluminum, it casts more shadow on greenhouse plants. This type of greenhouse is also difficult to add onto as a garden expands.

A wood frame with plastic glazing

An aluminum frame with polycarbonate glazing

ALUMINUM

Advantages: The foremost advantage of aluminum framing is that it is low-maintenance. It is strong and lightweight, lasts longer than wood, and can easily accommodate different glazing systems and connectors. Aluminum is used for most greenhouse kits (see page 78) and can be powder-coated or anodized in various colors, usually brown, green, or white. Kits are typically easy to assemble and come with predrilled holes for attachments. Some manufacturers offer thermally broken aluminum framing, which sandwiches a thermal barrier between two layers of extruded aluminum to decrease heat loss.

Disadvantages: Because aluminum loses heat at a faster rate than wood, this type of greenhouse is more expensive to heat. In addition, a cheaply made frame can be too flimsy to withstand high winds or heavy snow. Aluminum framing can also present condensation problems.

GALVANIZED STEEL

Advantages: Galvanized steel framing, mostly used for commercial greenhouses, is extremely sturdy, strong, and durable.

Disadvantages: Steel greenhouses are very heavy and expensive, not just to build but also to ship. Galvanized steel is subject to rusting if it is scratched, and the rust-resistant coating can eventually wear off.

A PVC plastic tube frame with plastic sheeting

PVC (POLYVINYL CHLORIDE)

Advantages: Inexpensive and easy to assemble from a kit, PVC framing is a good choice if you are just trying your hand at greenhouse gardening. It is lightweight, does not rust, and is ideal for portable or temporary greenhouses.

Disadvantages: High winds can easily damage PVC, so it's suitable only for small greenhouses, and glazing choices are restricted to plastic sheeting.

GLAZING & COVERS

Greenhouse glazing falls into two categories: glass and plastic, each with strengths and weaknesses. The ideal covering lets in maximum light and deters heat loss. It should also be durable and require minimal maintenance.

GLASS

Advantages: Glass is the material traditionally used for greenhouse glazing, and it remains popular today. It offers excellent light transmission, resists degradation due to ultraviolet (UV) light, and has a long lifespan. It is also nonflammable and, when layered, retains heat well. Double- and even triple-pane glass is available.

Disadvantages: Uninsulated single-pane glass offers very little heat retention. Glass is also breakable—playing children, tree branches, and hail are all threats to a glass greenhouse. For safety, tempered glass is recommended because it shatters into small, rounded "pebbles" rather than sharp, jagged pieces. Glass is heavy and requires a strong, square frame and foundation or the glass can crack. Although glass offers excellent light transmission, the light is harsh and direct, not diffused, and can easily burn plants. Insulated glass can be costly.

POLYCARBONATE

Advantages: Polycarbonate glazing is light, strong, and shatter-resistant, and when layered, it retains heat better than glass. It is available in corrugated, double-, and triple-wall panels. Corrugated polycarbonate provides excellent light transmission—equal to that of glass—but poor heat retention. Triple-wall polycarbonate (16 mm) offers excellent insulation but reduced light transmission. Polycarbonate is impact-resistant and long-lasting (15 years or longer). Unlike glass, it transmits diffused light, which eliminates shadows on plants and protects them from burns. Using twin- or triple-wall polycarbonate roof panels can increase heat retention while still allowing good light transmission.

Disadvantages: Polycarbonate scratches easily, and double- and triple-wall panels reduce light transmission. As with other plastic coverings, polycarbonate is subject to condensation, although it can be coated to reduce this problem. Like glass, it can also be costly, especially layered panels.

ACRYLIC

Advantages: Acrylic offers clarity and light transmission similar to glass but is lightweight and more impact-resistant. Acrylic panels are UV-resistant and can easily be molded. The material is less expensive than polycarbonate and can be layered for extra strength and heat retention. It is easy to cut and can be shaped with ordinary hand tools. Like polycarbonate, it can be coated to reduce condensation.

Disadvantages: Acrylic is not commonly used in home greenhouses. Less expensive types of acrylic can yellow, and even UV-coated acrylic will eventually need replacement. Unless it's coated, it suffers from condensation problems.

FIBERGLASS

Advantages: Fiberglass has improved since its debut as a replacement for glass. It is now more UV-resistant and resists yellowing. Its light transmission is almost equal to that of glass, but unlike glass, fiberglass diffuses light. It also offers better heat retention than glass and is much more durable. Good-quality fiberglass can last 20 years.

Disadvantages: Like other plastics, fiberglass tends to have condensation problems. If corrugated fiberglass is used, dirt can accumulate in the valleys, which detracts from its appearance. Inexpensive fiberglass may have a lifespan of no more than five years.

Water

All greenhouses need some kind of water supply system. This can be as simple as a hose connected to the nearest outdoor spigot or as complex as a frost-proof underground line extending from your basement to a special hydrant in the greenhouse. The latter is obviously more convenient, and the system can operate year-round. It's also a pretty big job that usually requires a plumber to make the final connections. A somewhat easier alternative is to install a shallow underground water line that you drain at the end of the growing season, similar to the supply line for a sprinkler system. Or, if your water demands are not too great and your greenhouse is located near your house, maintain a rainbarrel nearby.

A nearby rainbarrel provides a ready supply of water for your greenhouse. It's an easy water supply option but it lacks the convenience of linking the greenhouse to your house's water supply system.

An All-season Water Supply ▸

A dedicated all-season water line is certainly the ultimate setup for any freestanding greenhouse. To prevent the line from freezing during winter, the entire buried portion of the water line must be laid 6" below the frost line in your area. In the greenhouse, the water comes up through a freeze-proof yard hydrant (commonly used on farms), which drains itself of residual water each time it is shut off. The water drains into a gravel pit (installed per local code and the hydrant manufacturer).

In a typical installation, the supply line connects to a cold-water pipe in the house and includes a shutoff valve and backflow preventer (vacuum breaker). The line passes through the foundation wall (where it's protected by a sleeve of rigid pipe) at the burial depth then runs underground to the hydrant. For most applications, flexible PE (polyethylene) tubing is the best all-around option for the buried portion of the supply line. As always, all connections and devices must follow local code requirements.

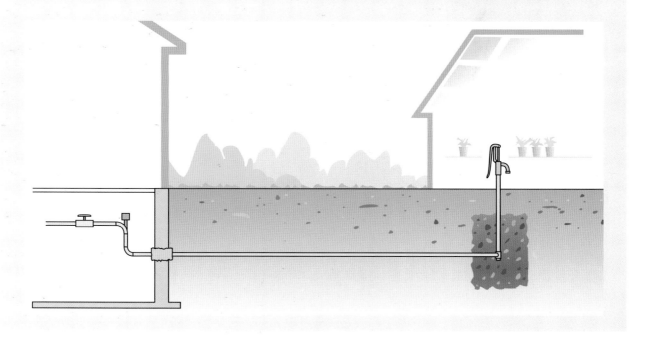

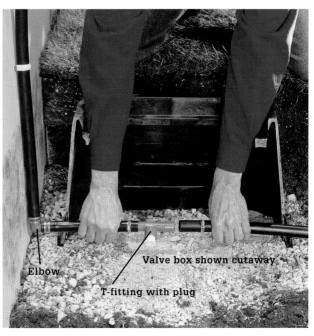

Elbow

Valve box shown cutaway

T-fitting with plug

A seasonal water supply line is similar to an all-season setup but somewhat easier to install and is just as convenient for everyday use. The supply line connects to a cold-water pipe inside the house and runs through an exterior wall above the foundation, then down into a trench (left photo). At the house-end of the trench, the initial supply run connects to the underground line (typically PE tubing) inside a valve box. The box provides easy access to a T-fitting necessary for freeze-proofing the line each fall. The supply run is buried in a 10"-deep trench (or per local code) and connects to copper tubing and a standard garden spigot inside the greenhouse.

Winterize a seasonal supply line using a shutoff valve with an air nipple. With the valve closed and the greenhouse spigot open, blow compressed air (50 psi max.) into the line to remove any water in the tubing. Then, remove the plug from the T-fitting inside the valve box (photo, top right, this page) and store it for the winter.

Adding a sink to a greenhouse can be fairly simple, provided it's for cold water only and drains into a dry well. A dry well can be made with an old trash can or other container perforated with holes and filled with coarse rock. The well sits in a pit about 2 ft. in diameter by about 3 ft. deep and is covered with landscape fabric and soil. Dry wells are for draining gray water only—no animal waste, food scraps, or hazardous materials.

Watering & Misting Systems

If your greenhouse is fairly small and you enjoy tending plants daily—pinching off a spent bloom here, propping up a leaning stem there—you might enjoy watering by hand, either with a watering can (which is laborious, no matter how small the greenhouse) or with a wand. Hand-watering helps you to pay close attention to plants and cater to their individual needs. You'll quickly notice signs of over- or under-watering and can adjust accordingly.

However, hand-watering isn't always practical. Many gardeners use an automatic system such as overhead sprinkling and drip irrigation. This approach is convenient, especially when you are out of town, and it lets you meet individual plant-watering needs if you group those with similar requirements together. Greenhouse suppliers sell kits as well as individual parts for automated watering systems. Be sure your system includes a timer that can be set to deliver water at specific times of the day, for a set duration, and on specific days of the week. You can also incorporate water heaters and fertilizer injectors into your system.

Overhead-sprinkler systems are attached to the main water supply and use sprinkler nozzles connected to PVC pipes installed above the benches. The system usually includes a water filter, which prevents the nozzles from clogging, and a pressure regulator. Set the system to water in the morning and during the hottest part of the day. Avoid watering late in the day so the plants will be dry before nightfall, when the temperature drops and dampness can cause disease.

Drip-irrigation systems use drip emitters to water plants slowly, a drop at a time, when moisture is needed. Each plant has an emitter attached to feeder lines that connect to a drip line of PVC tubing or pipe, which runs along the benches and back to the main water supply. Unlike overhead sprinklers, drip irrigation ensures that the plant leaves stay dry. It also helps to conserve water.

If you prefer to water plants from underneath, consider capillary mats. These feltlike mats are placed on top of the bench (which is first lined with plastic)

This automatic drip watering system is fed by a garden hose that connects to the mixing tank. In the tank, water and fertilizer are blended to a custom ratio and then distributed to plants at an adjustable rate via a network of hoses, drip pins and Y-connectors (See Resources, page 236). NOTE: The spiral trellis supports hanging from the greenhouse roof are not part of the watering system.

and under the plants, with one end of the mat set into a reservoir attached to the bench. The reservoir ensures that the mat is constantly moist. Moisture from the mat is drawn up into the soil and to the plant roots when water is needed. Unlike drip irrigation and overhead sprinkling, capillary-mat watering systems do not require electricity, pipes, or tubing. However, unless they are treated, the mats will need regular cleaning to prevent mildew and bacteria buildup. To ensure that the system works properly, it's important that the bench be level.

Regardless of the watering system you choose, use lukewarm water. Cold water can shock the roots, especially if the soil is warm. If you're hand-watering, let the water sit in the greenhouse so it warms up to ambient temperature. (Keep it out of the sun, though—you don't want it to get too hot). Wand watering and automatic systems can benefit from an installed water heater.

MISTING

When the temperature inside the greenhouse rises and the vents open, they release humidity. Misting increases humidity, which most plants love—levels of about 50 percent to 65 percent are ideal—and dramatically decreases the temperature by as much as 20° F. Misting systems are available through greenhouse suppliers. You can buy a complete system, which might include nozzles, tubing, PVC pipe, a humidistat, and sometimes a hard-water filter and a pressure gauge, or you can buy the parts separately to create a customized system. The size of the greenhouse will determine the size of the system: Larger greenhouses need more nozzles and in turn more tubing and pipe.

Humidistats can automatically turn on misters and humidifiers when the humidity drops below a set level. You might also want to invest in a device to boost the water pressure. Higher pressure produces a finer mist, which cools more quickly. Suppliers recommend placing the nozzles about 2 ft. apart around the perimeter of the greenhouse, between the wall and the benches. Place the nozzles underneath the benches so the mist doesn't drench the plants. As with watering, avoid misting late in the day. Wet leaves and cold, humid air can encourage disease.

Misting is a very gentle method of providing moisture to plants. Misting heads mounted on spray poles (inset) can be controlled manually or automatically. In addition to maintaining a constant state of moistness for plants, a misting system will give your greenhouse a tropical environment that many gardeners enjoy.

Lighting

If you've placed your greenhouse in a sunny, south-facing location, well away from shade, plants should get adequate sunlight during the summer. But if the greenhouse faces north or is shaded during the day, plants may need additional light. And no matter where the greenhouse is located, you'll likely need to rely on supplemental lighting during winter.

Supplementing natural light with artificial light can be tricky. Natural light is made up of a spectrum of colors that you can see (the red, orange, yellow, green, blue, indigo, and violet colors of the rainbow) and those you can't see (infrared and ultraviolet). Plants absorb light from the red and blue ends of the spectrum—blue light promotes plant growth; light from the red end of the spectrum encourages plants to flower and bud. The red-blue light combination is easily achieved when the source is the sun but a little more difficult when you're using artificial lighting. Intensity is also important: Lights that are set too far away or that don't provide enough brightness (measured in lumens or foot-candles) will produce weak, spindly plants.

Three basic types of lights are available: incandescent bulbs, fluorescent tubes, and high-intensity discharge (HID) lights, which include metal halide (MH) or high-pressure sodium (HPS). Each has advantages and disadvantages, which is why greenhouse gardeners often use a combination of two or more types to achieve light that is as close to natural as possible.

INCANDESCENT

Ordinary tungsten incandescent bulbs are inexpensive, readily available, and a good source of red rays, but they are deficient in blue light. They can be useful for extending daylight for some plants and for supplementing low light levels, but they are not an efficient primary source of light. Incandescent lights produce a lot of heat—hanging them too close to plants can burn foliage, but if you hang them at a safe distance, they don't provide enough intensity for plant growth. The average life span of an incandescent bulb is about 1,000 hours.

FLUORESCENT

Fluorescent tubes are more expensive than incandescent bulbs, but the higher cost is amply offset by their longevity and efficiency: bulb life for fluorescents is about 10,000 hours, and they provide the same amount of light as incandescents with only ¼ to ⅓ the amount of energy. They also produce much less heat than incandescent bulbs.

Adding lighting fixtures allows you to extend the growing hours during the early days of the growing season.

Fluorescent bulbs (or "lamps," as they're called by the lighting industry) come in a variety of colors and temperature ranges, including full-spectrum light. Cool white lamps, which produce orange, yellow-green, blue, and a little red light, are the most popular choice. To provide seedlings and plants with a nearly full spectrum of light, many growers combine one cool white lamp and one soft (or warm) white lamp in the same fixture.

Due to their energy efficiency and low heat output, fluorescent-tube fixtures are great for ambient lights that you might leave running for long periods, as well as for task lighting. They're also the best all-around choice for starting seedlings and growing small plants. The downside to using fluorescents as grow lights is that they must be hung very close to the plant—from 2 to 8", depending on the plant—to be effective. This makes them most useful for propagation and low-growing plants.

HID

High-intensity discharge (HID) lights work by sending an electrical charge through a pressurized-gas tube. There are two types: high-pressure sodium (HPS), which casts light in the yellow, orange, and red end of the spectrum, and metal halide (MH), which leans more toward the blue end, casting blue/violet light. MH lamps are often recommended as the primary light source for greenhouse growing, with HPS lights as a secondary light source. MH light mimics spring light and encourages early plant growth; HPS light resembles the type cast by the sun during fall and promotes fruiting and flowering. Greenhouse gardeners often start plants out under MH lamps and then switch to HPS. This requires switching fixtures during the growing season, which can be a nuisance. Convertible fixtures house both types of bulbs so that they can be used in tandem or succession.

HID lights are very expensive, but their lifespan is long: A standard 400-watt bulb can last 20,000 hours. They also cover a large area: a 400-watt lamp lights 16 sq. ft. of space. HID lights produce heat, so they should be hung higher in the greenhouse. If you use them, be sure to provide plenty of ventilation during summer.

Fluorescent is a better source of growth-stimulating light for your greenhouse. It must, however, be hung relatively close to plants in order to benefit their growth.

Ordinary incandescent lights aren't particulary good sources of growth-promoting light, but they can help heat a greenhouse. And their attractive warm light also turns a greenhouse into a nighttime landscape design feature.

Lighting Considerations ▶

The best lighting for growing greenhouse plants mimics natural light. Invest in lamps that resemble natural light in intensity and color (or combine lamps to provide a broad spectrum, as described above). Use lights when days are short and cloudy.

Heating

Once you understand your greenhouse heating requirements (see Calculating Heat Needs, opposite), you'll need to determine what type of heater to use and whether you'll need to run a gas line and power to the greenhouse. The two main types of greenhouse heaters are electric and fuel-fired (gas, propane, kerosene, or oil).

Electric heaters are inexpensive and easy to install. They provide adequate heat for a small greenhouse in a temperate climate and are useful for three-season greenhouses. However, they are expensive to operate (although relative costs are constantly changing) and do not provide sufficient heat for use in cold regions. Electric units can also distribute heat unevenly, making it too warm in some areas of the greenhouse and too cold in others. Placing a heater at each end of the greenhouse can help. If you use an electric heater, be sure the fan doesn't blow warm air directly on the plant leaves; they will scorch.

Gas heaters usually cost more than electric and most areas require that a licensed professional hook them up, but heating bills will be lower than if you use an electric heater. Gas heaters operate much like a furnace: a thermostat turns on the heat when the temperature drops below its setting. You can help to distribute the heat by using a fan with the heater. If you plan to use a gas heater, install the gas line when you're building the foundation. It is also important to ensure that the heater is vented to the outside and that fresh air is available for combustion. Poor ventilation can cause dangerous carbon-monoxide buildup.

Propane, oil, and kerosene heaters also need to be vented, and if you're using kerosene, be sure it's high-grade. Another option is hot-water heating, in which the water circulates through pipes set around the perimeter of the greenhouse under the benches. You can also consider overhead infrared heat lamps and soil-heating cables as sources of heat.

In most climates, an electric heater with an automatic thermostat will be sufficient to protect tender plants on cold nights. Electricity is an expensive heating option, however, so it's best reserved for moderate heating needs.

A portable space heater may be all the supplemental heat your greenhouse requires. Use it with caution, and make sure yours shuts off automatically if it overheats or is knocked over.

Calculating Heat Needs

Heat is measured in British thermal units (Btu), the amount of heat required to raise one pound of water one degree Fahrenheit. To determine how many Btu of heat output are required for your greenhouse, use the following formula:

Area (the total square footage of the greenhouse panels) × Difference (the difference between the coldest nighttime temperature in your area and the minimum nighttime temperature required by your plants) × 1.1 (the heat-loss factor of the glazing; 1.1 is an average) equals Btu.

Calculate the area by multiplying the length by the height of each wall and roof panel in the greenhouse and adding up the totals. Here's an example, using 380 sq. ft. for the greenhouse area and 45° F as the difference between the coldest nighttime temperature (10° F) and the desired nighttime greenhouse temperature (55° F).
380 sq. ft × 45 × 1.1 = 18,810 Btu.

If the greenhouse is insulated or uses double-glazed glass or twin-wall polycarbonate, you can deduct 30 percent from the total Btu required; if it's triple-glazed, deduct 50 percent. You can deduct as much as 60 percent if the greenhouse is double-glazed and attached to a house wall.

Heating Requirements ▸

- Oil, gas, kerosene, and other fuel-operated heaters must be vented to the outside and have a source of fresh air for combustion.
- Heaters must be equipped with an automatic shut-off switch.
- Position several thermometers at bench level throughout the greenhouse so you can check that heat is evenly distributed.

- Do not place thermometers or thermostats in direct sunlight.
- Install an alarm to warn you if the temperature drops dangerously low. Set the temperature warning high enough to give you time to remedy the problem before plants die.
- Use a backup generator to supply power to electric heaters during power outages.

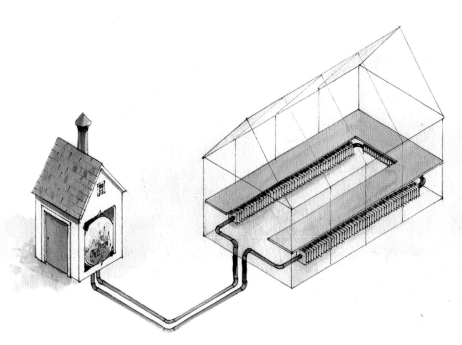

The stove for a wood-fired heating system is normally located in a remote spot near the greenhouse. In a typical set-up, the wood stove heats water that is pumped through a pipe into the greenhouse and distributed through a series of radiators.

Conserving Heat

On cold, cloudy days and at night, solar heat is lost. Even if you have supplemental heating, holding onto that heat is essential to maintaining an optimal climate. Insulating the greenhouse and making use of heat sinks are the most effective means of conserving heat, but don't overlook heat thieves such as cracks and gaps. Be sure the glazing is tight, and seal any opening that lets in cold air.

If you built a concrete foundation, it may have polystyrene board installed between the concrete and the soil. Concrete rapidly loses heat if the ground around it is cold, and polystyrene insulation helps to reduce this heat loss. You can use polystyrene board or bubble insulation (similar to bubble wrap used for shipping) to temporarily insulate the walls of the greenhouse: Simply attach the material to the greenhouse frame beneath the benches before winter and remove it in the summer. You can also insulate the greenhouse from the outside. Plant low-growing plants around the foundation, or prop hay bales or burlap bags filled with dry leaves against the walls.

HEAT SINKS

Heat sinks absorb solar energy during the day and radiate it back into the greenhouse at night. Stone, tile, and brick floors and walls are good collectors of heat, but to be really effective, they should be insulated from underneath. Piles of rocks can act as heat sink, but the best option is a blue- or black-painted barrel or drum full of water. Place a few of them around the greenhouse. If you have an attached greenhouse, painting the house wall a dark color can cause it to radiate solar heat back into the greenhouse at night. A light-colored wall, on the other hand, can help reflect heat and light back into the greenhouse during the day.

This heat sink system uses solar energy to heat the greenhouse. Air heated by the sun is drawn in by the fan and blown into the rock pile, which also absorbs solar heat. Heat is radiated back into the greenhouse after the sun goes down.

Smart Heat Conservation ▶

- Reduce the temperature by 5°. Growth may be slowed, but plants will survive.
- Make sure the greenhouse is as airtight as possible.
- To prevent drafts, add a storm door.
- Mulch the soil in raised benches to insulate it during cool seasons, consider watering tropical foliage plants and other warm-season plants with water warmed to 65° F.
- Insulate all water- or steam-heating supply lines.
- At night, hang black cloth horizontally from the greenhouse ceiling as close to the plants and benches as possible to prevent the warm air from escaping through the roof.

- If the greenhouse uses automatic vents that are controlled by a separate thermostat, set that thermostat 5° or 10° higher than the heater thermostat to keep the vents from opening when the heat is on.
- Install an alarm system that will go off when the temperature goes above or below the safe range or when there is a power failure.
- Make use of the heat exhausted by your clothes dryer by running the vent into your greenhouse.
- Plant a "shelter belt" of evergreens on the windward side of the greenhouse to reduce heating costs. (But be sure it is far enough away that it doesn't cast shade on the greenhouse.)

Microclimates ▶

When you landscape your property, you consider its microclimates: the sunny, sheltered corner; the cool, shady spot beneath the trees; that strip along the back that always catches the breeze. Your greenhouse has microclimates, too: It's warmer near the roof and cooler at floor level; some spots are shaded and others receive strong, direct light; and down near the wall vents, it's cool and breezy. Like the plants in a garden, greenhouse plants have differing light, heat, soil, and moisture requirements. Before you place them in the greenhouse, take stock of its microclimates, and group plants according to their needs.

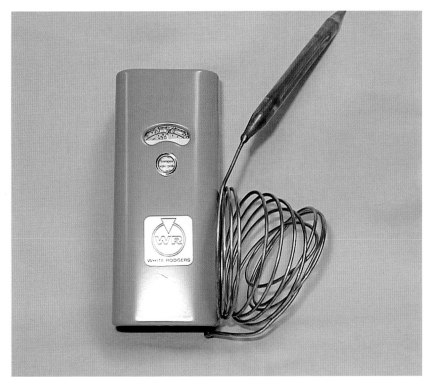

A heating and cooling thermostat is perhaps the most important greenhouse control device. The thermostat will control both heat sources, as well as automatic ventilaters to cool the greenhouse when temperatures climb into the danger zone for overheating plants.

Ventilation

Whether your plants thrive depends on how well you control their environment. Adequate sunlight is a good start, but ventilation is just as important: It expels hot air, reduces humidity, and provides air circulation, which is essential even during winter to move cold, stagnant air around, keep diseases at bay, and avoid condensation problems. You have two main options for greenhouse ventilation: vents and fans.

Because hot air rises, roof vents are the most common choice. They should be staggered on both sides of the ridgeline to allow a gentle, even exchange of air and proper circulation. Roof vents are often used in conjunction with wall vents or louvers. Opening the wall vents results in a more aggressive air exchange and cools the greenhouse much faster than using roof vents alone. On hot days, you can open the greenhouse door to let more air inside. Also consider running small fans to enhance circulation.

Vents can be opened and closed manually, but this requires constant temperature monitoring, which is inconvenient and can leave plants wilting in the heat if you are away. It's far easier—and safer—to use automatic vent openers. These can be thermostat-controlled and operated by a motor, which turns on at a set temperature, or they can be solar-powered. Unlike thermostat-controlled vent openers, which require electricity, solar-powered openers use a cylinder filled with wax, which expands as the temperature rises and pushes a rod that opens the vent. When the temperature drops, the wax shrinks and the vent closes. How far the vent opens is dictated by temperature: the higher the temperature, the wider the vent opens to let in more air.

A fan ventilator is a good idea if you have a large greenhouse. The fan is installed in the back opposite the greenhouse door, and a louvered vent is set into the door wall. At a set temperature, a thermostat mounted in the middle of the greenhouse activates the fan, and the louvered vent opens. Cool air is drawn in through the vent, and the fan expels the warm air. The fan should be powerful enough to provide a complete air exchange every 1 to 1.5 minutes.

Calculating Ventilation Requirements ▸

Greenhouse manufacturers rarely include enough vents in kits, so be sure to buy more. To determine the square footage of venting your greenhouse should have, multiply the square footage of the floor by 0.2.

Automatic openers sense heat build-up and open vents. Some openers are controlled by standard thermostats, while others are solar-powered.

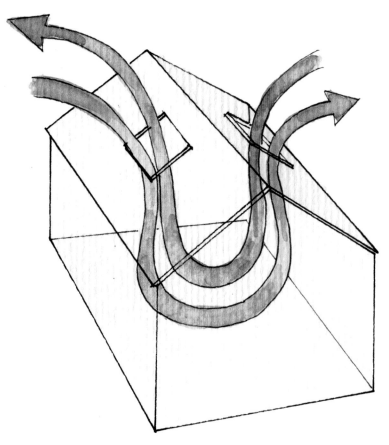

Venting your greenhouse–Installing at least one operable roof vent on each side of the ridgeline creates good air movement within the structure. Adding lower intake vents helps for cooling. Adding fans to the system greatly increases air movement.

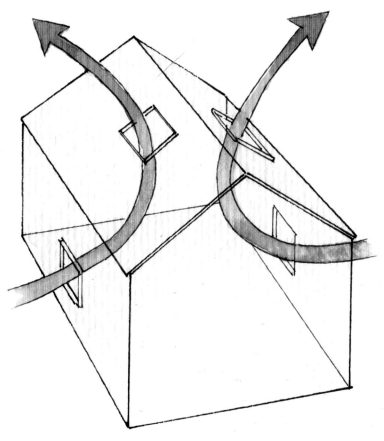

Cooling

Although vents and fans are the first line of defense when the temperature inside the greenhouse starts to climb, other cooling methods such as misting, humidifying, evaporative cooling, and shading can also help to maintain the ideal growing environment. Cooling is crucial during summer, but it can be just as important on a sunny winter day.

SHADES

By blocking direct sunlight, shades protect plants from sunburn and prevent the greenhouse from getting too hot. They can be installed on the exterior or hung from cables inside the greenhouse. Both methods block the sun, but only exterior shades prevent solar energy from penetrating the glazing, thereby keeping the air inside the greenhouse cooler.

When choosing shades, be sure they are UV-stabilized for longevity.

Two types of shades are available: cloth and roll-up. Shade cloth is usually woven or knitted from fiberglass or polyethylene and is available in many colors, although green, black, gray, and white are most common. You can also find shade cloth in silver, which, like white, reflects heat and sunlight and keeps the greenhouse cooler than darker colors. Shade cloth also varies in density, usually from 20 percent to 80 percent. The higher the density of the cloth, the more light it blocks (60 percent density blocks 60 percent of the light). Be careful when choosing shade density; too little light will slow plants' growth.

Shade cloth can be simply thrown over the greenhouse and tied down when shading is needed, but this hampers airflow through the vents (unless you cut the cloth to size and install it in sections). Better ventilation is achieved by suspending the cloth 4 to 9 in. above the exterior glazing. Be sure the vents are open when you do this. Greenhouse shade suppliers can provide framework kits.

Greenhouse Shading Compound ▸

Professional greenhouse growers with large operations typically apply greenhouse shading compound to the glazing of their structures so they can control heat entry and protect their plants. Similar to paint, shading compound contains ground pigments that reflect the sun's rays. The compound is sprayed onto the glazing with an airless sprayer (you can use a hand-sprayer for a small greenhouse). Sold in 5-gallon buckets, it is diluted with water at an 8 to 1 ratio for plenty of coverage. Some types are designed to be easily removed with water and a fine nylon broom so you can make adjustments as needed. Other formulations are intended to be permanent. For more information, ask about the product at your greenhouse supply store or do an online search for Greenhouse Shading Compound.

Roof shades, along with vents, help prevent a greenhouse from overheating in direct sunlight. Here, a combination of circulating fans and cloth shades mounted on the interior of the south-facing glass helps protect plants.

Louvered and roll-up shades help to block the sun in this greenhouse.

In addition to cloth, roll-up greenhouse shades may be constructed from aluminum, bamboo, or wood. They are convenient because you roll them up when they're not needed, and they last longer than shade cloth, but they are more expensive.

EVAPORATIVE COOLERS

Evaporative coolers (also called swamp coolers) cool the air by using a fan to push or pull air through a water-saturated pad. A portable cooler might be sufficient for a small greenhouse; larger greenhouses will benefit from a unit cooler placed outside. Used when the humidity outside is less than 40 percent, these units draw dry outside air through the saturated pad, where it is cooled. The air travels through the greenhouse and exits via a vent on the opposite side. It's a good idea to use an algaecide with these coolers.

LIQUID SHADING

Some greenhouse gardeners choose to paint liquid-shading compounds (sometimes called whitewashing) over the outside glazing. These compounds are inexpensive and easy to apply, but they can be unattractive and tend to wash off in the rain. Liquid shading can be thinned or layered to the level desired,

and the residue can be brushed off at the end of summer. (It is often almost worn off by that point anyway). Some liquid-shading compounds become transparent during rainy weather to let in more light and then turn white when they dry.

Roof vents that are triggered to open automatically by sensor alerts are far and away the most important component of a greenhouse cooling system. But additional cooling devices may be necessary.

Benches & Storage

Every greenhouse needs benches to support plants and provide space for potting. Because plants can be heavy, it's important that benches be sturdy.

How you lay out benches depends on your needs and the size of your greenhouse. Most average-size greenhouses can accommodate a bench along each wall, with an aisle down the middle for access. If you have enough space along one end wall, you can install more benches to create a U shape. Another option is to arrange the benches in a peninsula pattern. Shorter benches are set at right angles to the outside walls, with narrow aisles in between, leaving space for a wider aisle down the middle. You can also use a single, wider bench along a side wall and leave space for portable benches and taller plants against the other wall. A larger greenhouse can accommodate three benches with two aisles.

Regardless of the layout you choose, it's best to orient benches along a north-south line so plants receive even light distribution throughout the day. Use the space as efficiently as possible, and don't inadvertently block the door. Allow enough room in the aisles to move around comfortably; make them wider if you need to accommodate a garden cart or wheelbarrow. Set benches about 2 in. from the greenhouse walls to provide airflow, and avoid placing benches near any heat source.

Bench width is determined by the length of your reach, so if you are short, you may want benches to be narrow. The same concept applies to height: Although the average bench is about 28 to 32 in., yours can be higher or lower to suit your height and reach. (If they need to be wheelchair-accessible, lower them even more.) If you have access to benches from both sides, you can double their width.

Several options are available for bench tops. Wood slats are sturdy and attractive, and they provide good drainage and airflow. Be sure to use pressure-treated or rot-resistant wood, such as cedar, keeping in mind that cedar benches can be expensive. Wire mesh costs less, is low-maintenance, and also provides good airflow, but be sure that it is strong enough to support heavy plants. Plastic-coated wire-mesh tops are available. These are similar to (if not the same as) the closet shelving found in home stores. Usually white, they have the advantage of reflecting light within the greenhouse.

Sturdy benches that are easy to clean and withstand moisture are a critical part of a greenhouse that's pleasant to work in.

For space efficiency, potting benches can double as storage containers. Here, the potting benches include spaces for mixing and storing soils for potting. Slatted covers make it easy to keep the bench-tops tidy.

You can also choose solid tops made of wood, plastic, or metal. Solid wood tops should be made from pressure-treated wood, and metal tops should be galvanized to prevent rust. Solid tops provide less air circulation than slatted or mesh tops, but they retain heat better in winter and are necessary if you use a capillary-mat watering system.

The greenhouse framing material will determine whether you can install shelves. Shelves can easily be added to a wood-framed greenhouse, and many aluminum greenhouse kit manufacturers provide predrilled framing, along with optional accessories for installing shelves. Keep in mind that even if shelves are wire mesh, they can cast shade onto the plants below.

If you plan on potting inside the greenhouse, you can use part of the benches or dedicate a separate space for a potting bench in a shady corner or along an end wall. For convenience, consider building or

buying a potting tray that you can move around and use as needed.

Unless you have a separate place to store tools and equipment, you'll need to find room for them in the greenhouse. To determine how much space you'll need, first list all of the equipment necessary to operate the greenhouse: everything from labels, string, and gardening gloves to bags of soil, pots, trash cans, and tools. If you will use harmful chemicals, be sure to include a lockable storage area.

Just as in your home, finding storage space in the greenhouse can be a challenge. Look first to shady areas. If the greenhouse has a knee wall, the area under the benches can provide a good deal of storage space. Shelves can also provide storage space for lightweight items. Be creative and make efficient use of any area where plants won't grow to create accessible yet tidy storage for equipment.

Potting Materials

If you're a container gardener, you are already familiar with the vast array of pots available at garden centers. For greenhouse gardening, however, pot choices are narrowed to two types: terra cotta and plastic.

Terra cotta pots are attractive and heavier than plastic, which means they are less likely to be knocked over. In addition, they are porous—because water evaporates through the clay, the risk of overwatering is lower. However, you will have to water plants more often and clean the pots regularly to remove deposits caused by minerals from water and soil leaching through the sides. Glazed terra cotta pots hold moisture better than unglazed pots and don't show mineral deposits. Terra cotta pots are more expensive than plastic pots.

Practical and inexpensive, plastic pots hold moisture better than terra cotta pots, so you don't have to water plants as often. Gardeners who plan to start seeds and propagate plants often use plastic trays, flats, and cell packs, although peat pots, cubes, and plugs are also available for starting seeds.

Terra cotta containers are preferable if your plants will live in the pot permanently. If you are only starting plants for transplant, inexpensive plastic pots and trays are a good choice.

Hydroponics ▶

Hydroponics, the process of growing plants without soil, has become popular with greenhouse gardeners, especially for growing vegetables. Hydroponic growing medium, which holds plants in place, can be made of polystyrene balls, expanded clay pellets, gravel, pea stone, perlite, vermiculite, rock wool, or coconut fibers. The simplest method is to place growing medium into a pot and add a nutrient solution once or twice a day. A more complex system involves using computer-controlled pumps to automatically flush plants' roots with nutrient solution as necessary for maximum growth.

Lettuces are probably the most common hydroponically grown vegetable. They often are shipped with the root system intact for greater longevity.

Root systems grow through the plant support medium and down into the water below. Here, the water is contained in a child's plastic wading pool.

Many vegetables and herbs that are suitable for greenhouse growing are also good candidates for a hydroponic environment. Testing different species and judging their success can be a fun process.

Custom Victorian Greenhouse

One objection to most kit greenhouses is that they tend to have little going for them on the style front: a plain metal framework supporting clear panels. If you're looking for a greenhouse project that blends with the look and character of your home, your best bet is to design and build one yourself.

The custom greenhouse seen in this project is designed and scaled to fit lean-to-style against a south-facing wall on an 1890's era Victorian house. The principal design details that make it blend are the kneewall, which uses the same narrow wood lapsiding as the house, and the custom windows and door, which feature an arch element that is also present in the house trim. At roughly 6 × 9 ft. in floorplan, the greenhouse is on the small side. But a space-conserving built-in-bench helps the gardener who designed the greenhouse get maximum usage from this small space.

The glazing on the greenhouse is ¼"-thick clear polycarbonate (See Resources, page 236). The roof panels are also clear ¼" polycarbonate, but with a hollow twin-wall construction that resists shattering and limits condensation. The roof vents are operated by lift arms with integral thermometers. When the air temperature inside the greenhouse hits around 85° the vents pop open automatically. The windows and the door are custom-made by sandwiching polycarbonate panels between wood frames. To allow for movement of the materials, the frames are bolted together through oversized bolt holes. All but one of the windows are hinged on the tops so they can swing open to enhance ventilation.

Construction note: The greenhouse seen here features a poured concrete slab that is set apart from the house by an isolation joint. The back wall studs and roof panels are not connected to the house either, thus the greenhouse is technically a freestanding structure. Gaps between the greenhouse and the house are covered with various flashings, each of which is connected to one of the structures only. This has several advantages: primarily, it allows the structure to move and shift slightly (thereby avoiding cracking of glazing and roof panels) as the soil conditions and temperature change. And if the structure is small enough and has adequate setback distance from your property lines, you likely will not need a building permit. If the greenhouse were connected to the house, you would be required to dig full frost footings, as well.

Tools & Materials ›

Shovel	Circular saw	Concrete nails or screws	8d finish nails
Garden rake	Jigsaw	Skew joist hangers	Exterior-rated butt hinges
Hand tamper	Power miter saw	Joist hanger nails	Door pulls and eyehooks
Drill/driver	Pen	Paint and paint brush	Door stop moldings
Framing square	Drywall saw	Seaming strip	Garage door sweep
Level	Sandpaper	Pole barn screws	
Concrete mixer	Straightedge guide	Metal flashing	
Mallet	Compactible gravel	Roof vent covers	
Float	Deck screws (2 ½", 3")	Piano hinges	
Sheet plastic	Metal re-mesh	Automatic window vent opener (optional)	
Powder-actuated tool	Concrete	Bolts	
Clamps	J-bolts	Wood glue	
Pencil	Post anchors		
Tape measure	Socket wrench		

Framing

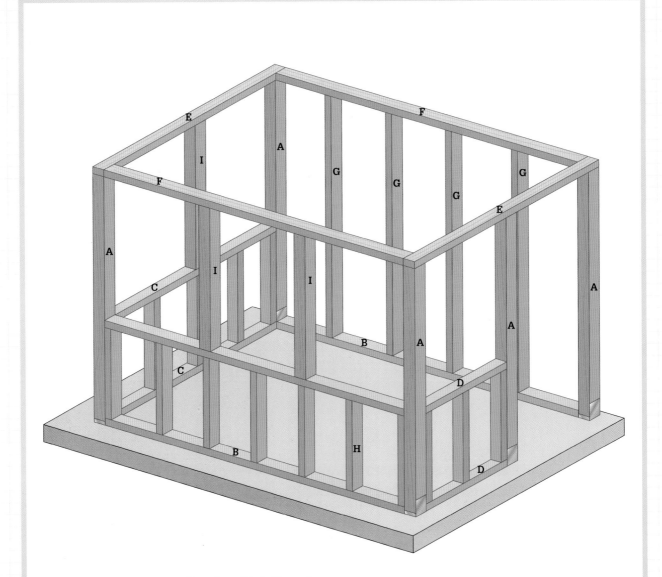

Cutting List-Framing

KEY	PART	NO.	DIMENSION	MATERIAL
A	Post	5	3½ × 3½ × 78"	4 × 4
B	Front/back plate	2	1½ × 3½ × 84½"	PT 2 × 4
C	End plate	2	1½ × 3½ × 56"	PT 2 × 4
D	Door wall plate	2	1½ × 3½ × 26"	PT 2 × 4
E	End cap-bottom	2	1½ × 3½ × 63"	2 × 4
F	F/B cap-bottom	2	1½ × 3½ × 84½"	2 × 4
G	Back wall stud	4	1½ × 3½ × 76½"	2 × 4
H	Kneewall stud	15	1½ × 3½ × 33"	2 × 4
I	Upper stud	3	3½ × 3½ × 42"	4 × 4

Roof

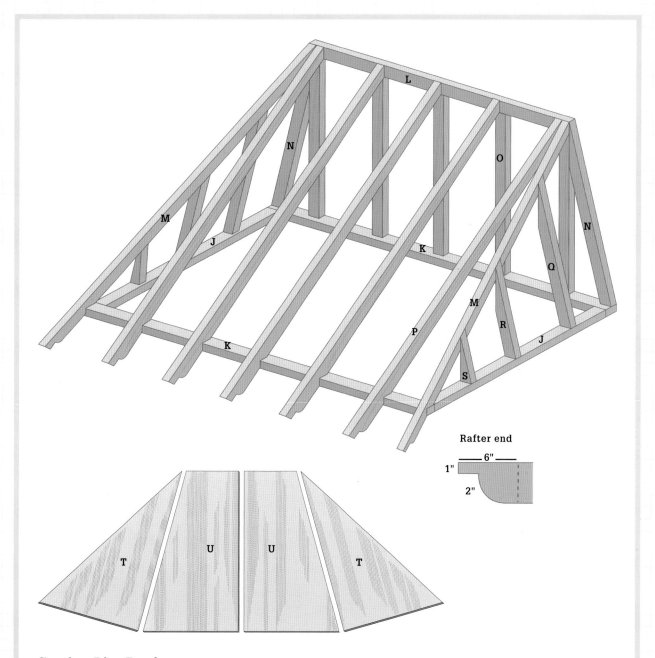

Rafter end

6"
1"
2"

Cutting List-Roof

KEY	PART	NO.	DIMENSION	MATERIAL
J	End cap-top	2	$1\frac{1}{2} \times 3\frac{1}{2} \times 56"$	2×4
K	F/B cap-top	2	$1\frac{1}{2} \times 3\frac{1}{2} \times 91\frac{1}{2}"$	2×4
L	Roof ridge	1	$1\frac{1}{2} \times 3\frac{1}{2} \times 64"$	2×4
M	Skew rafter	2	$1\frac{1}{2} \times 3\frac{1}{2} \times 79"$	2×4
N	Roof leg	2	$1\frac{1}{2} \times 3\frac{1}{2} \times 39\frac{1}{2}"$	2×4
O	Roof support	5	$1\frac{1}{2} \times 3\frac{1}{2} \times 34"$	2×4
P	Rafter	5	$1\frac{1}{2} \times 3\frac{1}{2} \times 81"$	2×4
Q	Cripple rafter	2	$1\frac{1}{2} \times 3\frac{1}{2} \times 30"$	2×4
R	Cripple rafter	2	$1\frac{1}{2} \times 3\frac{1}{2} \times 22"$	2×4
S	Cripple rafter	2	$1\frac{1}{2} \times 3\frac{1}{2} \times 12"$	2×4
T	Roof panel-side	2	$\frac{1}{4} \times 42 \times 63"$	Suntuf
U	Roof panel-main	2	$\frac{1}{4} \times 47 \times 79"$	Suntuf

Window

Cutting List-Window (1@ 26 × 40½")

KEY	PART	NO.	DIMENSION	MATERIAL
W1	Rail-A	2	¾ × 3½ × 26"	1 × 4
W2	Stile-A	2	¾ × 3½ × 33½"	1 × 4
W3	Rail-B	2	¾ × 3½ × 19"	1 × 4
W4	Stile-B	2	¾ × 3½ × 40½"	1 × 4
W5	Insert	2	¾ × 5¼ × 19"	1 × 4
W6	Glazing	1	¼ × 26 × 40½"	Palsun

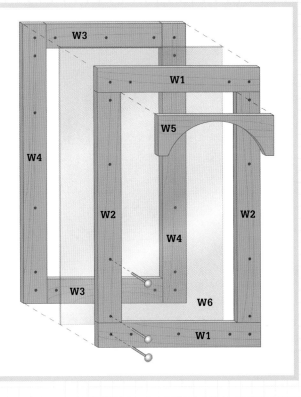

Door

Cutting List-Door (26 × 77½")

KEY	PART	NO.	DIMENSION	MATERIAL
D1	Rail-A	1	¾ × 3½ × 26"	1 × 4
D2	Rail-B	1	¾ × 5½ × 26"	1 × 6
D3	Rail-C	1	¾ × 3½ × 19"	1 × 4
D4	Rail-D	1	¾ × 5½ × 19"	1 × 6
D5	Stile-A	2	¾ × 3½ × 68½"	1 × 4
D6	Stile-B	2	¾ × 5½ × 77½"	1 × 4
D7	Insert	16	¾ × 5½ × 7¾"	1 × 6
D8	Glazing	1	¼ × 26 × 77½"	Palsun

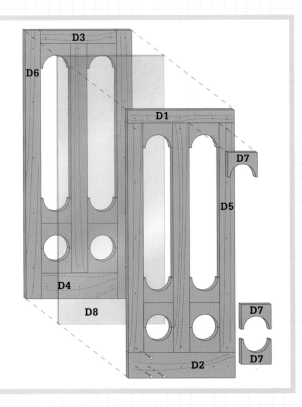

Materials for Building Custom Greenhouses

The glazing and roof panels in this custom greenhouse are made from Sunlite brand ¼"-thick polycarbonate panels (See Resources, page 236). The roof panels have vertical walls and are hollow, which makes them more dimensionally stable and less likely to crack than clear panels (a big benefit for roof). The ¼"-thick, clear polycarbonate used for the window and door glazing is very durable too, and offers 100% light penetration and clear sightlines. Standard ⅛"-thick clear acrylic can be used for roofs or glazing. It is relatively inexpensive and sold at most building centers. But it has a shorter lifespan than polycarbonate.

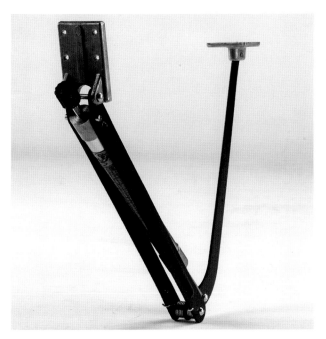

An automatic lifter arm contains a sensor that causes your roof window vents to raise when the interior temperature reaches a preset level—usually around 100 degrees.

Products for joining and fastening panels include a panel seam trim, which has wide flanges on both edges to accept two panels that butt together; 100% silicon caulk for sealing seams (check with the panel manufacturer for compatibility of adhesives and caulks); and rubber-gasket pole barn screws for fastening panels to rafters or purlins.

How to Build a Custom Greenhouse

Stake out the installation area for the greenhouse. Strip off vegetation and then excavate for the subbase material and that portion of the slab you want to be underground. For drainage reasons, plan your slab so at least 1 to 2" of the concrete is above grade.

Install a 4 to 6" thick layer of compactible gravel to create a stable subbase. Tamp the gravel with a hand tamper or rental compactor. The tamped surface should slope away from the house at a very shallow rate—about ¹⁄₁₆" per foot. Insert an isolation board strip (usually made of asphalt-impregnated fiberboard) between the slab area and the foundation wall to keep the structures separate.

Build the three-sided concrete form and position it on top of the subbase. Screw the three 2 × 4s together with deck screws and then tack a 1 × 4 or 2 × 4 across the top, back ends of the sides. Square and level the forms and then drive wood stakes outside the 2 × 4 members. Attach the form to the stakes with deck screws driven through the stakes and into the form boards. *Note: The slab seen here is sized so there is a concrete apron of 2 to 3" around the structure, resembling a foundation wall. Some builders prefer to size the slab so the corner posts are flush with the slab edges, allowing you to cover the gap at the concrete surface with siding.*

Add reinforcement in the concrete area. For most DIYers, metal re-mesh is an easy reinforcement material to work with. It is sold in 5 × 50 ft. rolls and in 4 × 8-ft. sheets. Prop the re-mesh on some small stones or bolsters. The edges of the reinforcement should be at least 4 to 6" away from the sides, and no closer than 1" to the concrete surface.

5

Isolation board

Pour concrete into the form. For a slab of the dimensions shown (4" thick by 68 × 84") approximately 15 cubic feet (one half yard) of concrete is required (thirty 60-pound bags of dry mix). Settle the concrete by rapping the forms lightly with a mallet, and then strike off the material before floating.

6

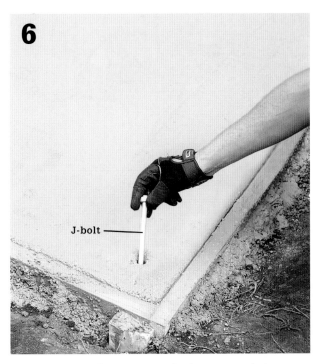

J-bolt

Set J-bolts into the concrete after it sets up and after you have rounded the edges with an edger tool. Make sure to follow your plan closely for the J-bolt positions. Cover the concrete with sheet plastic and allow it to dry overnight before removing the forms.

7

Install post anchors at the corners and at the door jamb location. Standoff posts that elevate the post bottom slightly will greatly reduce the amount of water the post end will wick up from the footing.

8

Ear protection

Cut the 2 × 4 sill plates to fit between the posts, using pressure-treated lumber. Install the sill plates by fastening with a powder-actuated tool and concrete nails. Or, you can drill guide holes and install masonry anchor sleeves or simply drive concrete screws into the concrete.

(continued)

Tack the posts in the standoff post bases with a couple of deck screws, making sure they are resting cleanly on the standoff pads. Also brace the posts with 2 × 4 braces so they are plumb. Tack all the posts in position and plumb them and then mark level cutting heights using a laser level or level for reference.

Remove the posts for trimming to final height, making sure to note which post belongs in which base. Marking and cutting in this manner ensures that the tops of all posts will be level even though the slab slopes away from the house. Pre-cutting posts to the same length will result in a roof structure that is not flat. Reinstall the posts in the anchors and fasten with joist hanger nails or 16d galvanized nails.

Cut the 2 × 4 endwall cap plates to length and screw them to the tops of the corner posts with 3" deck screws. Test frequently to make sure the corners are square and the edges are flush with the post edges.

Clamp the doubled front and back wall cap plates together so the top plate overhangs the lower plate by 3½" on each end. Screw the top plates to the endwall cap plates and then fasten the front and back wall plates together with 2½" deck screws. Fasten the top cap plate on each end.

Build stud walls for the knee walls between posts. Space the knee wall studs so they will be positioned beneath the intermediate posts (See Diagram). Attach cap plate to the tops of the studs.

Add 1 × 6 sills to the tops of the 2 × 4 knee walls. The sills will cover the edges of the exterior siding, so make the interior edges flush with interior wall studs and cap plate.

Add intermediate 4 × 4 posts between the sills and the undersides of the doubled cap plates. These posts should be situated directly above kneewall studs. The posts are spaced so the distances between posts will create uniform width bays for the windows.

Install back wall studs between the back sill plate and the back cap plates, spaced 16" O.C. Do not attach these studs to the house—they must remain isolated from it structurally.

Construct and attach the roof ridge support wall, featuring a 2 × 6 on edge at the top of the wall. It is easiest to build this wall on the ground and then erect it as a unit. Use a pair of 2 × 4 braces to keep the support wall stable while you attach the rafters.

(continued)

Position a 2 × 4 so it spans from the ridge pole and past the header. Transfer cutting lines onto the workpiece and then cut the outer support legs to length at the marked angle. Attach the legs with deck screws.

Cut the rafters. Set workpieces in position against the 2 × 6 ridge pole and mark the point where they meet the header. Make a birdsmouth cutout in each rafter so it will rest flush on the header (top photo). Cut a decorative profile on each rafter end according to the Diagram on page 55 (bottom photo).

Install the corner rafters. First, attach skew joist hangers to the ends of the ridge pole for the skewed rafters that extend out to the front corners. Nail the rafters into the hangers with joist hanger nails. Toenail them (or drive screws toenail style) to the header.

Fill in the remaining rafters. If you wish you can use joist hanger hardware to attach the rafters to the ridge pole. Or, you can nail or screw them. Spacing between rafters should be uniform.

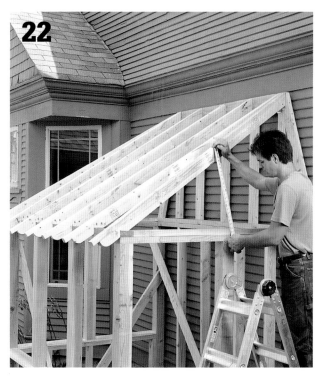

22

Measure from the corner rafters to the end wall headers to find the lengths for the side rafters in the hip wall configuration. Cut 2 × 4 workpieces to length for each rafter.

23

Clamp the side rafter workpieces to a sturdy worksurface and cut the top and bottom angles with a circular saw or jigsaw. The side rafters in this design do not overhang the wall headers. Attach the side rafters with screws driven through pilot holes.

24

Cut kneewall sheathing panels from exterior plywood and attach the panels to the kneewall studs with deck screws.

25

Cut and install trim boards and corner boards according to your plan for siding the kneewall. The tops of the trim boards should butt against the undersides of the sills.

(continued)

Install the siding on the kneewall. Generally, it is a good idea to install siding that matches the house siding. However, a well-chosen contrasting material also can have a pleasing design impact.

Paint the structure prior to adding roof panels and windows with glazing. Two coats of exterior paint is an adequate finish for an exterior lumber product, such as this cedar siding. A base coat of primer is always a good idea.

Also seal the roof structure with paint before installing the roof panels. The charcoal colored paint seen here recalls the color of wrought iron, which was used frequently to construct greenhouses and related Victorian structures, such as orangeries.

Seaming strip

Begin to fasten the roof panels. The twin-wall corrugated polycarbonate panels seen here are fastened directly to the rafters. A panel seaming strip with channels on each edge is fastened to the center rafter to create a transition between the two abutting panels. Install the strip first so you can take more accurate width measurements for cutting the panels.

30

Cut the first roof panel to rough size using a circular saw fitted with a fine-tooth panel-cutting blade. Use a straightedge cutting guide. Or, use a tablesaw if you have access to one.

31

Set one edge of the panel into the slot in the seam strip so it is in the exact position you'll install it. Use a marking pen to trace a cutting line onto the panel, flush with the edge of the end wall. Remove the panel and cut it to size.

32

Set the panel into position and test the fit.

Protecting Panel Ends ▸

Use foil tape to cover the top edges of corrugated panels, protecting the edges from moisture and insects (spiders love to lay eggs in channels like these). The edge on the bottom of the panel can be covered with foil tape also, but you'll need to poke a small weephole at the end of each channel so condensation can drain out. Or, you can use an alternate method such as L-shaped trim to protect the open panel ends (see step 54).

(continued)

33

34

Fasten the roof panels with rubber-gasket equipped pole barn screws driven every 12" at each rafter or purlin. Take care not to overdrive the screws, but be sure they penetrate far enough to create a tight seal.

Cut the side roof panels to fit and attach them with rubber gasket screws. The hip seams will be covered with flashing (see step 37).

35

36

Frame openings for the roof vent cutouts. Install a pair of parallel framing members at the top and bottom of each opening. The tops of the frames should be flush against the roof panel.

Cut out the openings in the roof panels. Drill a starter hole at each corner and then use a drywall saw to make the cuts. Clean up the cut edges with sandpaper.

Install flashing over the hip roof seams. Here, common drip cap flashing is being fastened with rubber-gasket screws driven into the roof rafters.

Cover the gap between the standalone greenhouse structure and the house with metal flashing. Aluminum handy flashing (12" width) can be fastened to the house and lightly creased so it extends over the gap and forms a seal without any physical connection to the greenhouse.

Install roof vent covers. (Here, the installation of the covers was postponed to allow access through the vent holes for installing flashing.) Use a piano hinge to attach each roof vent cover to the roof.

Attach an automatic window vent opener to each roof vent cover, according to the hardware manufacturer's instructions. These devices have internal sensors that lift the vent cover when the greenhouse overheats.

(continued)

Make the greenhouse windows. First, cut the window glazing panels (¼" clear polycarbonate is used here) using a circular saw and a straightedge guide. The glazing should equal the full height and width of the window. For convenience, this greenhouse was designed with all six windows exactly the same size.

Cut the rails and stiles for the window frame to length from 1 × 4 pine stock. Assemble the frame parts around the glazing panel, clamping them together temporarily. Use the glazing panel as an alignment reference: if the panel is square and the frame edges are flush with the glazing all around, your window is square.

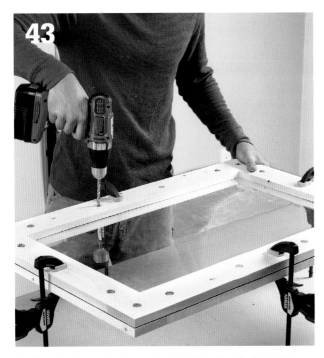

Drill guide holes for the bolts that draw the window parts together. Use a bit that's slightly larger than the diameter of the bolt shafts. This allows for slight expansion and contraction of the window parts as the temperature and humidity level change. Counterbore the bolt holes slightly.

Cut the arched inserts to fit at the top of the window frame opening. Install the inserts in the frame with glue and a couple of brads or pin nails. Install an insert on both the interior and the exterior sides of the window.

45

Attach window stop molding on the perimeter of each window opening, set so the window will be flush with the framed openings. Install fixed windows (if any) by centering the window unit in the opening side to side and driving a few 8d finish nails through pilot holes in the window and into the posts. Angle the pilot holes so the nail will not contact the glazing.

46

Install operable windows by centering the window unit in the opening, using shims to center it side-to-side and top-to-bottom. Hang the windows with exterior-rated pairs of butt hinges.

47

Install door pulls and eyehooks on the interior side of the window. Locate the pulls so they are centered and near the tops of the bottom window frame rails. Locate the eyehooks so there will be slight tension when the hook is in the screw eye—this will limit any rattling of the window.

48

Assemble the door frame. The center stiles should be attached to the frame rails with pocket screws or with deck screws driven toenail style. Clamp the parts together, sandwiching a piece of ¼" polycarbonate between the frames.

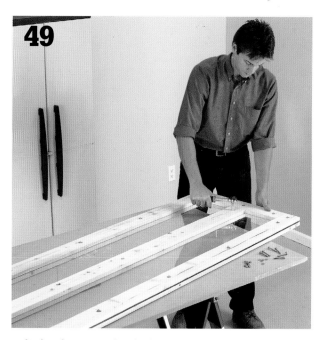

49

Bolt the door together in the same manner as the window, drilling over-sized guide holes and counterboring slightly for the nuts. Install two or three bolts in the center stile area to keep the frame and glazing from separating.

(continued)

50

Cut the door panel inserts with a jigsaw and sand them smooth. Insert them into the framed openings as shown in the Diagram. Secure them on both sides of the glazing, using glue and brads or pin nails.

51

Hang the door. You may find it easier to paint it first. Door stop moldings should be installed so the door is flush with the outside greenhouse wall when closed. Add a latch and a handle. If you want to be able to lock the greenhouse, add a hasp and padlock.

52

Attach a garage door sweep (or comparable weatherstripping product) to cover the gaps between the greenhouse and the house. Flashing, such as drip cap, may be used to cover the gaps on the downsloping sides of the hip roof.

53

Make sure the foundation is clean and dry, then fill the gap between the concrete and the siding with clear silicon caulk.

Add trim elements to complete the roof. Parts of the roof trim system include: Flashing over ridge (A); Clear vent panel (B) attached with piano hinge (C) and automatic closer (D); Seaming strip (E); Metal drip cap for edges (F); ¼ x 1½" wood battens at rafter locations (G); vinyl cap molding at eave edges (H).

Finish the interior. You may add interior wallcoverings if you wish, but the exposed stud bays are good spots for adding shelving. For instructions on building this built-in potting bench, see pages 134 to 137.

DIY Gabled Greenhouse

A greenhouse can be a decorative and functional building that adds beauty to your property. A greenhouse also can be a quick-and-easy, temporary structure that serves a purpose and then disappears. The wood-framed greenhouse seen here fits somewhere between these two types. The sturdy wood construction will hold up for many seasons. The plastic sheeting covering will last one to four or five seasons, depending on the materials you choose, and it is easy to replace when it starts to degrade.

The 5-ft.-high kneewalls in this design provide ample space for installing and working on a conventional-height potting table. The walls also provide some space for plants to grow. For a door, this plan simply employs a sheet of weighted plastic that can be tied out of the way for entry and exit. If you plan to go in and out of the greenhouse frequently, you can purchase a prefabricated greenhouse door from a greenhouse materials supplier. To allow for ventilation in hot weather, we built a wood-frame vent cover that fits over one rafter bay and can be propped open easily.

You can use hand-driven nails or pneumatic framing nails to assemble the frame if you wish, although deck screws make more sense for a small structure like this.

A wood-frame greenhouse with sheet-plastic cover is an inexpensive, semipermanent gardening structure that can be used as a potting area as well as a protective greenhouse.

Tools, Materials & Cutting List

(1) 20 × 50-ft. roll 4- or 6-mil
   polyethylene sheeting
(12) 24"-long pieces of No. 3 rebar
(8) 8" timber screws
Compactable gravel (or drainage gravel)
Excavation tools
Level
Circular saw
Drill
Reciprocating saw
Maul
3" deck screws
Jigsaw
Wire brads
Brad nailer (optional)
Scissors
Utility knife
Tape measure

KEY	NO.	PART	DIMENSION	MATERIAL
A	2	Base ends	3½" × 3½" × 96"	4 × 4 landscape timber
B	2	Base sides	3½" × 3½" × 113"	4 × 4 landscape timber
C	2	Sole plates end	1½" × 3½" × 89"	2 × 4 pressure-treated
D	2	Sole plates side	1½" × 3½" × 120"	2 × 4 pressure-treated
E	12	Wall studs side	1½" × 3½" × 57"	2 × 4
F	1	Ridge support	1½" × 3½" × 91"	2 × 4
G	2	Back studs	1½" × 3½" × 76" *	2 × 4
H	2	Door frame sides	1½" × 3½" × 81" *	2 × 4
I	1	Cripple stud	1½" × 3½" × 16"	2 × 4
J	1	Door header	1½" × 3½" × 32"	2 × 4
K	2	Kneewall caps	1½" × 3½" × 120"	2 × 4
L	1	Ridge pole	1½" × 3½" × 120"	2 × 4
M	12	Rafters	1½" × 3½" × 60" *	2 × 4

*Approximate dimension; take actual length and angle
measurements on structure before cutting.

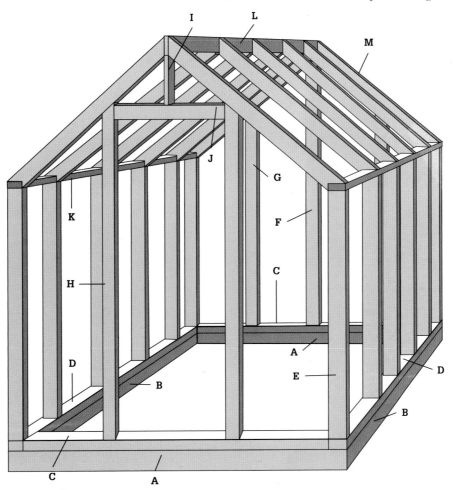

How to Build a Gabled Greenhouse

Prepare the installation area so it is flat and well drained (see page 88); then cut the base timbers (4 × 4 landscape timbers) to length. Arrange the timbers so they are flat and level and create a rectangle with square corners. Drive a pair of 8" timber screws at each corner, using a drill/driver with a nut-driver bit.

Cut 12 pieces of #3 rebar to length at 24" (if necessary), using a reciprocating saw or hacksaw. Drill a ⅜"-dia. pilot hole through each timber, near both ends and in the middle. Confirm that the timber frame is square by measuring diagonally between opposing corners (the measurements must be equal). Drive a rebar spike through each hole, using a sledgehammer, until the bar is flush with the timber.

Cut the sole plates, caps, and studs for the two kneewalls. Mark the stud layouts onto the plates and caps, spacing the studs at 24" on center. Assemble each kneewall by driving 3" deck screws through the sole plates and caps and into the ends of the studs.

Install the kneewalls onto the timber base. Set each wall onto a side timber so the sole plate is flush with the ends and side edges of the timber frame. Fasten the sole plate to the timber with 3" deck screws.

5

Temporary post

Begin the end walls by cutting and installing the end sole plates to fit between the side plates, using 3" deck screws. Cut the ridge support posts to length. Install one post at the center of each end sole plate, using screws or nails driven at an angle (toenailed). Check the posts with a level to make sure they're plumb before fastening. *Note: The front post will be cut later to create the door opening.*

6

Ridge pole

Set the ridge pole on top of the support posts and check it for level. Install temporary cross braces between the outer kneewall studs and each support post, making sure the posts are plumb before fastening the braces. Double-check the posts and ridge for plumb and level, respectively.

7

Create a template rafter by cutting a 2 × 4 at about 66" long. Hold the board against the end of the ridge and the top outside corner of a kneewall cap. Trace along the face of the ridge and the cap to mark the cutting lines for the rafter. Cut along the lines, then test-fit the rafter and make any necessary adjustments for a good fit.

8

Mark and cut the remaining rafters, using the template to trace the cutting lines onto each piece of stock. *Tip: A jigsaw or handsaw is handy for making the bottom-end cuts without having to over-cut, as you would with a circular saw.*

(continued)

Install the rafters, using the deck screws driven at an angle into the kneewall caps and the ridge. The rafters should be aligned with the studs and perpendicular to the ridge.

Mark the two door frame studs by holding them plumb and tracing along the bottom edge of the rafter above. Position the studs on-the-flat, so the inside edge of each is 16" from the center of the support post (for a 32"-wide door, as shown). Install the studs with angled screws. Cut and install two studs on the rear end wall, spacing them evenly between the kneewalls and support post.

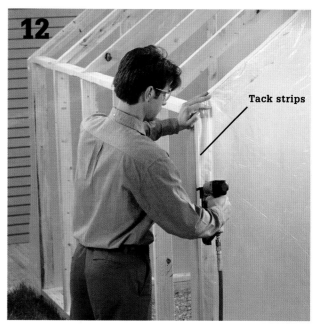

Tack strips

Complete the door frame: Mark the front support post 78" (or as desired) up from the sole plate. Make a square cut at the mark, using a circular saw or cordless trim saw (inset), then remove the bottom portion of the post. Cut the door header (from the post waste) to fit between the door studs. Fasten the header to the door studs and remaining post piece with screws.

Begin covering the greenhouse with the desired cover material (6-mil poly sheeting shown here), starting at the end walls. Cut the sheeting roughly to size and secure it to the framing with wood tack strips fastened with wire brads. Secure the sheeting at the top first, the sides next, and the bottom last. Trim the excess material along the edges of the strips with a utility knife.

13

Attach sheeting to the edges of the sole plate on one side of the greenhouse, then roll the sheeting over the top and down the other side. Draw it taut, and cut it a little long with scissors. Secure the sheeting to the other sole plate (using tack strips), then attach it to the outside edges of the corner studs.

14

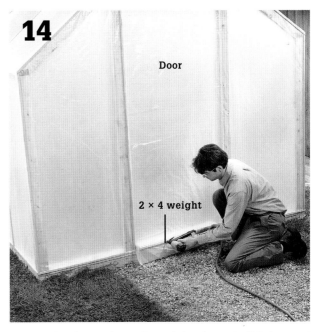

Door

2 × 4 weight

Create the door, using a piece of sheeting cut a little larger than the door opening (or purchase a door kit; see photo below). Secure the top of the door to the header with a tack strip. Weight the door's bottom end with a 2 × 4 scrap cut to length.

Option: Make a vent window. First, cut a hole in the roof in one rafter bay and tack the cut edges of the plastic to the faces (not the edges) of the rafters, ridge pole and wall cap. Then build a frame from 1 × 2 stock that will span from the ridge to the top of the kneewall and extend a couple of inches past the rafters at the side of the opening. Clad the frame with plastic sheeting and attach it to the ridge pole with butt hinges. Install a screw-eye latch to secure it at the bottom. Make and attach props if you wish.

Greenhouse Doors ›

Plastic door kits, available from greenhouse suppliers, include self-adhesive zipper strips and are easy to roll up and tie for access or ventilation. You can also create your own roll-up door with zipper strips and plastic sheeting purchased from a building center.

Freestanding Kit Greenhouse

Building a greenhouse from a prefabricated kit offers many advantages. Kits are usually very easy to assemble because all parts are prefabricated and the lightweight materials are easy to handle. The quality of kit greenhouses varies widely, though, and buying from a reputable manufacturer will help ensure that you get many years of service from your greenhouse.

If you live in a snowy climate, you may need to either provide extra support within the greenhouse or be ready to remove snow whenever there is a significant snowfall because the lightweight aluminum frame members can easily bend under a heavy load. Before buying a kit, make sure to check on how snowfall may affect it.

Kit greenhouses are offered by many different manufacturers, and the exact assembly technique you use will depend on the specifics of your kit. Make sure you read the printed instructions carefully, as they may vary from this project.

The kit we're demonstrating here is made from aluminum frame pieces and transparent polycarbonate panels and is designed to be installed over a subbase of gravel about 5" thick. Other kits may have different subbase requirements.

When you purchase your kit, make sure to uncrate it and examine all the parts before you begin. Make sure all the pieces are there and that there are no damaged panels or bent frame members.

A perfectly flat and level base is crucial to any kit greenhouse, so make sure to work carefully. Try to do the work on a dry day with no wind, as the panels and frame pieces can be hard to manage on a windy day. Never try to build a kit greenhouse by yourself. At least one helper is mandatory, and you'll do even better with two or three.

Construction of a kit greenhouse consists of four basic steps: laying the base, assembling the frame, assembling the windows and doors, and attaching the panels.

Kit greenhouses come in a wide range of shapes, sizes, and quality. The best ones have tempered-glass glazing and are rather expensive. The one at left is glazed with corrugated polyethylene and is at the low end of the cost spectrum.

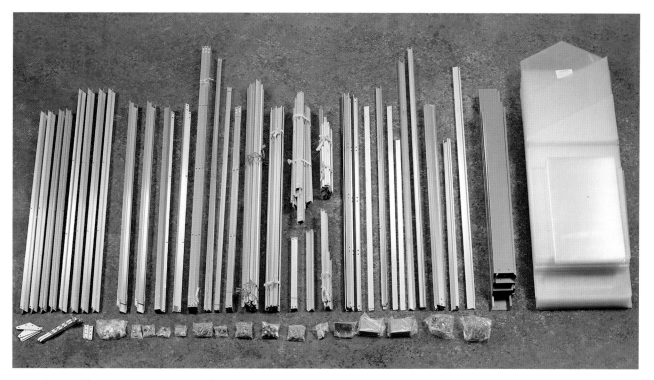

Organize and inspect the contents of your kit cartons to make sure all of the parts are present and in good condition. Most manuals will have a checklist. Staging the parts makes for a more efficient assembly. Just be sure not to leave any small parts loose, and do not store parts in high-traffic areas.

A cordless drill/driver with a nut-driver accessory will trim hours off of your assembly time compared with using only hand tools.

Rent outdoor power equipment if you need to do significant regrading to create a flat, level building base. Be sure to have your local utility company inspect for any buried utility lines first. (You may prefer to hire a landscaping company to do re-grading work for you.)

How to Build a Freestanding Kit Greenhouse

Establish layout lines for the gravel subbase, using stakes or batterboards and mason's string. The excavation area for the subbase should be at least 2" wider and longer than the outside dimensions of the greenhouse kit base. Make sure the layout is perfectly square (the lines are perpendicular to one another) by measuring diagonally between opposing corners: the layout is square when the measurements are equal.

Excavate the site to a depth of 5", using the layout strings as a guide. As you work, use a straight 2 × 4 and a 4-ft. level to check the excavation to make sure it is level and flat. Tamp any loose soil with a plate compactor or hand tamp. Cover the excavation with commercial-grade landscape fabric (do not use plastic; the membrane must be water-permeable). Fill the area with 2 or 3" of compactible gravel, grade and level it, then tamp it thoroughly. Add more gravel, level, and tamp for a final subbase depth of 5".

Assemble the greenhouse base, using the provided corner and end connectors. Set the base onto the subbase and make sure the base is level. Measure the diagonals to check for square, as before. Add a top dressing of gravel or other fill material inside the base, up to about 1" below the base's top lip. Smooth and level the gravel as before.

Attach the bottom wall plates to the base pieces so that the flanged edges face outside the greenhouse. In most systems, the floor plates will interlock with one another, end to end, with built-in brackets.

Fasten the four corner studs to the bottom wall plates, using hold-down connectors and bolts. In this system, each corner stud is secured with two connectors.

Install the ceiling plates: Assemble the pieces for each side ceiling plate. Attach each side plate against the inside of the two corner studs along each side of the greenhouse, making sure the gutter is positioned correctly. Attach the front ceiling plate to the outsides of the corner studs at the front of the building.

(continued)

Attach the other side ceiling plate
along the other side, flat against the inside of the corner studs. Then attach corner brackets to the rear studs, and construct the back top plate by attaching the rear braces to the corners and joining the braces together with stud connectors.

Corner bracket

Stud connectors

Fasten the left and right rear studs
to the outside of the rear floor plate, making sure the top ends are sloping upward, toward the peak of the greenhouse. Attach the center rear studs to the rear floor plate, fastening them to the stud connectors used to join the rear braces.

Backwards and Forwards ▸

With some kits you need to go backward to go forward. Because the individual parts of your kit depend upon one another for support, you may be required to tack all the parts together with bolts first and then undo and remake individual connections as you go before you can finalize them. For example, in this kit you must undo the track/ brace connections one at a time so you can insert the bolt heads for the stud connectors into the track.

9 Install the doorway studs at either side of the greenhouse door, on the front end of the building. Install the side studs along both side walls of the greenhouse.

10 Add diagonal struts, as directed by the manufacturer. The struts help to stiffen and square up the walls. As you work, take diagonal measurements between opposing corners at the tops of the walls, to make sure the structure remains square.

11 Fasten the gable-end stud extensions to the front and back walls of the greenhouse. The top ends of the studs should angle upward, toward the peak of the greenhouse.

12 Assemble the roof frame on a flat area near the wall assembly. First assemble the crown-beam pieces; then attach the rafters to the crown, one by one. The end rafters, called the crown beams, have a different configuration, so make sure not to confuse them.

(continued)

With at least one helper, lift the roof into place onto the wall frames. The gable end studs should meet the outside edges of the crown beams, and the ends of the crown beams rest on the outer edge of the corner bracket. Fasten in place with the provided nuts and bolts.

Attach the side braces and the roof-window support beams to the underside of the roof rafters, as specified by the manufacturer's instructions.

Build the roof windows by first connecting the two side window frames to the top window frame. Slide the window panel into the frame; then secure it by attaching the bottom window frame. Slide the window into the slot at the top of the roof crown; then gradually lower it in place. Attach the window stop to the window support beam.

Assemble the doors, making sure the top slider/roller bar and the bottom slider bar are correctly positioned. Lift the door panels up into place onto the top and bottom wall plates.

Install the panels one-by-one, using panel clips. Begin with the large wall panels. Position each panel and secure it by snapping a clip into the frame, at the intervals specified by the manufacturer's instructions.

Add the upper panels. At the gable ends, the upper panels will be supported by panel connectors that allow the top panel to be supported by the bottom panel. The lower panels should be installed already.

Install the roof panels and roof-window panels so that the top edges fit up under the edge of the crown or window support and the bottom edges align over the gutters.

Test the door and window operation, and make any necessary adjustments so they open and close smoothly.

PVC Hoophouse

The hoophouse is a popular garden structure for two main reasons: it is cheap to build and easy to build. In many agricultural areas you will see hoophouses snaking across vast fields of seedlings, protecting the delicate plants at their most vulnerable stages. Because they are portable and easy to disassemble, they can be removed when the plants are established and less vulnerable.

While hoophouses are not intended as inexpensive substitutes for real greenhouses, they do serve an important agricultural purpose. And building your own is a fun project that the whole family can enjoy.

The hoophouse shown here is essentially a Quonset-style frame of bent ¾" PVC tubing draped with sheet plastic. Each semicircular frame is actually made from two 10-ft. lengths of tubing that fit into a plastic fitting at the apex of the curve. PVC tubes tend to stay together simply by friction-fitting into the fittings, so you don't normally need to solvent glue the connections (this is important to the easy-to-disassemble and store feature). If you experience problems with the frame connections separating, try cutting 4- to 6"-long pieces of ½" (outside diameter) PVC tubing and inserting them into the tubes and fittings like splines. This will stiffen the connections.

A hoophouse is a temporary agricultural structure designed to be low-cost and portable. Also called Quonset houses and tunnel houses, hoophouses provide shelter and shade (depending on the film you use) and protection from wind and the elements. They will boost heat during the day, but are less efficient than paneled greenhouses for extending the growing season.

PVC Hoophouse

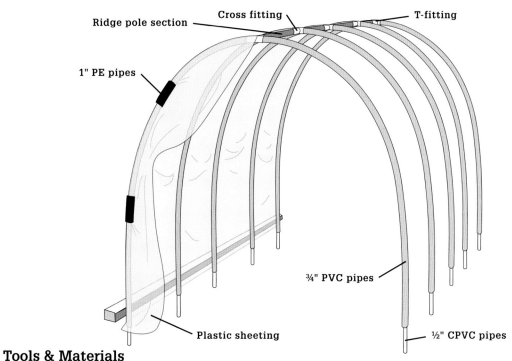

Ridge pole section — Cross fitting — T-fitting

1" PE pipes

¾" PVC pipes

Plastic sheeting

½" CPVC pipes

Tools & Materials

Hand sledge
Plastic tubing cutter or hacksaw
Wood or rubber mallet
Circular saw
Stapler
Drill
Utility knife
Stakes and mason's string
Eye and ear protection
Tape measure

Work gloves
(5) ½" × 10 ft. CPVC pipes
(14) ¾" × 10 ft. PVC pipes
(3) ¾" PVC cross fittings
(2) ¾" PVC T-fittings
16 × 24 ft. clear or translucent plastic sheeting
(4) 16-ft. pressure-treated 2 × 4s
2½" deck screws
(1) 1" × 6 ft. PE tubing (black, flexible)

Building a Hoophouse ▸

- Space frame hoops about 3 ft. apart.
- Leave ridge members a fraction of an inch (not more than ¼") shorter than the span, which will cause the structure to be slightly shorter on top than at the base. This helps stabilize the structure.
- Orient the structure so the wall faces into the prevailing wind rather than the end openings.
- If you are using long-lasting greenhouse fabric for the cover, protect the investment by spray-painting the frame hoops with primer so there is no plastic-to-plastic contact.

- Because hoophouses are temporary structures that are designed to be disassembled or moved regularly, you do not need to include a base.
- Hoophouses can act a lot like boat sails and will fly away if they're not anchored securely. Be sure to stake each hoop to the ground at both ends (with 30"-long or longer stakes), and carefully weight down the cover with boards (as shown here) or piles of dirt.
- Clip the hoophouse covers to the end frames. Clips fastened at the intermediate hoops will either fly off or tear the plastic cover in windy conditions.

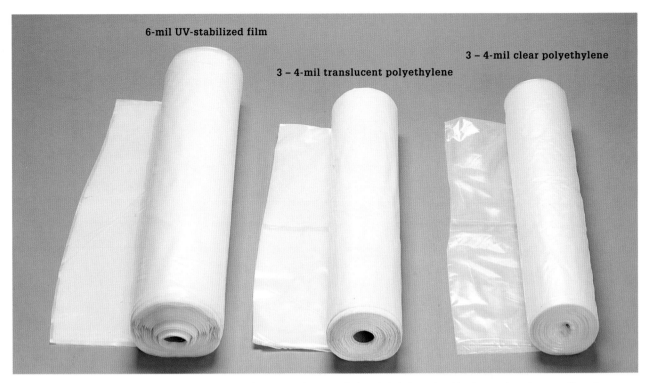

6-mil UV-stabilized film

3 – 4-mil translucent polyethylene

3 – 4-mil clear polyethylene

Sheet plastic is an inexpensive material for creating a greenhouse. Obviously, it is less durable than polycarbonate, fiberglass or glass panels. But UV-stabilized films at least 6-mil thick can be rated to withstand four years or more of exposure. Inexpensive polyethylene sheeting (the kind you find at hardware stores) will hold up for a year or two, but it becomes brittle when exposed to sunlight. Some greenhouse builders prefer to use clear plastic sheeting to maximize the sunlight penetration, but the cloudiness of translucent poly makes it effective for diffusing light and preventing overheating. For the highest quality film coverings, look for film rated for greenhouse and agricultural use.

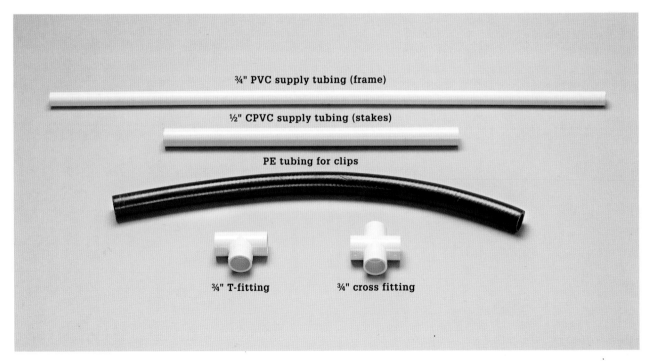

¾" PVC supply tubing (frame)

½" CPVC supply tubing (stakes)

PE tubing for clips

¾" T-fitting   **¾" cross fitting**

Plastic tubing and fittings used to build this hoophouse include: Light duty ¾" PVC tubing for the frame (do not use CPVC—it is too rigid and won't bend properly); ½" CPVC supply tubing for the frame stakes (rigidity is good here); Polyethylene (PE) tubing for the cover clips; T-fittings and cross fittings to join the frame members.

How to Build a PVC Hoophouse

Lay out the installation area, using stakes and mason's string. Stake the four corners to create a rectangle that is 10 ft. wide and 15 ft. long. To make sure the layout is square (the strings are perpendicular), measure diagonally between opposing corner stakes: when the measurements are equal, the layout is square.

Cut a 30"-long stake from ½" CPVC pipe for each leg of each frame hoop. Plastic pipe is easy to cut with a plastic tubing cutter or a hacksaw. Mark the layout strings at 36" intervals, using tape or a marker. Drive a stake at each marked location, using a hand sledge or hammer. Keep the stakes plumb and drive them in 20" deep, so only 10" is above ground.

Join the two legs for each frame hoop with a fitting. Use a tee fitting for the end hoop frames and a cross fitting for the intermediate hoop frames. No priming or solvent gluing is necessary. (The friction-fit should be sufficient, but it helps if you tap on the end of the fitting with a mallet to seat it.)

(continued)

Slip the open end of one hoop-frame leg over a corner stake so the pipe is flush against the ground. Then bend the pipes so you can fit the other leg end over the stake at the opposite corner. If you experience problems with the pipes pulling out of the top fitting, simply tape the joints temporarily until the structure frame is completed.

Continue adding hoop frames until you reach the other end of the structure. Wait until all the hoop frames are in place before you begin installing the ridge poles. Make sure the cross fittings on the intermediate hoop frames are aligned correctly to accept the ridge poles.

Add the ridge pole sections to tie together the hoop frames. The correct length for the ridge poles depends on the socket depth of the fitting you use, so you'll have to measure the fittings and calculate length of the ridge pieces. If necessary, tap the end of each ridge piece with a wood or rubber mallet to seat it fully in the fitting socket.

Cut four 2 × 4s to length (15 ft. as shown). Cut the cover material to length at 16 ft. (or as needed so it is several inches longer than the house at both ends). Staple one edge of the cover to one of the 2 × 4s, keeping the material taut and flat as you work from one end to the other

8

Lay another 2 × 4 over the first so their ends and edges are flush and the cover material is sandwiched in between. Fasten the two boards together with 2½" deck screws driven every 24" or so. Position the board assembly along the base of the hoops and pull the free end of the material over the tops of the hoops to the other side.

9

Pull the cover taut on the other side of the house, and repeat the process of stapling it to one board then sandwiching with the other.

10

Secure the cover at the ends with 6" lengths of 1" PE tubing. Cut the tubing pieces to length, then slit them lengthwise to create simple clips. Use at least six clips at each end of the house. Do not use clips on the intermediate hoops.

Option: Make doors by clipping a piece of cover material to each end. (It's best to do this before attaching the main cover.) Then cut a slit down the center of the end material. You can tie or tape the door material to the sides when you want it open and weigh down the pieces with a board or brick to keep the door shut. This solution is low-tech but effective.

Shed-style Greenhouse

This unique outbuilding is part greenhouse and part shed, making it perfect for a year-round garden space or backyard sunroom, or even an artist's studio. The front facade is dominated by windows—four 29 × 72" windows on the roof, plus four 29 × 18" windows on the front wall. When appointed as a greenhouse, two long planting tables inside the shed let you water and tend to plants without flooding the floor. If gardening isn't in your plans, you can omit the tables and cover the entire floor with plywood, or perhaps fill in between the floor timbers with pavers or stones.

Some other details that make this 10 × 12-ft. shed stand out are the homemade Dutch door, with top and bottom halves that you can open together or independently, and its traditional saltbox shape. The roof covering shown here consists of standard asphalt shingles, but cedar shingles make for a nice upgrade.

Because sunlight plays a central role in this shed design, consider the location and orientation carefully. To avoid shadows from nearby structures, maintain a distance between the shed and the structure that's at least 2½ times the height of the obstruction. With all of that sunlight, the temperature inside the shed is another important consideration. You may want to install some roof vents to release hot air and water vapor.

Building the Shed-style Greenhouse involves a few unconventional construction steps. First, the side walls are framed in two parts: You build the square portion of the end walls first, then move onto the roof framing. After the rafters are up, you complete the "rake," or angled, sections of the side walls. This makes it easy to measure for each wall stud, rather than having to calculate the lengths beforehand. Second, the shed's 4 × 4 floor structure also serves as its foundation. The plywood floor decking goes on after the walls are installed, rather than before.

Tools & Materials ▶

Circular saw	Level	Eye & ear protection	Caulk
Power miter saw	Hand tamper	Framing square	Caulk gun
Hammer	Ladder	Plumb bob	Screw driver

With slight modifications, many ordinary sheds can be redesigned as greenhouses. The addition of glass roof panels turns this shed design into an effective greenhouse.

Cutting List

DESCRIPTION	QUANTITY/SIZE	MATERIAL
Foundation/Floor		
Foundation base & interior drainage beds	5 cu. yds.	Compactible gravel
Floor joists & blocking	7 @ 10'	4 × 4 pressure-treated landscape timbers
4 × 4 blocking	1 @ 10' 1 @ 8'	4 × 4 pressure-treated landscape timbers
Box sills (rim joists)	2 @ 12'	2 × 4 pressure-treated
Nailing cleats & 2 × 4 blocking	2 @ 8'	2 × 4 pressure-treated
Floor sheathing	2 sheets @ 4 × 8'	¾" ext.-grade plywood
Wall Framing		
Bottom plates	2 @ 12', 2 @ 10'	2 × 4 pressure-treated
Top plates	4 @ 12', 2 @ 10'	2 × 4
Studs	43 @ 8'	2 × 4
Door header & jack studs	3 @ 8'	2 × 4
Rafter header	2 @ 12'	2 × 8
Roof Framing		
Rafters — A & C, & nailers	10 @ 12'	2 × 4
Rafters — B & lookouts	10 @ 10'	2 × 4
Ridge board	1 @ 14'	2 × 6
Exterior Finishes		
Rear fascia	1 @ 14'	1 × 6 cedar
Rear soffit	1 @ 14'	1 × 8 cedar
Gable fascia (rake board) & soffit	4 @ 16'	1 × 6 cedar
Siding	10 sheets @ 4 × 8'	⅝" Texture 1-11 plywood siding
Siding flashing	10 linear ft.	Metal Z-flashing
Trim*	4 @ 12' 1 @ 12'	1 × 4 cedar 1 × 2 cedar
Wall corner trim	6 @ 8'	1 × 4 cedar
Roofing		
Sheathing	5 sheets @ 4 × 8'	½" exterior-grade plywood roof sheathing
15# building paper	1 roll	
Drip edge	72 linear ft.	Metal drip edge
Shingles	2⅔ squares	Asphalt shingles — 250# per sq. min.

DESCRIPTION	QUANTITY/SIZE	MATERIAL
Windows		
Glazing	4 pieces @ 31¼ × 76½" 4 pieces @ 31¼ × 20¾"	¼"-thick clear plastic glazing
Window stops	12 @ 10'	2 × 4
Glazing tape	60 linear ft.	
Clear exterior caulk	5 tubes	
Door		
Trim & stops	3 @ 8'	1 × 2 cedar
Surround	4 @ 8'	2 × 2 cedar
Z-flashing	3 linear ft.	
Plant Tables (Optional)		
Front table, top & trim	6 @ 12'	1 × 6 cedar or pressure-treated
Front table, plates & legs	4 @ 12'	2 × 4 pressure-treated
Rear table, top & trim	6 @ 8'	1 × 6 cedar or pressure-treated
Rear table, plates & legs	4 @ 8'	2 × 4 pressure-treated
Fasteners & Hardware		
16d galvanized common nails	5 lbs.	
16d common nails	16 lbs.	
10d common nails	1½ lbs.	
8d galvanized common nails	2 lbs.	
8d galvanized box nails	3 lbs.	
10d galvanized finish nails	2½ lbs.	
8d galvanized siding nails	8 lbs.	
1" galvanized roofing nails	7 lbs.	
8d galvanized casing nails	3 lbs.	
6d galvanized casing nails	2 lbs.	
Door hinges with screws	4 @ 3½"	Corrosion-resistant hinges
Door handle	1	
Sliding bolt latch	1	
Construction adhesive	1 tube	

Note: The 1 × 4 trim bevel at the bottom of the sloped windows can be steeper (45° or more) so the trim slopes away from the window if there is concern that the trim may capture water running down the glazing (see WINDOW DETAIL, page 100).

Building Section

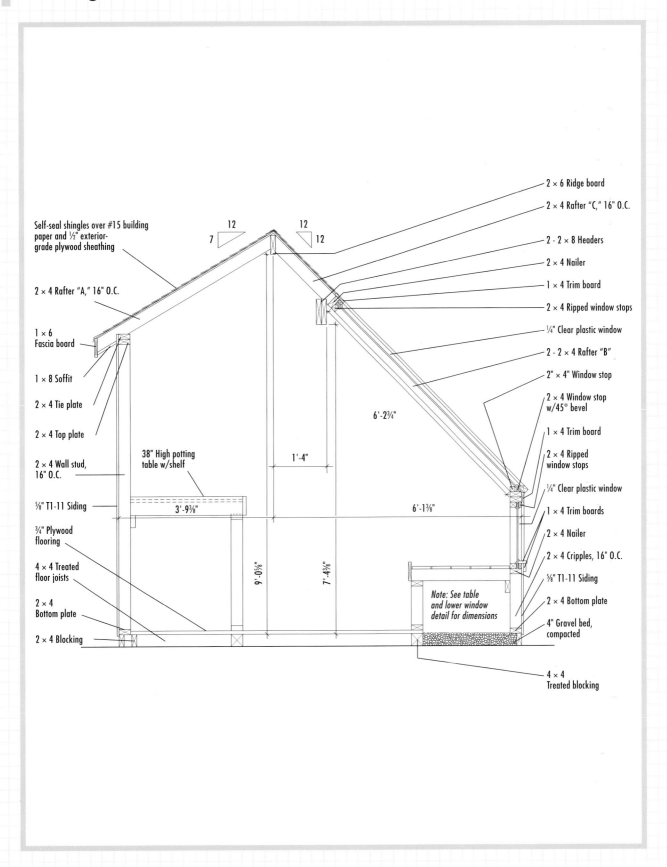

Self-seal shingles over #15 building paper and ½" exterior-grade plywood sheathing

2 × 4 Rafter "A," 16" O.C.

1 × 6 Fascia board

1 × 8 Soffit

2 × 4 Tie plate

2 × 4 Top plate

2 × 4 Wall stud, 16" O.C.

⅝" T1-11 Siding

¾" Plywood flooring

4 × 4 Treated floor joists

2 × 4 Bottom plate

2 × 4 Blocking

38" High potting table w/shelf

3'-9⅜"

9'-0⅝"

7'-4⅜"

1'-4"

12
7

12
12

6'-2¾"

6'-1⅜"

Note: See table and lower window detail for dimensions

2 × 6 Ridge board

2 × 4 Rafter "C," 16" O.C.

2 - 2 × 8 Headers

2 × 4 Nailer

1 × 4 Trim board

2 × 4 Ripped window stops

¼" Clear plastic window

2 - 2 × 4 Rafter "B"

2" × 4" Window stop

2 × 4 Window stop w/45° bevel

1 × 4 Trim board

2 × 4 Ripped window stops

¼" Clear plastic window

1 × 4 Trim boards

2 × 4 Nailer

2 × 4 Cripples, 16" O.C.

⅝" T1-11 Siding

2 × 4 Bottom plate

4" Gravel bed, compacted

4 × 4 Treated blocking

Floor Framing Plan

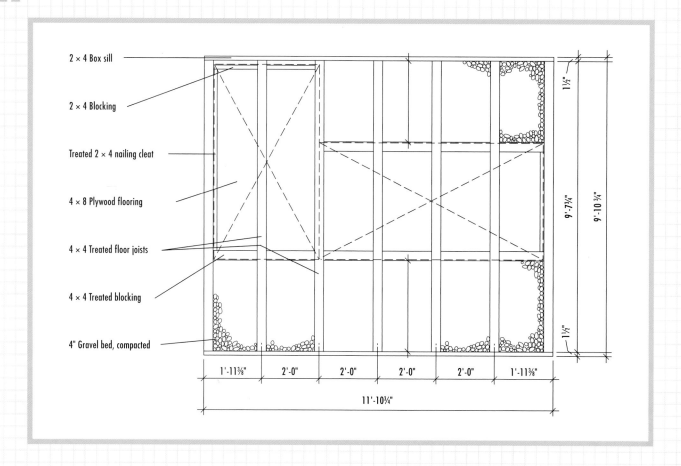

2 × 4 Box sill

2 × 4 Blocking

Treated 2 × 4 nailing cleat

4 × 8 Plywood flooring

4 × 4 Treated floor joists

4 × 4 Treated blocking

4" Gravel bed, compacted

1½"

9'-7¾"

9'-10¾"

1½"

1'-11⅜" 2'-0" 2'-0" 2'-0" 2'-0" 1'-11⅜"

11'-10¾"

Left Side Framing

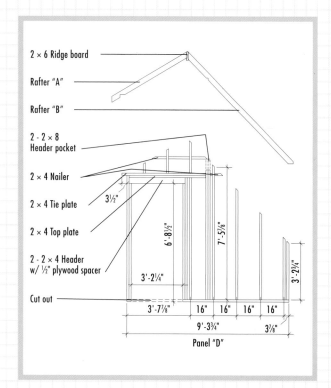

2 × 6 Ridge board

Rafter "A"

Rafter "B"

2 - 2 × 8 Header pocket

2 × 4 Nailer

2 × 4 Tie plate

2 × 4 Top plate

2 - 2 × 4 Header w/ ½" plywood spacer

Cut out

3½"

6'-8½"

7'-5⅝"

3'-2¼"

3'-2¾"

3'-7⅞" 16" 16" 16" 16"

9'-3¾" 3⅞"

Panel "D"

Right Side Framing

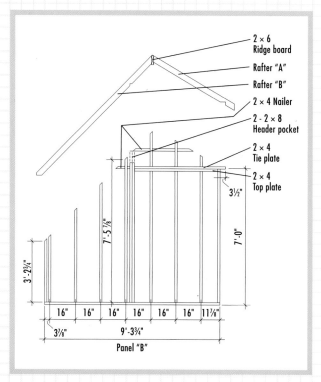

2 × 6 Ridge board

Rafter "A"

Rafter "B"

2 × 4 Nailer

2 - 2 × 8 Header pocket

2 × 4 Tie plate

2 × 4 Top plate

3½"

7'-5⅞"

7'-0"

3'-2¾"

16" 16" 16" 16" 16" 16" 1⅞"

3⅞" 9'-3¾"

Panel "B"

Front Framing

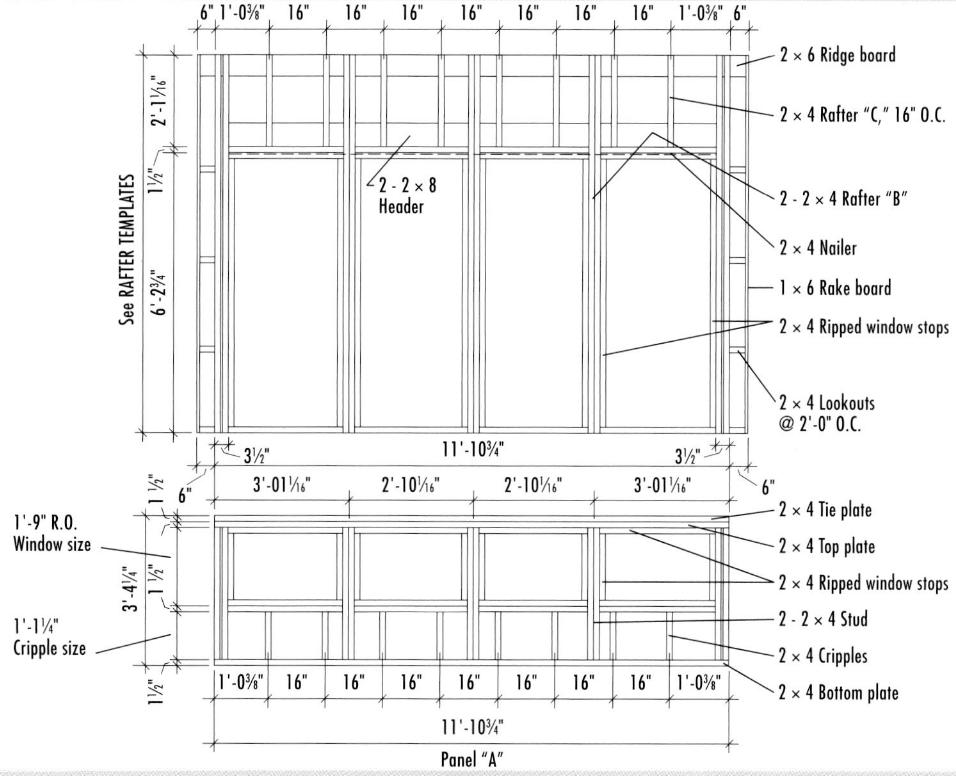
6" 1'-0⅜" 16" 16" 16" 16" 16" 16" 16" 1'-0⅜" 6"
2 × 6 Ridge board
2 × 4 Rafter "C," 16" O.C.
2 - 2 × 4 Rafter "B"
2 × 4 Nailer
1 × 6 Rake board
2 × 4 Ripped window stops
2 × 4 Lookouts @ 2'-0" O.C.
2 - 2 × 8 Header
See RAFTER TEMPLATES
2'-1 1/16"
1½"
6'-2¾"
3½"
11'-10¾"
3½"
6"
3'-01/16"
2'-101/16"
2'-101/16"
3'-01/16"
6"
2 × 4 Tie plate
2 × 4 Top plate
2 × 4 Ripped window stops
2 - 2 × 4 Stud
2 × 4 Cripples
2 × 4 Bottom plate
1'-9" R.O. Window size
1'-1¼" Cripple size
1½"
3'-4¼"
1½"
1½"
1'-0⅜" 16" 16" 16" 16" 16" 16" 16" 1'-0⅜"
11'-10¾"
Panel "A"

Rear Framing

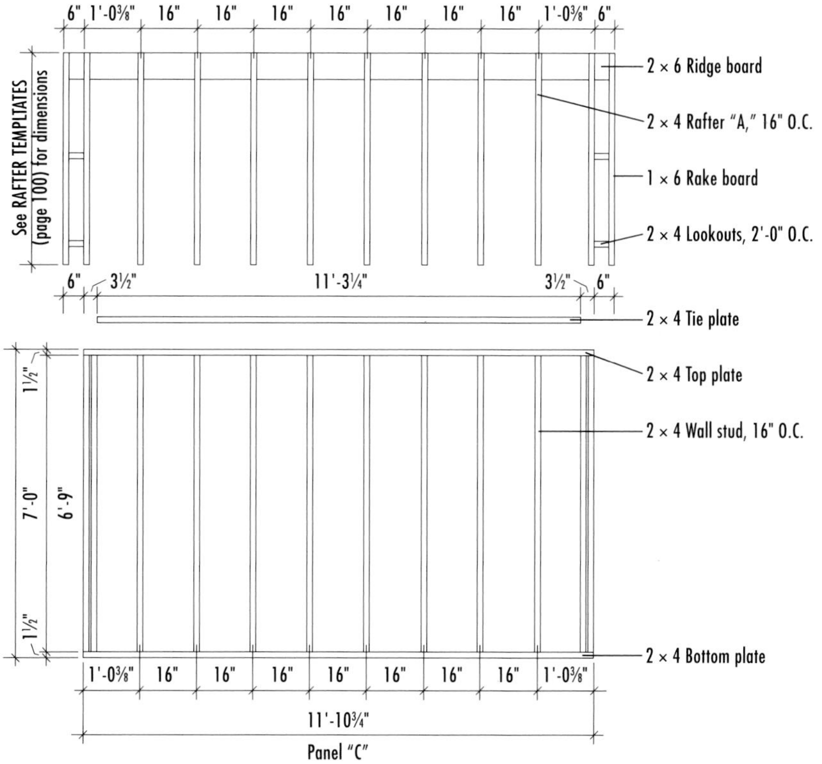
6" 1'-0⅜" 16" 16" 16" 16" 16" 16" 16" 1'-0⅜" 6"
2 × 6 Ridge board
2 × 4 Rafter "A," 16" O.C.
1 × 6 Rake board
2 × 4 Lookouts, 2'-0" O.C.
See RAFTER TEMPLATES (page 100) for dimensions
6" 3½" 11'-3¼" 3½" 6"
2 × 4 Tie plate
2 × 4 Top plate
2 × 4 Wall stud, 16" O.C.
2 × 4 Bottom plate
1½"
7'-0"
6'-9"
1½"
1'-0⅜" 16" 16" 16" 16" 16" 16" 16" 1'-0⅜"
11'-10¾"
Panel "C"

Front Elevation

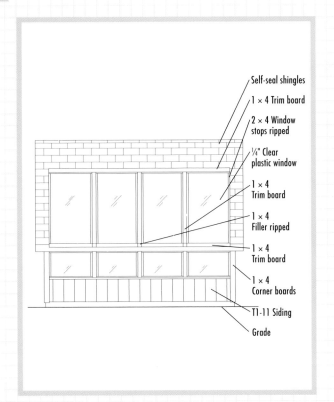

Self-seal shingles

1 × 4 Trim board

2 × 4 Window stops ripped

¼" Clear plastic window

1 × 4 Trim board

1 × 4 Filler ripped

1 × 4 Trim board

1 × 4 Corner boards

T1-11 Siding

Grade

Rear Elevation

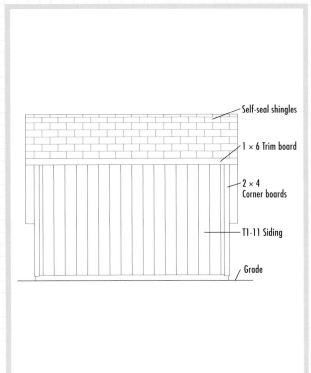

Self-seal shingles

1 × 6 Trim board

2 × 4 Corner boards

T1-11 Siding

Grade

Right Side Elevation

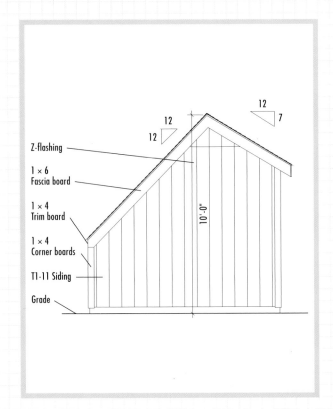

12
12
12
7

Z-flashing

1 × 6 Fascia board

1 × 4 Trim board

1 × 4 Corner boards

T1-11 Siding

Grade

10'-0"

Soffit Detail

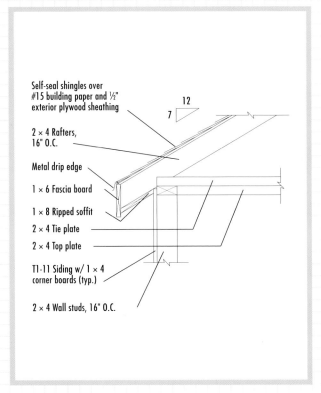

Self-seal shingles over #15 building paper and ½" exterior plywood sheathing

2 × 4 Rafters, 16" O.C.

Metal drip edge

1 × 6 Fascia board

1 × 8 Ripped soffit

2 × 4 Tie plate

2 × 4 Top plate

T1-11 Siding w/ 1 × 4 corner boards (typ.)

2 × 4 Wall studs, 16" O.C.

12
7

Front & Side Door Construction

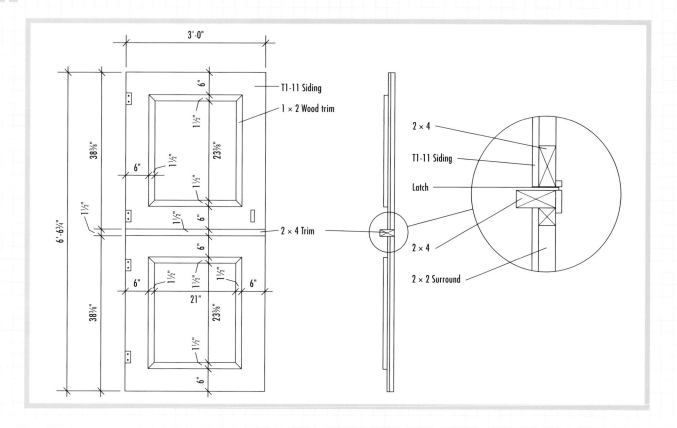

Front & Side Door Construction (Door Jamb, Rear, Door Header)

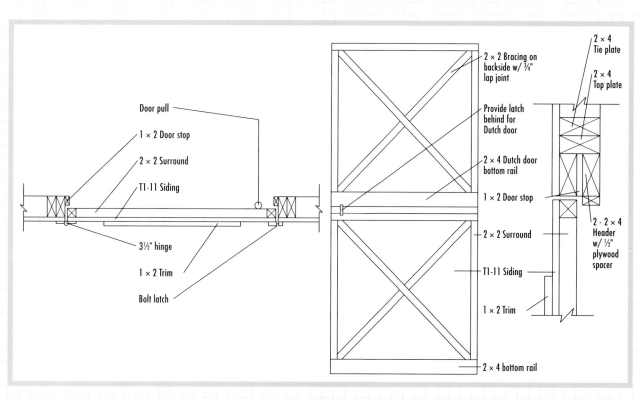

Header & Window Detail

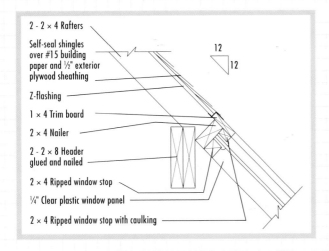

2 - 2 × 4 Rafters

Self-seal shingles over #15 building paper and ½" exterior plywood sheathing

Z-flashing

1 × 4 Trim board

2 × 4 Nailer

2 - 2 × 8 Header glued and nailed

2 × 4 Ripped window stop

¼" Clear plastic window panel

2 × 4 Ripped window stop with caulking

12
12

Window Section

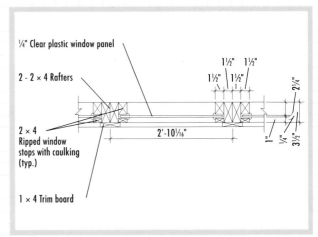

¼" Clear plastic window panel

2 - 2 × 4 Rafters

2 × 4 Ripped window stops with caulking (typ.)

1 × 4 Trim board

1½" 1½"
1½" 1½"
2¼"

2'-10¹⁄₁₆"

1" ¼" 3½"

Window Detail

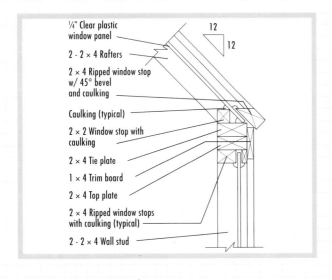

¼" Clear plastic window panel

2 - 2 × 4 Rafters

2 × 4 Ripped window stop w/ 45° bevel and caulking

Caulking (typical)

2 × 2 Window stop with caulking

2 × 4 Tie plate

1 × 4 Trim board

2 × 4 Top plate

2 × 4 Ripped window stops with caulking (typical)

2 - 2 × 4 Wall stud

12
12

Table & Lower Window Detail

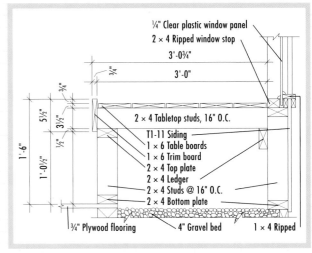

¼" Clear plastic window panel

2 × 4 Ripped window stop

3'-0¾"

3'-0"

¾"

5½"

3½"

½"

1'-6"

1'-0½"

2 × 4 Tabletop studs, 16" O.C.

T1-11 Siding

1 × 6 Table boards

1 × 6 Trim board

2 × 4 Top plate

2 × 4 Ledger

2 × 4 Studs @ 16" O.C.

2 × 4 Bottom plate

¾" Plywood flooring

4" Gravel bed

1 × 4 Ripped

Rafter Templates

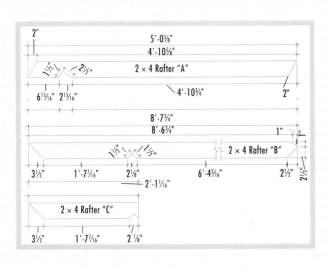

2"

5'-0⅝"

4'-10⅝"

2 × 4 Rafter "A"

1½" 2½"

4'-10¾"

2"

6¹⁵⁄₁₆" 2¹⁵⁄₁₆"

8'-7¾"

8'-6¾"

1"

1½" 1½"

2 × 4 Rafter "B"

2½"

3½" 1'-7⁷⁄₁₆" 2⅛" 6'-4³⁄₁₆" 2½" 2½"

2'-1¹⁄₁₆"

2 × 4 Rafter "C"

3½" 1'-7⁷⁄₁₆" 2⅛"

Rake Board Detail

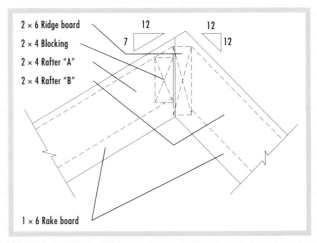

2 × 6 Ridge board

2 × 4 Blocking

2 × 4 Rafter "A"

2 × 4 Rafter "B"

1 × 6 Rake board

12 12
7 12

How to Build the Shed-style Greenhouse

Build the foundation, following the basic steps used for a wooden skid foundation. First, prepare a bed of compacted gravel. Make sure the bed is flat and level. Cut seven 4 × 4" × 10 ft. pressure-treated posts down to 115¾" to serve as floor joists. Position the joists as shown in the FLOOR FRAMING PLAN. Level each joist, and make sure all are level with one another and the ends are flush. Add rim joists and blocking: Cut two 12-ft. 2 × 4s (142¾") for rim joists. Fasten the rim joists to the ends of the 4 × 4 joists (see the FLOOR FRAMING PLAN) with 16d galvanized common nails.

Cut ten 4 × 4 blocks to fit between the joists. Install six blocks 34½" from the front rim joist, and install four blocks 31½" from the rear. Toenail the blocks to the joists. All blocks, joists, and sills must be flush at the top.

To frame the rear wall, cut one top plate and one pressure-treated bottom plate (142¾"). Cut twelve studs (81"). Assemble the wall following the layout in the REAR FRAMING (page 97). Raise the wall and fasten it to the rear rim joist and the intermediate joists, using 16d galvanized common nails. Brace the wall in position with 2 × 4 braces staked to the ground.

For the front wall, cut two top plates and one treated bottom plate (142¾"). Cut ten studs (35¾") and eight cripple studs (13¼"). Cut four 2 × 4 window sills (311⁄16"). Assemble the wall following the layout in the FRONT FRAMING (page 97). Add the double top plate, but do not install the window stops at this time. Raise, attach, and brace the front wall.

(continued)

Cut lumber for the right side wall: one top plate (54⅞"), one treated bottom plate (111¾"), four studs (81"), and two header post studs (86⅞"); and for the left side wall: top plate (54⅞"), bottom plate (111¾"), three studs (81"), two jack studs (77½"), two posts (86⅞"), and a built-up 2 × 4 header (39¼"). Assemble and install the walls as shown in the RIGHT SIDE FRAMING and LEFT SIDE FRAMING (page 96). Add the doubled top plates along the rear and side walls. Install treated 2 × 4 nailing cleats to the joists and blocking as shown in the FLOOR FRAMING PLAN (page 96) and BUILDING SECTION (page 95).

Trim two sheets of ¾" plywood as needed and install them over the joists and blocking as shown in the FLOOR FRAMING PLAN, leaving open cavities along the front of the shed and a portion of the rear. Fasten the sheets with 8d galvanized common nails driven every 6" along the edges and 8" in the field. Fill the exposed foundation cavities with 4" of gravel and compact it thoroughly.

Construct the rafter header from two 2 × 8s cut to 142¾". Join the pieces with construction adhesive and pairs of 10d common nails driven every 24" on both sides. Set the header on top of the side wall posts, and toenail it to the posts with four 16d common nails at each end.

Cut one of each "A" and "B" pattern rafters using the RAFTER TEMPLATES (page 100). Test-fit the rafters. The B rafter should rest squarely on the rafter header, and its bottom end should sit flush with outside of the front wall. Adjust the rafter cuts as needed, then use the pattern rafters to mark and cut the remaining A and B rafters.

Cut the 2 × 6 ridge board (154¾"). Mark the rafter layout onto the ridge and front and rear wall plates following the FRONT FRAMING and REAR FRAMING. Install the A and B rafters and ridge. Make sure the B rafters are spaced accurately so the windows will fit properly into their frames; see the WINDOW SECTION (page 100).

Cut a pattern "C" rafter, test-fit, and adjust as needed. Cut the remaining seven C rafters and install them. Measure and cut four 2 × 4 nailers (311/16") to fit between the sets of B rafters (as shown). Position the nailers as shown in the HEADER & WINDOW DETAIL (page 100) and toenail them to the rafters.

Complete the rake portions of each side wall. Mark the stud layouts onto the bottom plate, and onto the top plate of the square wall section; see the RIGHT and LEFT SIDE FRAMING. Use a plumb bob to transfer the layout to the rafters. Measure for each stud, cutting the top ends of the studs under the B rafters at 45° and those under the A rafters at 30°. Toenail the studs to the plates and rafters. Add horizontal 2 × 4 nailers as shown in the framing drawings.

Create the inner and outer window stops from 10-ft.-long 2 × 4s. For stops at the sides and tops of the roof windows and all sides of the front wall windows, rip the inner stops to 2¼" wide and the outer stops to 1" wide; see the WINDOW SECTION and WINDOW DETAIL (page 100). For the bottom of each roof window, rip the inner stop to 1½"; bevel the edge of the outer stop at 45°.

(continued)

13

Install each window as follows: Attach inner stops as shown in the drawings, using galvanized finish nails. Paint or varnish the rafters and stops for moisture protection. Apply a heavy bead of caulk at each location shown on the drawings (HEADER & WINDOW DETAIL, WINDOW SECTION/DETAIL, TABLE & LOWER WINDOW DETAIL). Set the glazing in place, add another bead of caulk, and attach the outer stops. Cover the rafters and stop edges with 1 × 4 trim.

14

Cover the walls with T1-11 siding, starting with the rear wall. Trim the sheets as needed so they extend from the bottom edges of the rafters down to at least 1" below the tops of the foundation timbers. On the side walls, add Z-flashing above the first row and continue the siding up to the rafters.

15

Install 1 × 6 fascia over the ends of the A rafters. Keep all fascia ½" above the rafters so it will be flush with the roof sheathing. Using scrap rafter material, cut the 2 × 4 lookouts (5¼"). On each outer B rafter, install one lookout at the bottom end and four more spaced 24" on center going up. On the A rafters, add a lookout at both ends and two spaced evenly in between. Install the 1 × 6 rake boards (fascia) as shown in the RAKE BOARD DETAIL (page 100).

16

Soffit

Rip 1 × 6 boards to 5¼" width (some may come milled to 5¼" already) for the gable soffits. Fasten the soffits to the lookouts with siding nails. Rip a 1 × 8 board for the soffit along the rear eave, beveling the edges at 30° to match the A rafter ends. Install the soffit.

Deck the roof with ½" plywood sheathing, starting at the bottom ends of the rafters. Install metal drip edge, building paper, and asphalt shingles. If desired, add one or more roof vents during the shingle installation. Be sure to overlap shingles onto the 1 × 4 trim board above the roof windows, as shown in the HEADER & WINDOW DETAIL.

Construct the planting tables from 2 × 4 lumber and 1 × 6 boards, as shown in the TABLE & LOWER WINDOW DETAIL and BUILDING SECTION. The bottom plates of the table legs should be flush with the outside edges of the foundation blocking.

Build each of the two door panels using T1-11 siding, 2 × 2 bracing, a 2 × 4 bottom rail, and 1 × 2 trim on the front side; see the DOOR CONSTRUCTION drawings (page 99). The panels are identical except for a 2 × 4 sill added to the top of the lower panel. Install 1 × 2 stops at the sides and top of the door opening. Hang the doors with four hinges, leaving even gaps all around. Install a bolt latch for locking the two panels together.

Complete the trim details with 1 × 4 vertical corner boards, 1 × 4 horizontal trim above the front wall windows, and ripped 1 × 4 trim and 1 × 2 trim at the bottom of the front wall windows (see the TABLE & LOWER WINDOW DETAIL). Paint the siding and trim, or coat with exterior wood finish.

Garden Projects

In this section you'll find thirty DIY projects to meet your gardening needs and make your hobby a more pleasant pursuit. You'll also find that each project remains true to the homegrown spirit of gardening in more than one way: Not only are the materials and construction simple and inexpensive, but most of the designs are also highly customizable, so you can alter the given dimensions and details to suit your needs. If the trellis we show is better sized for pole beans than for the melons you want to grow, simply change the dimensions of the parts that matter to create something that fits just right.

In this chapter:

Seed Starter Rack

A seed starter rack provides a spot for you to germinate seeds and grow seedlings indoors, any time of the year (in particular, immediately before the start of the outdoor growing season). Starting your own seeds can save money over buying established plants each growing season. And in many cases, it also lets you grow less-common varieties that might not be locally available in plant form.

This simple starter rack is perfect for a basement or utility room. The basic structure is built with 2 × 4s and has shelves made from ½" plywood. Plants that need the warmest temperatures should go on the upper shelf.

Each shelf of the rack measures 24 × 48"—plenty of room for four full-size seedling flats. Two fluorescent shop lights illuminate each shelf and are fully height-adjustable so you can raise or lower them as needed to provide plants with the right amounts of light and

heat at different stages of development (see page 38 for tips on choosing light bulbs for your fixtures). Because seeds and seedlings can require as much as 20 hours of light per day, it's most convenient to control the lights with an automatic timer. This should be plugged into a GFCI-protected receptacle, due to all of the water used in the area. Even so, it's best to remove flats before misting or watering, to keep water away from the lights.

As with many projects in this book, you can easily modify the dimensions of the rack as shown to suit your specific needs. For a smaller unit, switch to 2-ft. or 3-ft. lights and re-size the shelves accordingly, or make the shelves half as deep and use a single fixture for each. For a larger rack, you can make the shelves square and hang four 4-ft. lights over each shelf. Another option is to bypass the construction and use a store-bought shelving unit for the basic structure (see Variation, below).

This easy-to-build starter rack (left) holds up to 12 full-size seedling flats or trays and can be located practically anywhere with an accessible electrical outlet. The top shelf offers a handy space for storing extra flats and other supplies. Wire utility shelving (above) offers an easy-to-assemble alternative to building your own rack. Most inexpensive units are only 14" deep and can accommodate one row of seedling flats per shelf. Use one or two light fixtures above each shelf, as appropriate for your needs.

Seed Starter Rack

Tools & Materials

Circular saw
Drill/driver
Framing square
(2) 10-ft. 2 × 4
(8) 8-ft. 2 × 4
(1) ½" × 4 × 8 ft. plywood
3½", 2½" and 1⅝" deck screws
(3) 48" fluorescent light fixtures
    with two 40W lamp capacity
    and plug-in cord
Chain (10 linear ft.)
(6) S-hooks
Grounded power strip
Grounded automatic timer
Eye and ear protection
Work gloves

Cutting List

KEY	PART	DIMENSION	PCS.	MATERIAL
A	Shelf frame side	1½ × 3½ × 50"	8	2 × 4
B	Shelf frame end	1½ × 3½ × 21"	8	2 × 4
C	Leg	1½ × 3½ × 79½"	4	2 × 4
D	Shelf	½ × 24 × 48"	4	Plywood

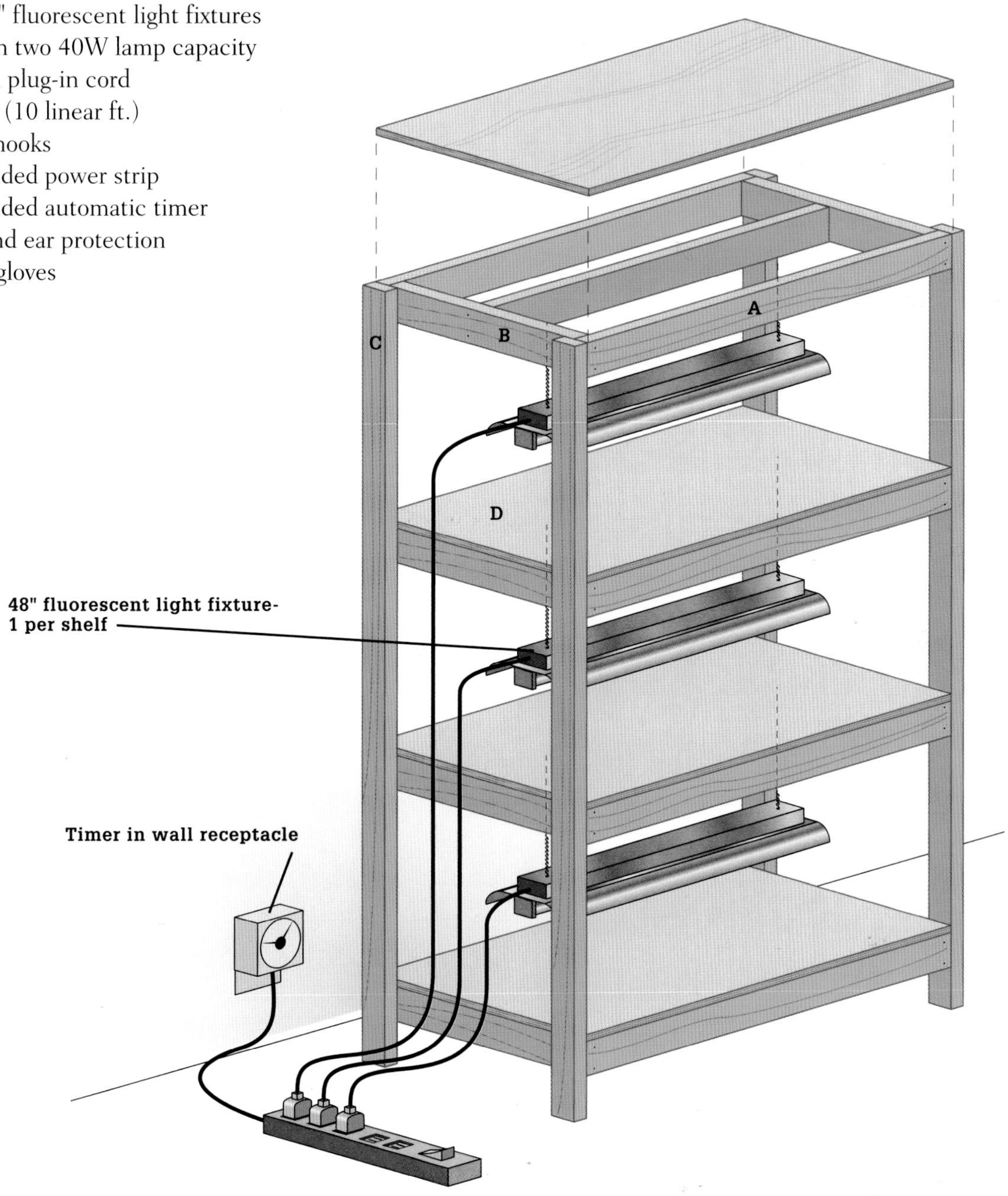

**48" fluorescent light fixture-
1 per shelf**

Timer in wall receptacle

How to Build a Seed Starter Rack

1

Cut all of the wood parts for the shelf frames, using a circular saw or power miter saw. Cut one shelf frame side and two shelf frame ends from each of four 8-ft. 2 × 4s, and cut the remaining four shelf frame sides from two 10-ft. 2 × 4s. Cut each of the four legs from an 8-ft. 2 × 4.

2

Assemble the shelf frames with 3½" deck screws. Position the side pieces of each frame over the ends of the end pieces and so their top edges are flush. Drill pilot holes and drive two screws through the sides and into the ends. Complete all four shelf frames using the same technique.

3

Add the shelves. Cut four shelves at 24 × 48", using a circular saw and straightedge cutting guide. Check each shelf frame with a framing square, then lay the shelf over the top so it's centered side-to-side and end-to-end. Fasten the shelf to the frame with 1⅝" deck screws.

4

Mark the shelf locations onto the legs. Measuring from the bottom of one leg, make marks at 7½", 31½", and 55½". These marks represent the top edges of the shelves; the top shelf is installed flush with the top ends of the legs. Use the framing square to transfer the layout marks to the remaining three legs.

Fasten the shelves to each leg with two 2½" deck screws driven through the shelf ends and into the legs. The top edges of each shelf should be on its layout marks (or flush with the ends of the legs), and the front and rear sides should be flush with the outside edges of the legs. Use a square to make sure the shelf and legs are perpendicular before fastening.

Hang the light fixtures, using chain and S-hooks. Cut the chain into 18" lengths, using wire cutters, and attach each to one end of each fixture, using S-hooks or wire, as applicable. Attach the other end of the chains to the plywood shelf above, using S-hooks.

Route the fixture cords to the nearest leg of the rack and secure them with zip ties or insulated cable staples. Be sure to leave enough slack in the cord to allow for moving the fixture up and down. If necessary, use an approved extension cord to extend a fixture cord to the power strip location.

Plug the light fixtures into an approved (grounded) power strip, and plug the power strip into a 24-hour timer installed in a GFCI-protected wall receptacle. If the circuit or receptacle is not GFCI-protected, replace the existing receptacle with a GFCI receptacle, following the manufacturer's directions.

Cold Frame Box

An inexpensive foray into greenhouse gardening, a cold frame is practical for starting plants six to eight weeks earlier in the growing season and for hardening off seedlings. Basically, a cold frame is a box set on the ground and topped with glass or plastic. Although mechanized models with thermostatically controlled atmospheres and sashes that automatically open and close are available, you can easily build a basic cold frame yourself from materials you probably already have around the house.

The back of the frame should be about twice as tall as the front so the lid slopes to a favorable angle for capturing sunrays. Build the frame tall enough to accommodate the maximum height of the plants before they are removed. The frame can be made of brick, block, plastic, wood, or just about any material you have on hand. It should be built to keep drafts out and soil in.

If the frame is permanently sited, position it facing south to receive maximum light during winter and spring and to offer protection from wind. Partially burying it takes advantage of the insulation from the earth, but it also can cause water to collect, and the direct soil contact will shorten the lifespan of the wood frame parts. Locating your frame near a wall, rock, or building adds additional insulation and protection from the elements. Keep an inexpensive thermometer in a shaded spot inside the frame for quick reference. A bright spring day can heat a cold frame to as warm as 100°, so prop up or remove the cover as necessary to prevent overheating. And remember, the more you vent, the more you should water. On cold nights, especially when frost is predicted, cover the box with burlap, old quilts, or leaves to keep it warm inside.

A cold frame is positioned over tender plants early in the growing season to trap heat and moisture so they get a good, strong start. This cold frame doesn't rely on finding old windows for the top, so anyone can build it.

Cold Frame Box

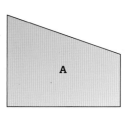

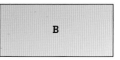

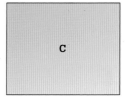

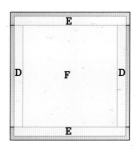

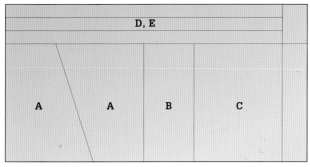

Tools & Materials

(2) 3 × 3" butt hinges (ext.)
Exterior paint
(2) 4" utility handles
2" or 2½" deck screws
(4) Corner L-brackets (¾ × 2½")
#8 × ¾" wood screws
(1) ¾" × 4 × 8 ft. plywood (ext.)
Circular saw
⅛ × 37 × 38" clear Plexiglas
Drill/driver
Exterior caulk/adhesive
Caulk gun
Pipe clamps
Exterior wood glue
Straightedge cutting guide
Eye and ear protection
Work gloves

Cutting List

KEY	PART	NO.	SIZE	MATERIAL
A	Side	2	¾ × 16/28 × 36"	Ext. Plywood
B	Front	1	¾ × 16 × 36"	Ext. Plywood
C	Back	1	¾ × 28 × 36"	Ext. Plywood
D	Lid frame	2	¾ × 4 × 31"	Ext. Plywood
E	Lid frame	2	¾ × 4 × 38"	Ext. Plywood
F	Cover	1	⅛ × 37 × 38"	Plexiglas

How to Build a Cold-frame Box

Cut the parts. This project, as dimensioned, is designed to be made entirely from a single 4 × 8 sheet of plywood. Start by cutting the plywood lengthwise to make a 36"-wide piece. *Tip: Remove material in 4" wide strips and use the strips to make the lid frame parts and any other trim you may want to add.*

Cut the parts to size with a circular saw or jigsaw and cutting guide. Mark the cutting lines first (See Diagram, previous page).

Assemble the front, back and side panels into a square box. Glue the joints and clamp them together with pipe or bar clamps. Adjust until the corners are square.

Reinforce the joints with 2" or 2½" deck screws driven through countersunk pilot holes. Drive screws every 4 to 6" along each joint.

Make the lid frame. Cut the 4"-wide strips of ¾" plywood reserved from step 1 into frame parts (2 @ 31" and 2 @ 38"). Assemble the frame parts into a square 38 × 39" frame. There are many ways to join the parts so they create a flat frame. Because the Plexiglas cover will give the lid some rigidity, simply gluing the joints and reinforcing with an L-bracket at each inside corner should be more than adequate structurally.

Paint the box and the frame with exterior paint, preferably in an enamel finish. A darker color will hold more solar heat.

Lay thick beds of exterior adhesive/caulk onto the tops of the frame and then seat the Plexiglas cover into the adhesive. Clean up squeeze-out right away. Once the adhesive has set, attach the lid with butt hinges and attach the handles to the sides.

Move the cold frame to the site. Clear and level the ground where it will set if possible. Some gardeners like to excavate the site slightly.

Raised Planting Bed

If you live on a rural homestead with ample acreage, siting your gardens usually comes down to choosing among many good options. But if you live in a home with a smaller lot, your foray into gardening will take more planning. It will require you to make extremely efficient use of your gardening space to achieve the volume of produce you want. In many cases, this challenge is addressed by sowing your plants in raised garden beds.

Raised garden beds offer several advantages over planting at ground level. When segregated, soil can be amended in a more targeted way to support high density plantings. Also, in raised garden beds, soil doesn't suffer compaction under foot traffic or machinery, so plant roots are free to spread and breathe more easily. Vegetables and flowers planted at high densities in raised beds are placed far enough apart to avoid overcrowding, but close enough to shade and choke out weeds. In raised beds, you can also water plants easily with soaker hoses, which deliver water to soil and roots rather than spraying leaves and inviting disease.

Raised garden beds can easily be customized to fit the space you have available. Just make sure you can reach the center easily. If you can only access your raised bed from one side, it's best to build it no wider than 3 ft. Beds that you can access from both sides can be as wide as 6 ft., as long as you can reach the center. You can build your raised bed as long as you'd like.

Tip: For low-growing plants, position the bed with a north-south orientation, so both sides of the bed will be exposed to direct sunlight. For taller plants, position the bed east-west.

Raised garden beds are easy to weed, simple to water, and the soil quality is easier to control, ensuring that your vegetable plants yield bountiful fresh produce. Your garden beds can be built at any height up to waist-level. It's best not to build them much taller than that, however, to make sure you can reach the center of your bed.

How to Build a Raised Bed with Timbers

This basic but very sturdy raised bed is made with 4 × 4 landscape timbers stacked with their ends staggered in classic log-cabin style. The corners are pinned together with 6" galvanized spikes (or, you can use timber screws). It is lined with landscape fabric and includes several weep holes in the bottom course for drainage. Consider adding a 2 × 8 ledge on the top row (see facing page). Corner finials improve the appearance and provide hose guides to protect the plants in the bed.

Outline a 3 × 5-ft area with stakes and mason's string. Remove all grass inside the area, then dig a 2"-deep × 6"-wide trench along the inside perimeter of the outline. Cut each of the four timbers into one 54" piece and one 30" piece, using a reciprocating saw or circular saw.

Set the first course of timbers in the trench. Check the timbers for level along their lengths and at the corners, adding or removing soil to adjust, as needed. Position the second course on top of the first, staggering the corner joints with those in the first course. Fasten the courses together at each corner with pairs of 6" nails driven through ¾₁₆" pilot holes.

Line the bed with landscape fabric to contain the soil and help keep weeds out of the bed. Tack the fabric to the lower part of the top course with roofing nails. Some gardeners recommend drilling 1"-dia. weep holes in the bottom timber course at 2-ft. intervals. Fill with a blend of soil, peat moss and fertilizer (if desired) to within 2 or 3" of the top.

Variation: How to Build a Raised Bed with a Kit

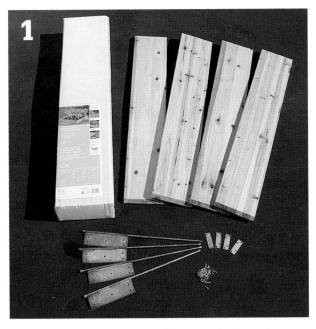

Raised garden bed kits come in many styles. Some have modular plastic or composite panels that fit together with grooves or with hardware. Others feature wood panels and metal corner hardware. Most kits can be stacked to increase bed height.

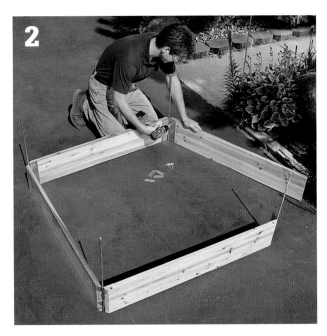

On a flat surface, assemble the panels and corner brackets (or hinge brackets) using the included hardware. Follow the kit instructions, making sure all corners are square.

Set the box down, experimenting with exact positioning until you find just the spot and angle you like. Be sure to observe the sun over an entire day when choosing the sunniest spot you can for growing vegetables. Cut around the edges of the planting bed box with a square-nose spade, move the box and then slice off the sod in the bed area.

Set the bed box onto the installation site and check it for level. Add or remove soil as needed until it is level. Stake the box to the ground with the provided hardware. Add additional box kits on top of or next to the first box. Follow the manufacturer's suggestion for connecting the modular units. Line the bed or beds with landscape fabric and fill with soil to within 2" or so of the top box.

Plant Compatibility ▸

VEGETABLE	LOVES	DOES NOT GET ALONG WITH	PLANTING SEASON
Asparagus	Tomatoes, parsley, basil		Early spring
Beans (bush)	Beets, carrots, cucumbers, potatoes	Fennel, garlic, onions	Spring
Cabbage & broccoli	Beets, celery, corn, dill, onions, oregano, sage	Fennel, pole beans, strawberries, tomatoes	Spring
Cantaloupe	Corn	Potatoes	Early summer
Carrots	Chives, leaf lettuce, onion, parsley, peas, rosemary, sage, tomatoes	Dill	Early spring
Celery	Beans, cabbage, cauliflower, leeks, tomatoes		Early summer
Corn	Beans, cucumbers, peas, potatoes, pumpkins, squash		Spring
Cucumbers	Beans, cabbages, corn, peas, radishes	Aromatic herbs, potatoes	Early summer
Eggplant	Beans	Potatoes	Spring
Lettuce	Carrots, cucumbers, onions, radishes, strawberries		Early spring
Onions & garlic	Beets, broccoli, cabbages, eggplant, lettuce, strawberries, tomatoes	Peas, beans	Early spring
Peas	Beans, carrots, corn, cucumbers, radishes, turnips	Chives, garlic, onions	Early spring
Potatoes	Beans, cabbage, corn, eggplant, peas	Cucumber, tomatoes, raspberries	Early spring
Pumpkins	Corn	Potatoes	Early summer
Radishes	Beans, beets, carrots, cucumbers, lettuce, peas, spinach, tomatoes		Early spring
Squash	Radishes	Potatoes	Early summer
Tomatoes	Asparagus, basil, carrots, chive, garlic, onions, parsley	Cabbages, fennel, potatoes	Dependent on the variety
Turnips	Beans, peas		Early spring

Raised Planting Bed & Cover

Raised planting beds solve a number of gardening challenges. A raised bed is much like a container garden in that it offers total control over the soil content and quality, without the worry of compaction from walking through the garden. Containment of the soil also prevents erosion, helps with weed encroachment, and improves water drainage. For many urban gardeners, a raised bed is the best—and often only—way to grow vegetables and other crop plants in tight spaces.

Another advantage of a raised bed is that the frame around the bed provides a structure for adding covers to protect plants from cold, wind, and snow, or to erect netting to keep out pests. The simple cover frame shown here is much like a hoophouse structure used by farmers to shelter rows of crops on a temporary basis. Ours is made with PVC pipe and is easy to disassemble for storage at the end of the season. The lightweight frame is perfect for a canopy of plastic sheeting (for warmth in colder weather), spun fleece (for insect protection), or deer netting (to deter deer or any other hungry critters).

The raised bed frame is made with a single course of 2 × 10 lumber. You can use smaller lumber for a shallower bed, or go higher with more courses and taller corner posts. Unless your bed will be used strictly for ornamental plants (not food), don't use pressure-treated lumber, due to the risk of chemical contamination. Instead, choose a naturally decay-resistant species such as all-heart redwood, cedar, cypress, or Douglas fir.

Filled with carefully prepared soil, a raised bed offers high yields in a relatively small space. This simple, inexpensive bed design includes wood cleats installed along its top edges—a handy feature for clamping down covers of all types.

Raised Planting Bed & Cover

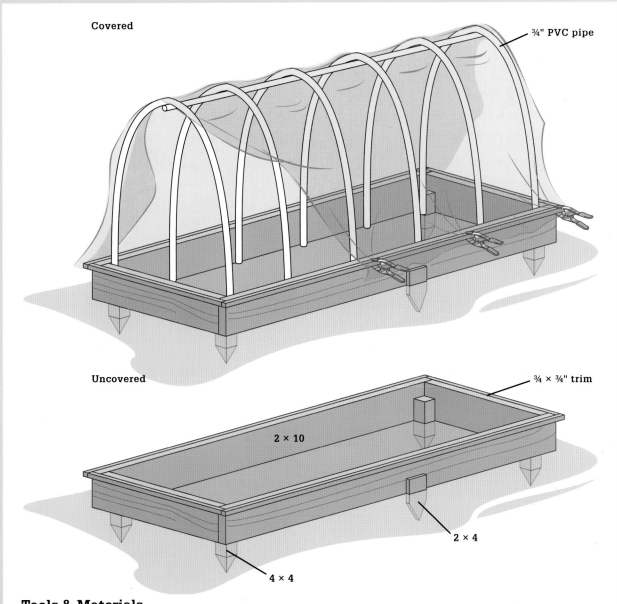

Covered

¾" PVC pipe

Uncovered

¾ × ¾" trim

2 × 10

2 × 4

4 × 4

Tools & Materials

Tape measure
Hammer
Circular saw
Square
Drill and countersink bit and ³⁄₁₆" twist bit
Reciprocating saw or handsaw
Hand sledge
Level
Permanent marker
Hacksaw or pipe cutter
Eye and ear protection

Work gloves
(2) 10-ft. 2 × 10
(1) 8-ft. 2 × 10
3½" and 1¼" deck screws
(1) 8-ft. 4 × 4
(1) 8-ft. 2 × 4
(1) 8-ft. 1 × 4
(7) ¾"-dia. × 10 ft. PVC pipe
(6) 1½" #8 stainless steel machine bolts and wing nuts
Cover material (8 × 14 ft.)
(12) spring clamps

How to Build a Raised Bed with Cover

Cut the two frame ends to length (45") from an 8-ft. 2 × 10, using a circular saw and a square or straightedge to ensure straight cuts. For the frame side pieces, trim the ends of the 10-ft. 2 × 10s, if necessary, so they are square and measure 120".

Assemble the frame by setting the sides over the ends of the end pieces so they are flush at the top and outside edges. Drill three evenly spaced pilot holes through the sides and into the end pieces and fasten the parts with 3½" deck screws.

Create the corner posts by cutting the 8-ft. 4 × 4 into four pieces roughly 24" each. Trim the ends of each post to a point, using a reciprocating saw or handsaw.

Set the bed frame into place, then measure diagonally between opposing corners to check for square: the frame is square when the measurements are equal. *Tip: For general soil preparation, turn over the soil beneath the bed and add compost or manure, as desired, before setting down the frame.*

Drive a post at each corner inside the frame, using a hand sledge and a wood block to prevent mushrooming the post top. Drive the posts until the tops are about 2" below the top of the bed frame. Check the frame for level, then drill pilot holes and fasten each side and end piece to a post with 3½" deck screws.

Add a 2 × 4 stake at the midpoint of each frame side, to help keep the lumber from bowing out over time. Cut the stake to a point and drive it down below the top edge of the frame. Tack the stake to the frame with a couple of screws.

Install the cleats: Rip a 1 × 4 into four ¾"-wide strips, using a circular saw or table saw (it's okay if the last strip isn't exactly ¾"). Fasten the strips along the perimeter of the bed frame, flush with the top edges, using 1¼" deck screws driven through pilot holes. Cut the strips to length as needed to complete each run. Fill the bed with soil and compost, as desired.

(continued)

Mark and drill the ridge pole for the cover frame, using one of the 10-ft. PVC pipes. Make a mark 1" from each end, then mark every 24" in between. The marks should form a straight line down the length of the pipe. At each mark, drill a ³⁄₁₆-dia. hole straight down through the pipe.

Prepare the cover frame ribs by cutting six ¾"-dia. PVC pipes to length at 96", using a hacksaw or tubing cutter. Then, make a mark at the midpoint (48") of each rib, and drill a ³⁄₁₆" hole straight through the pipe at each mark.

Assemble the cover frame, using 1½" machine bolts and wing nuts. Fit a rib over the top of the ridge pole at each hole location. Insert the bolt through the rib and ridge and secure with a wing nut. The wing nuts allow for quick disassembly of the frame.

Anchor the Frame ▸

For a more secure frame that is less likely to blow away, anchor the ¾" tubing onto pieces of ½" CPVC tubing that are set into holes drilled into the raised bed walls. A ¾" bit should makes holes that are sized just right for the CPVC tubes, but drill a hole in a scrap piece first and test the fit. For extra holding power and to prevent the holes from filling with water, squeeze caulk into the hole before inserting the CPVC pipe.

Install the cover frame into the bed by fitting one end of each rib against a frame side, inside the box area, and then bending the rib and fitting the other end inside the frame. It helps to have two people for this job, starting at one end of the frame and working down.

Add the cover material of your choice. Drape the cover over the cover frame, center it side-to-side and end-to-end, and secure it on all sides with clamps fitted over the cleats. To prevent overheating with plastic covers, you can roll up the cover at the ends and clamp it to the outside ribs.

Simple Potting Bench

A multi-functional workstation, like the High-low Potting Bench on pages 130 to 133, offers great versatility that makes it useful for a host of different gardening projects. But sometimes, all you really want from your work area is a big, broad surface with plenty of room to spread out and get busy. This workhorse of a bench is modeled after the most-used workspace in any home: the kitchen countertop. At 36" tall, the bench is the same height as most kitchen counters, and at 28" wide, it's slightly deeper than standard countertops—but not so deep that you can't easily reach across to the other side. The symmetrical configuration allows you to push any part of the bench against a wall or leave it out in the open for easy access to all sides.

There's also no need to worry about leaving the bench out in the rain. The understructure is made with moisture-resistant, pressure-treated lumber, and the top is made up of composite decking boards that won't split, rot, or splinter and require no protective finish.

Of course, if you've always wished your kitchen counters were a bit higher or lower, you can simply add or subtract a few inches from the given dimension for the bench legs. You can also change the length of the bench to fit a tight space, if necessary. Shortening the whole thing by 2 feet allows you to build it with standard 8-ft. lumber and decking instead of 12-ft. and 10-ft. pieces.

This potting bench has a 28 × 71" top and is built with four 2 × 4s and three standard-size decking boards. The handy pot shelf below the bench top is made with a cutoff from one of the deck boards.

Simple Potting Bench

¾" overhang all sides

Tools & Materials

Tape measure
Circular saw
Drill
Piloting-countersink bit
Framing square
Clamps
(3) 12-ft. pressure-treated 2 × 4
3½" and 2½" deck screws
(1) 10-ft. pressure-treated 2 × 4
(3) 12-ft. 1 × 6 composite decking boards
Sandpaper
Eye and ear protection
Work gloves

Cutting List

KEY	PART	DIMENSION	PIECES	MATERIAL
A	Top frame side	1½ × 3½ × 69½"	2	2 × 4
B	Top frame end	1½ × 3½ × 23½"	2	2 × 4
C	Top supports	1½ × 3½ × 23½"	4	2 × 4
D	Leg	1½ × 3½ × 35"	4	2 × 4
E	Leg support	1½ × 3½ × 16½" (field measure)	2	2 × 4
F	Stretcher	1½ × 3½ × 63½" (field measure)	1	2 × 4
G	Top decking	1 × 5½ × 71"	5	1 × 6 decking
H	Pot shelf	1 × 5½ × 68"	1	1 × 6 decking

How to Build the Simple Potting Bench

Cut the two top frame sides from one 12-ft. 2 × 4, using a circular saw or power miter saw. Cut the two top frame ends and the four top supports from another 12-ft. 2 × 4. Fit the side pieces over the ends of the end pieces so all top edges are flush. Drill countersunk pilot holes and fasten the pieces together with two 3½" deck screws at each joint.

Mark the layout for the top supports: Measuring from one end of the top frame, mark both frame sides every 13⅝". Check the top frame for square, using a framing square. Install the top supports between the frame sides with 3½" deck screws driven through the frame sides and into the supports. Make sure the supports and frame sides are flush across the top.

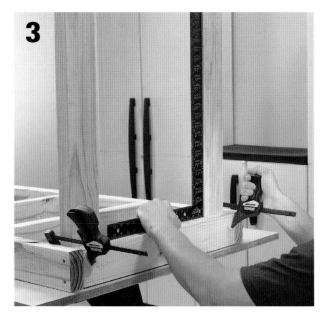

Cut the four legs from one 12-ft. 2 × 4. Round-over the edges on the bottom end of each leg, using sandpaper, a file, or a router and roundover bit; this prevents splintering if the table is slid around. Install the legs at the inside corners of the top frame, driving 2½" deck screws through the legs and into the top frame ends. Also screw through the top frame sides and into the legs. Make sure the legs are square to the frame before fastening.

Mark the inside edge of each leg, 10" up from its bottom end. Measure the distance between each leg pair and cut a leg support to fit snugly between the legs, using the 10-ft. 2 × 4. Install the leg supports with their bottom edges on the marks; drive 3½" screws toenail style through the top and bottom edges of the supports and into the legs.

5

Cut the 2 × 4 stretcher to fit snugly between the leg supports, using the remainder of the 10-ft. 2 × 4. Install the stretcher so it's centered side-to-side on each support, with the top edges flush. Drive 3½" screws through the outsides of the leg supports and into the stretcher ends.

6

Cut the top decking boards to length. Clamp the first board in place so it overhangs the front and ends of the top frame by ¾". If the deck boards are crowned (slightly curved across the face), make sure the convex side faces up. Drill two pilot holes at the center of each top frame end and top support location, countersinking the holes slightly. Fasten the board with 2½" deck screws.

7

Install the remaining deck boards so all of their ends are perfectly aligned and each board is gapped ⅛" from the next (without gaps, the joints would trap dirt). Use pieces of ⅛"-thick hardboard or two ⅛"-dia. drill bits to set the gaps. The last board should overhang the rear frame side by ¾".

8

Complete the pot shelf by cutting the remaining half-piece of deck board to length. Position the board so it is centered side-to-side over the stretcher and overhangs both leg supports by ¾". Fasten the board to the stretcher and leg supports with 2½" deck screws driven through pilot holes.

High-low Potting Bench

Working the soil is part of the fun of gardening, but crouching down all day can be exhausting. Many gardening tasks are easier if you can work at a standard workbench height instead of on the ground. That's where a potting bench comes in handy. A potting bench provides a comfortable and efficient place to work on gardening jobs that don't have to happen on the ground.

What makes this potting bench different from most other potting benches is that the work surfaces are at appropriate heights for gardening tasks. The work surface is 30" high, making it easier to reach down into pots. The low work surface is just over a foot high, so you won't have to lift heavy objects such as large pots or bags of soil. In addition to the high-low work surfaces, this bench also features a shelf and hook rail to keep small supplies and tools within reach, yet still off the main work area.

A potting bench gets wet and it gets dirty, so rot- and moisture-resistant materials were chosen to build this bench. The frame is made with pressure-treated pine lumber and the work surfaces are composite deck boards. The composite material provides a smooth surface that will not splinter and is easy to clean.

Tools & Materials ▶

Tape measure	Work gloves
Bandsaw or jigsaw	Eye and ear protection
Drill	(1) 1 × 2" × 8 ft. pine
Exterior-rated screws	(2) 1 × 4" × 8 ft. pine
(1¼", 2", 2½")	(4) 2 × 4" × 8 ft. pine
Cup hooks (4) ¾" × 8	(1) 1¼ × 5½" × 6 ft.
ft. deck boards	pine

Not all pots are the same height. With two different working heights, this bench is comfortable to use whether you're planting seeds in starter trays or planting a 5-gallon planter with tomatoes.

High-low Potting Bench

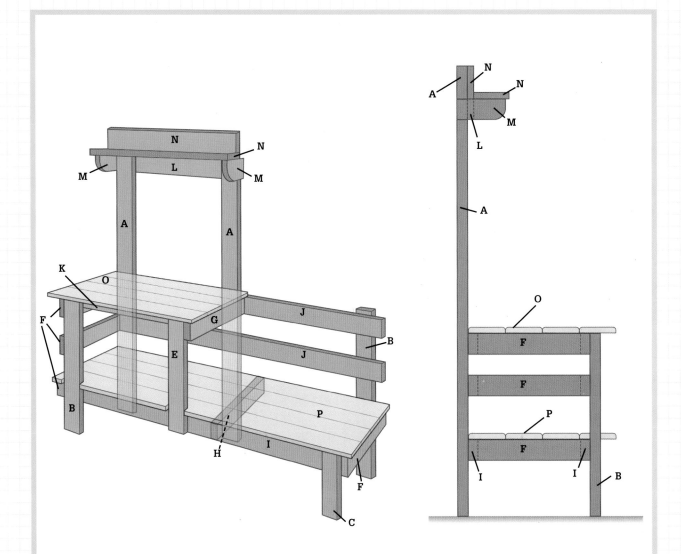

Cutting List

KEY	PART	DIMENSION	PCS.	MATERIAL
A	Long leg	1½ × 3½ × 62¾"	2	Treated pine
B	Mid length leg	1½ × 3½ × 29"	2	Treated pine
C	Short leg	1½ × 3½ × 12"	1	Treated pine
D	Back strut*	1½ × 3½ × 54¼"	1	Treated pine
E	Front strut	1½ × 3½ × 20½"	1	Treated pine
F	Outside cross supports	¾ × 3½ × 22"	4	Treated pine
G	Middle top cross support	1½ × 3½ × 19¾"	1	Treated pine
H	Middle bottom cross support	1½ × 3½ × 16"	1	Treated pine

KEY	PART	DIMENSION	PCS.	MATERIAL
I	Bottom rails	1½ × 3½ × 60"	2	Treated pine
J	Back rails	¾ × 3½ × 60"	2	Treated pine
K	Front rail	¾ × 1½ × 30"	1	Treated pine
L	Hook rail	¾ × 3½ × 30"	1	Treated pine
M	Shelf supports	¾ × 3½ × 7"	2	Treated pine
N	Shelf/shelf back	1¼ × 5½ × 31½"	2	Treated pine
O	High worktop	1¼ × 5½ × 33½"	4	Deck boards
P	Low worktop	1¼ × 5½ × 62½"	4	Deck boards

*Not Shown

High-low Potting Bench

CUT THE FRAME PARTS

Cut all of the frame and shelf parts to length. Draw a 3½" radius on the front bottom corner of each shelf support. Cut along the radius lines with a jigsaw or bandsaw (photo 1). Sand the profiles smooth. Apply a solid color exterior deck and siding stain to all sides of the frame and shelf parts. Staining these parts isn't mandatory, but it's an opportunity to customize your workbench and the stain will extend the life of the parts.

ASSEMBLE THE FRAME

Attach two back rails and one bottom rail to the long leg, back strut, and back right mid-length leg with 2" deck screws. Check that all of the parts intersect at 90-degree angles. Attach the front rail and one bottom rail to the left front mid-length leg, front strut, and short leg. Connect the back assembly and front assembly by attaching them to the cross supports (photo 2).

ATTACH THE WORKTOP PLANKS

Cut the deck boards that will be used to create the work surfaces to length. We used composite deck boards because they require little maintenance and are easy to clean. Place the front deck board for the lower work surface against the backside of the frontleft leg and front strut. Mark the point

Cut the shelf supports. Use a bandsaw or a jigsaw to make the 3½" radius roundovers on the ends of the shelf supports. Sand smooth.

Assemble the bench frame. Clamp the cross supports to the front and back assemblies. Attach the cross supports with 2" deck screws.

where the front leg and strut intersect the deck board. Using these marks, draw the 3¾" deep notch outlines and cut out the notches with a jigsaw (photo 3).

Place the top and bottom deck boards on the cross supports, leaving a ¼" space between the boards. Drill two pilot holes that are centered over the cross supports in each deck board. Attach the deck boards with 2" deck screws (photo 4). If you are using composite deck boards, use specially designed decking screws.

ATTACH THE SHELF & RACK

Attach the shelf back, shelf hook rail, and shelf supports to the long leg and back strut with 2½" deck screws. Attach the shelf to the shelf supports with 2" deck screws. Fasten the hooks to the shelf hook rail (photo 5).

Cut notches. Lay out notches in the front board for the low work surface where the board must fit around the front leg and front strut. Use a jigsaw to cut the notches.

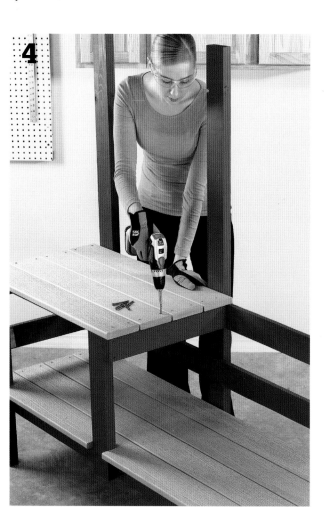

Install the worktop slats. Use composite screws to attach the composite deck boards that create the upper and lower worktops.

Install the shelf and hook rail. Attach the shelf to the shelf supports. Drill pilot holes for each screw to prevent splitting the shelf supports. Once the hook rail is installed twist in the cup hooks.

Built-in Potting Bench

If you have a greenhouse or shed that's dedicated to gardening and has adequate structural integrity, a built-in potting bench is a good way to create a sturdy worksurface that is efficient in its usage of materials and floor area. A built-in bench has the advantage of being easily customized both for size and for function. For example, if your chief gardener is taller or shorter than average, you can adjust the worsksurface height much easier than you can if you purchase a readymade potting bench. And if you plan on blending batches of amended potting soil, you can create a shelf beneath the removable section of worktop. The slats at the right of the bench

seen here, for example, can be removed to access a shelf that is just the right height for the rim of a typical 5-gallon bucket to be supported at working height.

This built-in bench is made of standard construction grade 2 × 4s and pressure-treated 1 × 6 deck boards. Because it is covered by a roof, leaving the bench unpainted will not materially affect its longevity. But greenhouses and gardening sheds usually aren't simple utility areas. Investing a little time and money in painting the bench is well worth it (technically, the potting bench seen here is coated with semi-transparent deck stain).

This potting bench uses the structural members of a greenhouse kneewall for support. The five slats at the right end can be removed to access a shelf for buckets and planters.

Built-in Potting Bench

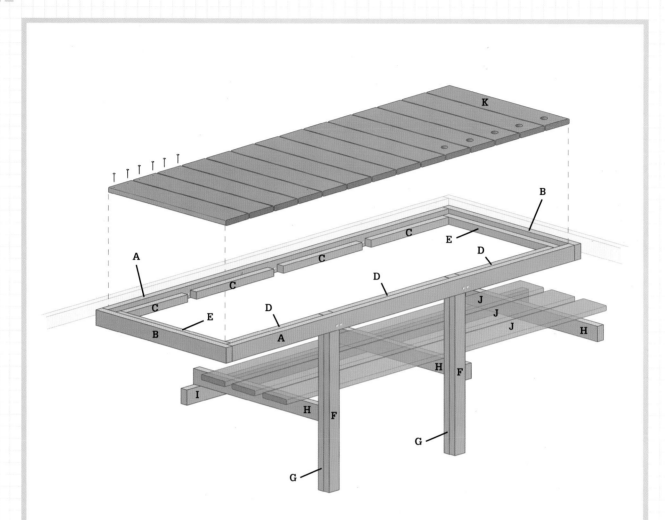

Tools & Materials

Tape measure
Deck screws (2½, 3½")
Lag screws (⅜ × 3")
Carriage bolts (½ × 3½")
Level
Exterior-rated wood glue
Drill/driver
Circular saw or power miter saw
Clamps
(6) 2 × 4" × 8 ft.
(3) 2 × 2" × 8 ft.
Eye and ear protection

Cutting List

KEY	PART	PCS.	DIMENSION	MATERIAL
A	Front/back frame	2	1½ × 3½ × 81"	2 × 4
B	Frame ends	2	1½ × 3½ × 22"	2 × 4
C	Cleats-back	4	1½ × 1½ × 16"	2 × 2
D	Cleats-front	3	1½ × 1½ × 22"	2 × 2
E	Cleats-side	2	1½ × 1½ × 19"	2 × 2
F	Leg half	2	1½ × 3½ × 31½"	2 × 4
G	Leg half	2	1½ × 3½ × 33½"	2 × 4
H	Shelf support	3	1½ × 3½ × 20½"	2 × 4
I	Back wall ledger	1	1½ × 3½ × 32"	2 × 4
J	Shelf board	3	4/4 × 5½ × 60"	Deckboard
K	Top slat	14	4/4 × 5½ × 18½"	Deckboard

How to Build a Built-in Potting Bench

Pre-assemble the frame that is the benchtop support. Cut the 2 × 4 front, back and ends to length and then join them with 3" deck screws and exterior-rated wood glue.

Attach the benchtop frame to the greenhouse wall studs using ⅜ × 3" lag screws. Before driving the lag screws, tack the back of the frame to the long wall with deck screws. The tops should be 36" above the floor. Then, clamp a 2 × 4 brace to the front rail of the frame and adjust it until level. Drill guide holes and drive one lag screw per wall stud at the back rail and on the ends.

Install the front legs. Each leg is created with a pair of 2 × 4s face-nailed or screwed together. The front 2 × 4 in each pair should fit between the frame and the floor. The back 2 × 4 in each pair is 2½" longer to provide a surface for attaching the frame and legs. Join the leg halves with glue and 2½" deck screws.

Attach each leg to the frame with a pair of ½" × 3½" carriage bolts. Drill guide holes for the bolt and counterbores for the nuts and washers in the back face of the frame. Do not use washers behind carriage bolt heads.

Attach a 2 × 4 ledger to the front wall studs to support the 2 × 4 shelf supports that run from the front of the bench to the wall. Use 3" deck screws driven at kneewall stud locations.

Attach 2 × 4 shelf supports to the legs and attach a 2 × 4 shelf support to the end wall. Then, fasten the shelving material to the tops of the supports. The best height for the shelf depends on the height of the containers you plan to set on the shelves beneath the removable section of the top.

Glue and screw 2 × 2 cleats around the inside perimeter of the benchtop frame. The cleats should be positioned so they are level and the top faces of the deckboard slats will be about ⅛" above the frame tops when they rest on the cleats. Install a full-length cleat along the back wall and fill in between the legs at the front.

Cut the benchtop slats from treated or cedar decking (or composite if you prefer). Attach the slats over the first two bays by driving a pair of deck screws into each slat end and the cleat below. Do not fasten the deckboards over the right end bay. Drill 1" finger holes near the end of each board and simply set them on the cleats so they can be removed to access the shelf below. If you wish, coat the bench with deck finish.

Greenhouse Tables

Good, sturdy worktables are indispensable tools for most greenhouse gardeners. That's why almost any sizable greenhouse is furnished with some kind of bench running down both long sides of the building. Benches hold plants at a comfortable level, saving your back and your knees during those many hours of tending and watering. They also make for healthier plants, keeping them above the cooler air near the floor and, with permeable bench tops, allowing airflow and even some light to reach them from below.

In this project, you'll learn how to build a basic, easily adaptable worktable, to which you can add the top and shelf surfaces of your choice. Made with 2 × 4 lumber, the bench frame is simple, inexpensive, and durable. And because it's put together with screws, you can easily disassemble the main parts for compact off-season storage (a great feature for temporary hoophouse gardeners). Several good options for top and shelf surfaces are shown on page 141.

Regarding adaptability, you might want to change the dimensions of the bench as shown to suit your needs and/or fit the available space in your greenhouse. Simply add or subtract whatever you need to modify the bench width, length, or height. You can also add a second shelf to double the storage space for seedling flats and other short items, or to keep garden tools conveniently close to the bench top.

A greenhouse bench should be practical, lightweight, and space-efficient. This simple bench is highly adaptable and easy to move around. The ample shelf below the top provides maximum storage area without taking up unnecessary floor space.

Greenhouse Tables

Galv. wire fencing
(or other surface)

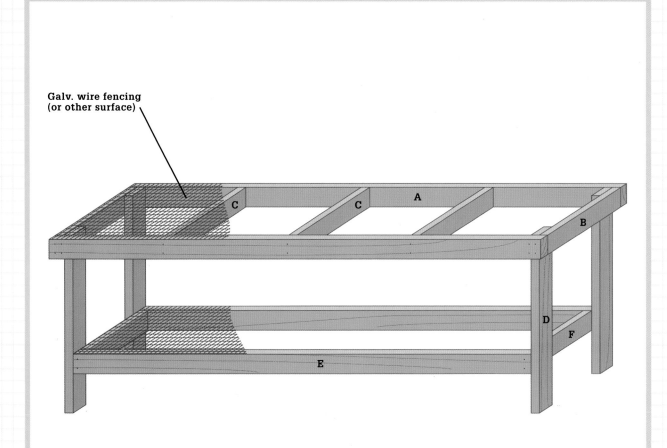

Tools & Materials

Tape measure
Hammer
Circular saw or power miter saw
Clamps
Drill/driver
Framing square
Aviation snips
Metal file
(8) 8-ft. cedar or PT 2 × 4
Deck screws (2½, 3½")
24"-wide steel mesh
   (or other tabletop material)
1½" galvanized horseshoe nails
Eye and ear protection
Work gloves

Cutting List

KEY	PART	DIMENSION	PIECES	MATERIAL
A	Top frame side	1½ × 3½ × 96"	2	2 × 4
B	Top frame end	1½ × 3½ × 22"	2	2 × 4
C	Top supports	1½ × 3½ × 22"	3	2 × 4
D	Leg	1½ × 3½ × 32"	4	2 × 4
E	Shelf frame side	1½ × 3½ × 90"	2	2 × 4
F	Shelf frame end	1½ × 3½ × 19"	2	2 × 4

How to Build a Greenhouse Table

Assemble the top frame by clamping the side pieces over the ends of the end pieces so they're flush along the top edges. Drill pilot holes and fasten each corner with two 3½" deck screws.

Install the top supports between the side pieces, spacing them 24" apart on center. First, mark layout lines onto both side pieces, then square the frame by measuring diagonally between opposing corners; the frame is square when the measurements are equal. Fasten the supports with pairs of 3½" deck screws.

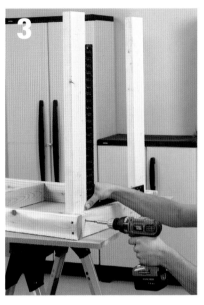

Attach the legs to the inside corners of the top frame, using 2½" deck screws. The top ends of the legs should be flush with the top edges of the frame. Use a framing square to make sure each leg is perpendicular to the frame before fastening.

Assemble the shelf frame in the same manner as the top frame. Mark the inside face of each leg 10" up from the bottom end. Position the shelf frame with its top edges on the marks, and fasten it to the legs with 2½" deck screws driven through the frame ends. The side frame pieces should be flush with the outside edges of the legs.

Add the top and shelf surface material. Galvanized wire mesh fencing is shown here (see next page for other options). Cut the 24"-tall fencing to length at 95", using aviation snips. Round over any sharp cut ends of wire with a metal file. Center the mesh over the top frame, leaving a ½" margin at all sides. Fasten the mesh with 1½" horseshoe nails. Trim and install the shelf mesh in the same fashion.

Options for Bench Top & Shelf Surfaces

Expanded steel mesh is stiffer and has smaller holes than metal wire fencing, offering a more solid surface while maintaining permeability. Fasten steel mesh to the frame parts with heavy-duty staples or horseshoe nails. Do not use stucco lath, which has a rough surface and sharp steel edges.

Exterior plywood offers a smooth, continuous surface for a bench top or shelf. One full 4 × 8-ft. sheet of ¾"-thick plywood will cover a full-size bench top and shelf. Fasten plywood to the frame parts with 1½" deck screws. Keep in mind that a plywood surface won't drain like a permeable material; you may want to pitch the bench slightly to one side for drainage. Coat it with deck stain or paint to make it easier to clean and more stain resistant.

1 × 4 or 1 × 6 cedar boards or decking boards make an attractive top surface and offer some runoff, depending on how widely the boards are gapped. For the bench top, run boards parallel to the length of the top frame; for the shelf, run them perpendicular to the length of the shelf frame.

Protect stored items from draining water with a simple "roof" made with a single panel of corrugated plastic or fiberglass roofing. Use 2 × 4s between the leg pairs to support the panel, sloping the panel down toward one end at ¼" per foot. Secure the panel at the top end with a couple of screws.

Compost Bin

The byproducts of routine yard maintenance can pile up. Consider the waste generated by your landscaping during a single year: grass clippings, deadheaded blossoms, leaves, branches, and weeds. All this can be recycled into compost and incorporated back into plant beds as a nutrient-rich soil amendment.

Compost is nature's own mulch, and it effectively increases soil porosity, improves fertility, and stimulates healthy root development. Besides, making your own mulch or soil amendment through composting is much less expensive than buying commercial materials. Kitchen waste and yard refuse are all the ingredients you need.

So how does garbage turn into plant food? The process works like this: Organisms such as bacteria, fungi, worms, and insects convert compost materials into humus, a loamy, nutrient-rich soil. Humus is the end goal of composting, and it can take as long as a couple of years or as short as a month to produce.

With the right conditions, you can speed up Mother Nature's course and yield several helpings of fresh compost for your yard each season. This is called managed composting, as opposed to passive composting, when you allow a pile of plant debris and such to decompose on its own. The conditions must be just right to manage compost and speed the process. You'll need a balance of carbon and nitrogen, the right temperature, good air circulation, and the right amount of water. By mixing, chopping materials, and monitoring conditions in your compost pile, you'll increase your yield each season.

Tools & Materials ▸

(8) Cedar 2 × 4	U-nails (or narrow crown staples)	Caulk	Hammer
(10) Cedar 1 × 2	(2) 2 × 2" galvanized butt hinges	Circular saw	Pneumatic stapler (optional)
(3 × 12 ft.) Galvanized hardware cloth (½")	Exterior wood glue	Table saw (optional)	Caulk gun
Deck screws (3")	Galvanized finish nails	Power miter saw	Work gloves
18-gauge brads (galvanized)	Exterior wood sealant	Clamps	
Eye and ear protection		Tape measure	
		Drill/driver	

Browns and Greens ▸

A fast-burning compost pile requires a healthy balance of "browns" and "greens." Browns are high in carbon, which is food energy microorganisms depend on to decompose the pile. Greens are high in nitrogen, which is a protein source for the multiplying microbes. A ratio of 3-to-1 brown-to-green materials is the best balance.

- Browns: Dry brown plant material, straw, dried brown weeds, wood chips, saw dust (used with caution)
- Greens: Grass clippings, kitchen fruit and vegetable scraps, green leaves, and manure (no pet droppings)

Note: If you use chemical lawn care products on your lawn, do not include grass clippings in your compost pile.

Compost Bin

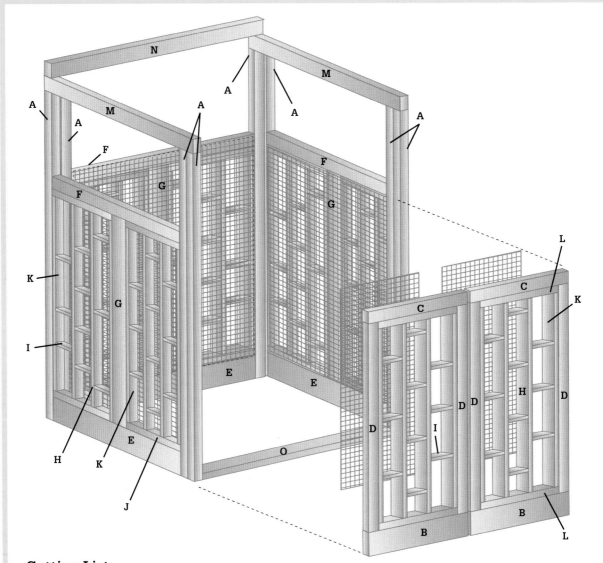

Cutting List

KEY	PART	NO.	DIM.	MATERIAL
A	Post	8	1½ × 1¾ × 48"	Cedar
B	Door rail	2	1½ × 3½ × 16"	Cedar
C	Door rail	2	1½ × 1¾ × 16"	Cedar
D	Door stile	4	1½ × 1¾ × 30½"	Cedar
E	Panel rail	3	1½ × 3½ × 32½"	Cedar
F	Panel rail	3	1½ × 1¾ × 32½"	Cedar
G	Panel stile	3	1½ × 3½ × 30½"	Cedar
H	Infill	16	¾ × 1½ × 30½"	Cedar

KEY	PART	NO.	DIM.	MATERIAL
I	Filler	80	¾ × 1½ × 4"	Cedar
J	Panel grid frame-h	12	¾ × 1½" × Cut to fit	Cedar
K	Grid frame-v	16	¾ × 1½" × Cut to fit	Cedar
L	Door frame-h	4	¾ × 1½" × Cut to fit	Cedar
M	Top rail-side	2	1½ × 1¾ × 39"	Cedar
N	Top rail-back	1	1½ × 1¾ × 32½"	Cedar
O	Front spreader	1	1½ × 3½ × 32½"	Cedar

How to Build a Compost Bin

Prepare the wood stock. At most building centers and lumber yards you can buy cedar sanded on all four sides, or with one face left rough. The dimensions in this project are sanded on all four sides. Prepare the wood by ripping some of the stock into 1¾" wide strips (do this by ripping 2 × 4s down the middle on a tablesaw or with a circular saw and cutting guide).

Cut the parts to length with a power miter saw or a circular saw. For uniform results, set up a stop block and cut all similar parts at once.

Assemble the door frames. Apply exterior-rated wood glue to the mating parts and clamp them together with pipe or bar clamps. Reinforce the joints with 3" countersunk deck screws (two per joint). Reinforce the bottom joints by drilling a pair of ¾"-dia. × 1" deep clearance holes up through the bottom edges of the bottom rails and driving 3" deck screws through pilot holes up into the stiles.

Assemble the side and back panels. Clamp and glue the posts and rails for each frame, making sure the joints are square. Then, reinforce the joints with countersunk 3" deck screws—at least two per joint.

(continued)

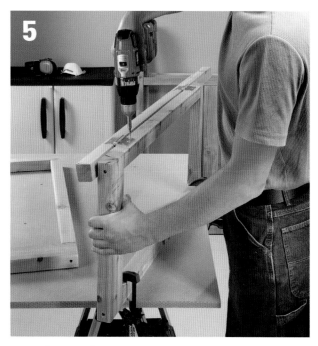

Hang the door frames. With the posts cut to length and oriented correctly, attach a door frame to each post with a pair of galvanized butt hinges. The bottoms of the door frames should be flush with or slightly higher than the bottoms of the posts. Temporarily tack a 1 × 4 brace across both door bottom rails to keep the doors from swinging during construction.

Join the panels and the door assembly by gluing and clamping the parts together and then driving 3" countersunk deck screws to reinforce the joints. To stabilize the assembly, fasten the 2 × 4 front spreader between the front, bottom edges of the side panels. Make sure the spreader will not interfere with door operation.

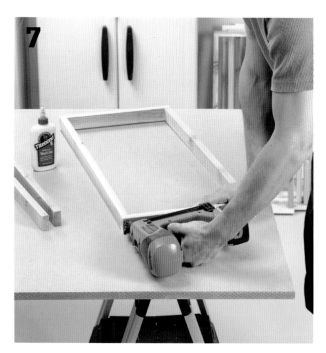

Make the grids for the panel infill areas. Use 1 × 2 cedar to make all parts (you may have to rip-cut cedar 2 × 4s for this, depending on availability in your area. Use exterior glue and 18-gauge brads (galvanized) to connect the horizontal filler strips to the vertical infill pieces. Vary the heights and spacing of the filler for visual interest and to make the ends accessible for nailing.

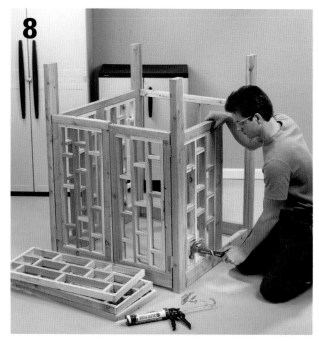

Frame the grids with 1 × 2 strips cut to the correct length so each frame fits neatly inside a panel or door opening. Install the grid frames in the openings, making sure all front edges are flush.

Attach the top rails that conceal the post tops and help tie the panels together. Attach the sides first using exterior glue and galvanized finish nails. Then, install the back rail on top of the side rails. Leave the front of the project open on top so you can load, unload, and turn over compost more easily.

Line the interior surfaces of the compost bin with ½" galvanized hardware cloth. Cut the hardware cloth to fit and fasten it with fence staple or galvanized U-nails driven every 6" or so. Make sure you don't leave any sharp edges protruding. Grind them down with a rotary tool or a file.

Set up the bin in your location. Apply a coat of exterior wood sealant to all wood surfaces—use a product that contains a UV inhibitor. *Tip: Before setting up your compost bin, dig a 12"-deep hole just inside the area where the bin will be placed. This will expand your bin's capacity.*

Easy Compost Corral

Composting yard debris is an increasingly popular practice that makes good environmental sense. Composting is the process of converting organic waste into rich fertilizer for the soil, usually in a compost bin. A well-designed compost bin has a few key features. It's big enough to contain the organic material as it decomposes. It allows cross-flow of air to speed the process. And the bin area is easy to reach whether you're adding waste, turning the compost, or removing the composted material. This compost bin has all these features, plus one additional benefit not shared by most compost bins: it's very attractive.

Grass clippings, leaves, weeds, and vegetable waste are some of the most commonly composted materials. Just about any formerly living organic material can be composted, but DO NOT add any of the following items to your compost bin:

- animal material or waste
- dairy products
- papers with colored inks

For more information on composting, contact your local library or agricultural extension office.

Tools & Materials ▸

Tape measure	Hook-and-eye
(4) 4 × 4" × 4 ft. cedar	latch mechanism
posts	3 × 3" brass butt
(5) 2 × 2" × 8 ft. cedar	hinges (one pair)
(8) 1 × 6" × 8 ft. cedar	Drill and
fence boards	counterbore bit
1½", 3" galvanized	Eye and ear protection
deck screws	Work gloves

Convert organic waste into garden fertilizer inside the confines of this easy-to-make cedar compost bin.

Easy Compost Corral

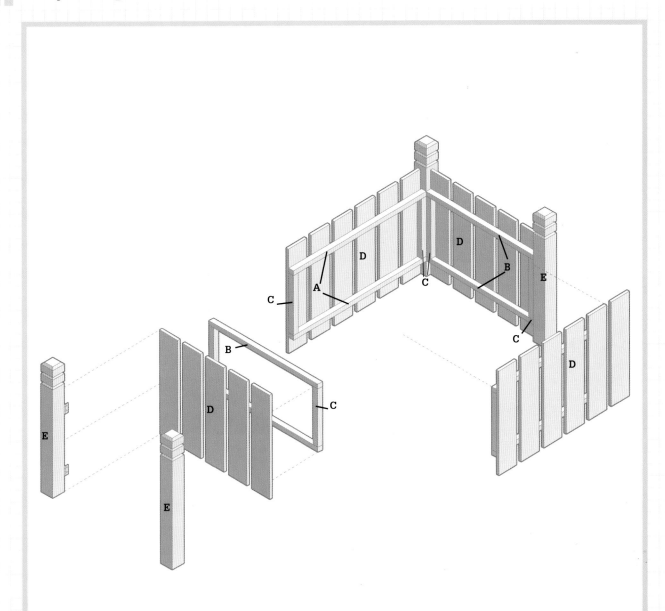

Cutting List

KEY	PART	DIMENSION	PCS.	MATERIAL
A	Side rail	1½ × 1½ × 40½"	4	Cedar
B	End rail	1½ × 1½ × 33½"	4	Cedar
C	Cleat	1½ × 1½ × 15"	8	Cedar
D	Slat	¾ × 5½ × 27"	22	Cedar
E	Post	3½ × 3½ × 30"	4	Cedar

Compost Bin

BUILD THE PANELS

The four fence-type panels that make up the sides of this compost bin are cedar slats that attach to panel frames. The panel frames for the front and back of the bin are longer than the frames for the sides. Cut the side rails, end rails, and cleats to length. Group pairs of matching rails with a pair of cleats. Assemble each group into a frame—the cleats should be between the rails, flush with the ends. Drill ⅛"-dia. pilot holes into the rails. Counterbore the holes ¼" deep using a counterbore bit. Fasten all four panel frames together by driving 3" deck screws through the rails and into each end of each cleat (photo 1).

Cut all of the slats to length. Lay the frames on a flat surface and place a slat at each end of each frame. Keep the edges of these outer slats flush with the outside edges of the frame and let the bottoms of the slats overhang the bottom frame rail by 4". Drill pilot holes in the slats. Counterbore the holes slightly. Fasten the outer slats to the frames with 1½" deck screws (photo 2).

When you have fastened the outer slats to all of the frames, add slats between each pair of outer slats to fill out the panels. Insert a 1½" spacing block between the slats to set the correct gap. This will allow air to flow into the bin. Be sure to keep the ends

of the slats aligned. Check with a tape measure to make sure the bottoms of all the slats are 4" below the bottom of the panel frame (photo 3).

ATTACH THE PANELS & POSTS

The four slatted panels are joined with corner posts to make the bin. Three of the panels are attached permanently to the posts, while one of the end panels is installed with hinges and a latch so it can swing open like a gate. You can use plain 4 × 4 cedar posts for the corner posts. For a more decorative look, buy prefabricated fence posts or deck rail posts with carving or contours at the top.

Cut the posts to length. If you're using plain posts, you may want to do some decorative contouring at one end or attach post caps. Stand a post upright on a flat work surface. Set one of the longer slatted panels next to the post, resting on the bottoms of the slats. Hold or clamp the panel to the post, with the back of the panel frame flush with the inside face of the post. Fasten the panel to the post by driving 3" deck screws through the frame cleats and into the posts. Space screws at roughly 8" intervals.

Stand another post on end, and fasten the other end of the panel frame to it, making sure the posts

Fasten the cleats between the rails to construct the panel frames.

Attach a slat at each end of the panel frame so the outer edges of the slats are flush with the outer edges of the frame.

are aligned. Fasten one of the shorter panels to the adjoining face of one of the posts. The back faces of the frames should meet at the inside corner of the post (photo 4). Fasten another post at the free end of the shorter panel. Fasten the other longer panel to the posts so it is opposite the first longer panel, forming a U-shaped structure.

ATTACH THE GATE

The unattached shorter panel is attached at the open end of the bin with hinges to create a swinging gate for loading and unloading material. Exterior wood stain or a clear wood sealer with UV protectant will keep the cedar from turning gray. If you are planning to apply a finish, it's easier to apply it before you hang the gate. Make sure all hardware is rated for exterior use.

Set the last panel between the posts at the open end of the bin. Move the sides of the bin slightly, if needed, so there is about ¼" of clearance between each end of the panel and the posts. Remove this panel gate and attach a pair of 3" butt hinges to a cleat, making sure the barrels of the hinges extend past the face of the outer slats. Set the panel into the opening, and mark the location of the hinge plates onto the post. Open the hinge so it is flat, and attach it to the post (photo 5). Attach a hook-and-eye latch to the unhinged end of the panel to hold the gate closed.

Continue to attach slats. The inner slats should be 1½" apart, with the ends 4" below the bottom of the frame.

Stand the posts and panels upright, and fasten the panels to the posts by driving screws through the cleats.

Attach exterior-rated hinges to the end panel frame and then fasten them to the post. Add a latch on the other side of the hinged panel.

Rain Barrel

Practically everything around your house that requires water loves the natural goodness that's provided with soft rainwater. With a simple rain barrel, you can collect rainwater to irrigate your garden or lawn, wash your car, or top off swimming pools and hot tubs.

Collecting rainwater runoff in rain barrels can save thousands of gallons of tap water each year. A typical 40 × 40-ft. roof is capable of collecting 1,000 gallons of water from only one inch of rain. A simple rain barrel system that limits collected water to outdoor (nonpotable) use, like the rain barrels described on the following pages, can have a big impact on the self-sufficiency of your home, helping you save on utility expenses and reduce the energy used to process and purify water for your lawn and garden. Some communities now offer subsidies for rain barrel use, offering free or reduced-price barrels and downspout connection kits. Check with your local water authority for more information. Get smart with your water usage, and take advantage of the abundant supply from above.

Tools & Materials ▸

Barrel or trash can (minimum 44 gallons)	¾" female pipe coupling
Tape measure	¾" bushing or bulkhead connector
Drill with spade bit	Channel-type pliers
Jigsaw	Fiberglass window screening
Hole saw	
Barb fitting for overflow hose	Hacksaw
1½" sump drain hose	Sheet metal screws
¾" hose bibb or sillcock	Screwdriver
	Cargo strap with ratchet, or bungee cord
Teflon tape	Eye and ear protection
Clear silicone caulk	Work gloves

How to Make a Rain Barrel

Cut a large opening in the barrel top or lid. Mark the size and shape of your opening—if using a bulk food barrel, mark a large semi-circle in the top of the barrel. If using a plastic garbage can with a lid, mark a 12"-dia. circle in the center of the lid. Drill a starter hole, and then cut out the shape with a jigsaw.

Install the overflow hose. Drill a hole near the top of the barrel for the overflow fitting. Thread the barb fitting into the hole and secure it to the barrel on the inside with the retainer nut and rubber washer (if provided). Slide the overflow hose into the barbed end of the barb elbow until the end of the hose seats against the elbow flange.

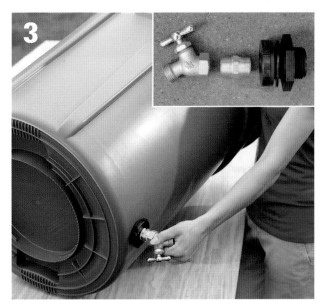

Drill the access hole for the spigot (either a hose bibb or sillcock, brass or PVC). There are many ways to make the spigot connection. We tightened the stem of the sillcock onto a threaded coupling which is inserted into the access hole. Inside the barrel, a rubber washer is slipped onto the coupling end and then a threaded bushing is tightened over the coupling to create a seal. Apply a strip of Teflon tape to all threaded parts before making the each connection. Caulk around the spigot flange with clear silicone caulk.

Screen over the opening in the top of the barrel. Lay a piece of fiberglass insect mesh over the top of the trash can and secure it around the rim with a cargo strap or bungee cord that can be drawn drum-tight. Snap the trash can lid over the top. Once you have installed the rain barrel, periodically remove and clean the mesh.

Strawberry Barrel

Container gardens aren't just for vegetables—fruit trees and berry bushes also thrive in a potted garden environment, and can produce enough fruit for a family to enjoy throughout the summer. Strawberries, which typically grow in long rows or patches in the ground, can also be grown in a converted wine or food barrel. Two recycled whiskey or wine barrels can be enough space to grow the equivalent of 25 feet of strawberry plants. For this project, make sure you choose everbearing strawberry varieties, and cut off runners for transplanting when they appear. Insulate your barrels with hay or straw during the winter, and you can enjoy a strawberry crop for several years. To keep your barrel going, start fresh every four or five years with new plants and new soil.

Tools & Materials ▸

Pry bar or jigsaw	Work gloves	4" dia. PVC Pipe	Gravel
Hole saw	Large, clean barrel	Window screen	Potting soil mix
Drill	(55 gallon plastic	or hardware cloth	Strawberry plants
Eye and ear protection	or wood)		

A strawberry barrel planter can grow the equivalent of 25 ft. of strawberry plants; choose everbearing varieties for best results.

How to Build a Strawberry Barrel

Prepare the barrel. If your barrel has a lid or closed top, remove it with a pry bar. If your barrel does not have a lid, cut a large opening in the top with a jigsaw. Beginning about one foot above the ground, use a hole saw to cut 3"-dia. planting holes around the barrel, about 10" apart. Stagger the holes diagonally in each row and space the rows about 10" apart. Leave at least 12" above the top row of holes. Flip the barrel over and drill about a half dozen ½"-dia. drainage holes in the bottom.

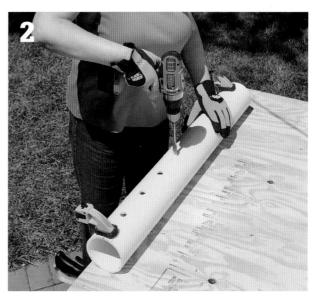

Prepare the watering pipe. Cut a section of 4"-dia. PVC pipe to fit inside the barrel from top to bottom. Punch or drill ¾"-dia. holes in the pipe every 4 to 6", all the way around. Cut a section of window screen or hardware cloth to fit inside the bottom of the barrel and place it inside. Cover the screen with 2" of gravel or small rocks.

Begin to fill the barrel with soil. Have a friend hold the watering pipe in the center of the barrel and fill the pipe with sand. Then, begin to add soil to the bottom of the barrel, packing it firmly around the watering pipe in the bottom with a piece of scrap lumber. Add water to help the soil settle. Continuing adding soil until you reach the bottom of your first row of planting holes.

Add soil and plants. Carefully insert your strawberry plants into the holes, spreading the roots into a fan shape. Add soil on top of the roots and lightly water. Continue to add soil and plants, packing soil gently and watering after each planting, until you reach the top of the barrel. Do not cover the watering pipe. Plant additional strawberries on top of the barrel. Insert a hose into the watering pipe and run water for several minutes to give the barrel a good soaking.

Solar Produce Dryer

A solar dryer is a drying tool that makes it possible to air-dry produce even when conditions are less than ideal. This dryer is easy to make, lightweight and is space efficient. The dryer makes a great addition to your self-sufficient home, allowing you to use your outdoor space for more than gardening. The dryer, which is made of cedar, utilizes a salvaged window for completion. But you will have to adjust the dimensions given here for the size window that you find. The key to successful solar drying is to check the dryer frequently to make sure that it stays in the sun. If the air becomes cool and damp, the food will become a haven for bacteria. In a sunny area, your produce will dry in a couple days. Add a thermometer to the inside of your dryer box, and check on the temperature frequently—it should stay between 95 and 145°F. You may choose to dry any number of different produce in the dryer, such as:

- Tomatoes
- Squash
- Peppers
- Bananas
- Apples

Based on the cold frame platform seen on pages 112 to 115, this solar dryer lets you dry fruit and vegetables quickly, naturally and in a more sanitary fashion than simply air-drying.

Solar Produce Dryer

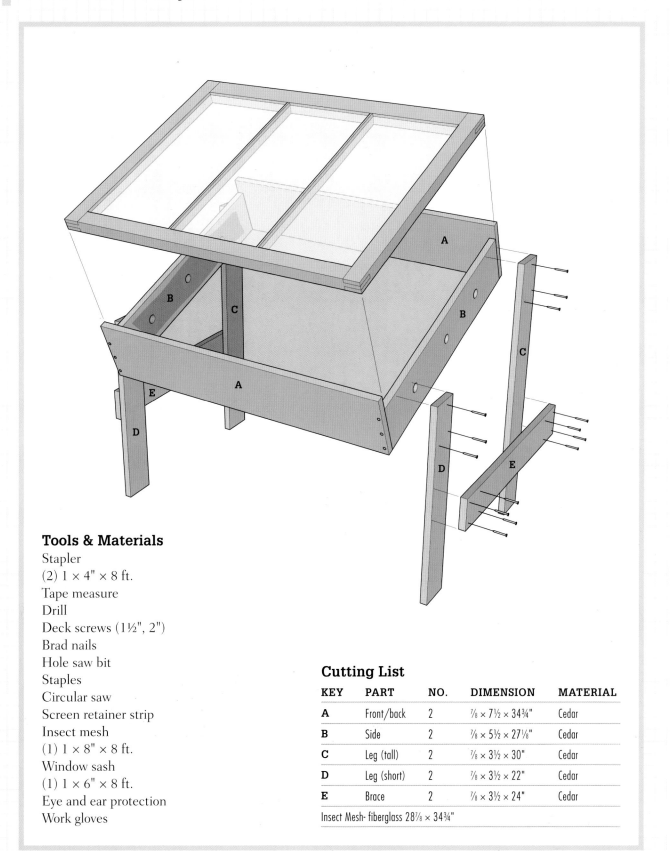

Tools & Materials
Stapler
(2) 1 × 4" × 8 ft.
Tape measure
Drill
Deck screws (1½", 2")
Brad nails
Hole saw bit
Staples
Circular saw
Screen retainer strip
Insect mesh
(1) 1 × 8" × 8 ft.
Window sash
(1) 1 × 6" × 8 ft.
Eye and ear protection
Work gloves

Cutting List

KEY	PART	NO.	DIMENSION	MATERIAL
A	Front/back	2	⅞ × 7½ × 34¾"	Cedar
B	Side	2	⅞ × 5½ × 27⅛"	Cedar
C	Leg (tall)	2	⅞ × 3½ × 30"	Cedar
D	Leg (short)	2	⅞ × 3½ × 22"	Cedar
E	Brace	2	⅞ × 3½ × 24"	Cedar

Insect Mesh- fiberglass 28⅞ × 34¾"

How to Build a Solar Dryer

Assemble the box. Attach the wider boards for the frame by driving 2" screws through the faces of the 1 × 8" boards into the ends of the 1 × 6" boards. There will be a difference in height between these pairs of boards so that the window sash can sit flush in the recess created.

Install the mesh. Staple the screen to the frame. Then tack the retainer strips over the screen to the frame with 3 to 4 brad nails per side. Trim off the excess mesh.

Build the stand. Attach each 24" board to a 30" board (in the back) and a 22" board (in the front) with 1½" deck screws. Then attach the finished posts to the frame with three 1½" deck screws in each post.

Drill three 1" holes for ventilation in each 1 × 6" board equally spaced along the length of the board, leaving 5" of room on each end for the posts. Staple leftover insect mesh behind the ventilation holes on the inside of the frame.

Finish the project by sliding the window sash into place.

Drying Produce on Trays ▸

If you live in an area with clean air, a dry climate, and consistently sunny weather around harvest-time, you can have some success sun-drying food. The chief ingredients you'll need are time and the right weather: 85 to 100° and low to moderate humidity for several consecutive days. You'll also need a place to set your food so it receives good air circulation but is not exposed to pollution from vehicles.

- Use either stainless steel or a nonmetallic material for your food-drying screens. Metal screen materials could be coated with chemicals that contaminate food.
- Spread your food on the trays in a single layer so the pieces do not touch one another.

- Protect your food from insects with cheesecloth—drape the cloth over wooden blocks to keep it from touching the food, and weigh down all of its edges with scrap lumber so it doesn't blow away.
- Place your trays on top of blocks at least six inches tall to promote air circulation on all sides.

Drying food outdoors will likely take at least two to three days, and perhaps longer. At dusk each day, bring the trays indoors. Cool nights can restore moisture, which not only slows down the drying process, it can also cause mold to grow. It's a good idea to keep the drying process going at night if you can. The food will dry much faster and this lessens the chance of mold growth.

Bamboo Trellis

Bamboo is an ideal material for building custom trellises and other structures to support climbing plants in your garden. Bamboo poles are lightweight, strong, and naturally decay-resistant. And because it's a giant grass and in its natural form, bamboo looks right at home in any garden setting.

In this easy project, you'll learn the traditional technique of constructing with natural bamboo poles and lashing twine. The trellis shown is freestanding and is held upright with rebar rods driven into the ground. You can apply the same techniques to create your own trellis designs, tailoring the height, length, and pole spacing to suit your plants and planting area.

Bamboo poles are sold through online retailers, local bamboo suppliers (where available), import stores and some garden centers. The poles come in sizes ranging from about ¼" to 5" in diameter and in lengths up to 20 ft. or so. Of course, the diameters are approximate and variable, since this is a natural product. For this project, the vertical supports are 1½" in diameter and the horizontal and vertical crosspieces are 1" in diameter.

While bamboo can survive many years of exposure to the elements, a bamboo trellis is lightweight enough that you can simply pull it off of its supports and store it over winter. Ground contact or burial of bamboo poles does lead to premature rot, so it's a good idea to prop up the trellis poles on stones or brick to prevent ground contact. A small pile of stones nicely hides the rebar and creates an attractive base around each support pole.

Tools & Materials ›

Tape measure
Hacksaw
Hammer
Scissors
Hand maul
Level
(3) 5-ft. 1½"-dia. bamboo poles
(2) 5-ft. 1"-dia. bamboo poles

(4) 4-ft. 1"-dia. bamboo poles
2-ft. length of #2 rebar or metal rod
(3) 3-ft. lengths of rebar
Waxed lashing twine
Stones
Eye and ear protection
Work gloves

A bamboo trellis like this is great for bolstering any climbing plant. You can build a taller version for pole beans and other aggressive climbers or add more crosspieces or weave kite string between poles to support delicate vines.

How to Build a Bamboo Trellis

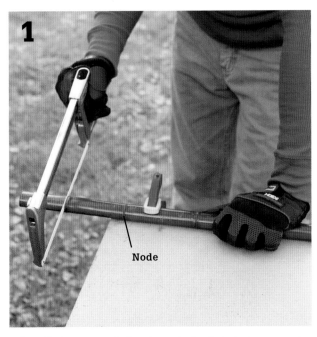

1

Node

Trim off the top end of each vertical pole just above a node, using a hacksaw. The solid membrane of the node will serve as a cap to prevent water from collecting inside the pole. Trim the three 1½"-dia. vertical support poles and four 1"-dia. vertical crosspieces.

2

Measuring from the trimmed top ends of the vertical poles, cut the two outer support poles to length at 48", and cut the four vertical crosspieces at 36". The middle support pole and horizontal crosspieces should be about 60" long; cut them to length only if necessary.

3

Break out the nodes in the bottom ends of the three vertical support poles, using a hammer and #2 rebar or other metal rod, shaking out the broken pieces as you work. Remove any nodes within the bottom 18" of each pole. *Tip: If the first node is close to the end, it might help to drill several holes through the node before breaking it out.*

4

Mark the poles for positioning, using a pencil; these are layout marks that represent the pole intersections. Mark the vertical support poles at 12" and 36" from the bottom ends. On each horizontal crosspiece, make a mark at the center and at 6", 14", and 22" from each end. Finally, make a mark at 6" from each end of the vertical crosspieces.

(continued)

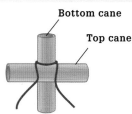 Bottom cane
Top cane

1. Fold a 4-ft.-long piece of waxed twine in half and wrap it around the bottom cane.

2. Pull both ends of the twine across the top cane and cross them underneath the bottom cane.

3. Pull the twine ends back up and cross them over the top cane.

4. Cross the twine underneath the joint, forming an X.

5. Lift the ends up and make an X across the top of the joint.

6. Wrap the bottom cane from below and then across the top, next to the joint.

7. Wrap the bottom cane on the other side of the joint.

8. Tie a square knot and then trim off the twine ends.

Lay out the poles onto a flat work surface, starting with the vertical support poles. To facilitate the lashing process, let the bottom ends of the poles overhang the edge of the work surface beyond the lower layout marks. Position the bottom horizontal crosspiece on top of the support poles using the layout marks for positioning.

Lash the crosspiece to each support pole, using a 60"-long piece of waxed lashing twine; see Lashing Technique, above. When each lashing is complete, trim the excess twine with scissors.

7

Lash the remaining horizontal crosspiece at the upper marks on the support poles. Position the vertical crosspieces on top of the horizontals, and lash the poles together at each intersection.

8

Position the completed trellis framework in the desired location of the garden or planting bed. The back sides of the vertical support poles should face away from the planting area. Press down on the framework so the vertical support poles make an impression in the soil, marking the locations of the rebar spikes.

9

Drive a 36" length of #3 rebar (or other size that fits snugly inside the vertical support poles) into the soil at each pole impression, using a hand maul. Use a level to check the bar for plumb as you work. Drive the bars 18" into the soil.

10

Set stones, bricks, or other bits of masonry material around each piece of rebar. Fit the ends of the vertical support poles over the rebar so they stand squarely on the stones. Check the trellis with a level and adjust for squareness or plumb, as needed, by adding or moving the stones.

Sandwich Board Trellis

Inspired by the ingeniously simple and stable structure of a sidewalk sandwich board sign, the A-frame trellis has, in one form or another, proved a trusty workhorse for many backyard gardeners. Its basic design offers several advantages. It's portable, so you can move it between beds and quickly set it up wherever plants need support, as well as store it away for winter. And, like a sidewalk sign, the trellis is hinged at the top, allowing you to spread the two frames any distance you need to fit a bed or accommodate plant growth.

This trellis design is incredibly easy to build and just as easy to customize. Simply change the lengths of the frame pieces to make your trellis taller or shorter, wider or narrower, or any combination to fit your needs. The other optional feature is the material used for the webbing within the frames. Here, jute or hemp twine is threaded through holes in the frame to create a roughly 6½" square grid for supporting climbing plants. What's nice about the twine is that you can snip it off at the end of the season and compost it with the old vines—there's none of that tedious work of picking off the dried tendrils from the webbing. Other popular webbing materials that you can use on this trellis are chicken wire and yard fencing, as shown below.

All of the trellis frame parts are made with 1 × 4 cedar boards (or other naturally decay-resistant wood). These can be rough or smooth and don't need to be high-grade. You can even use unstained fence planks, which come in 6-ft. lengths and tend to be cheaper than 1 × 4 dimension lumber.

Tools & Materials ▸

Tape measure	3"-long galvanized or
Circular saw	stainless steel butt
Framing square	hinges with screws
Clamps	Heavy jute or hemp
Drill and bits	twine (250 ft.)
Scissors	Marker
(6) 8-ft. cedar 1 × 4	Eye and ear protection
Deck screws	Work gloves
(1¼" and 2")	

Variation: You can substitute chicken wire for the twine for a permanent webbing. Cut each wire panel to size at 46 × 70", using wire cutters or aviation snips. Center the panel over the front face of the frame and secure it with staples along one stile (use galvanized, stainless steel, or other corrosion-resistant staples). Pull the panel taut and staple it along the other stile, then along both rails.

Variation: Vinyl-coated wire fencing on a short frame makes a great trellis for melons, tomatoes, and other sprawling varieties. Cut the fencing about 2" shorter and narrower than the outsides of the trellis frames, and fasten it to the outside faces with galvanized heavy-duty staples or poultry staples (U-shaped nails).

A sandwich board trellis is made with two identical frames held together with simple hinges. The pointed feet in this design keep the main frame parts off the ground (to forestall decay) and dig into the soil for added stability.

How to Build a Sandwich Board Trellis

Cut the frame parts to length from 1 × 4 lumber, using a circular saw or power miter saw. To make the 6-ft. version seen here, cut four stiles (side pieces) at 72", and cut four rails (top and bottom pieces) at 48".

Dry-fit the parts of one frame. Set the stiles facedown on your worksurface so they're about 48" apart. Set a rail across both stiles at the top and bottom ends of the stiles. Make sure the rail ends are flush with the ends and outside edges of the stiles. Check one of the corners with a framing square, and clamp the rail to the stile at that corner.

Drill four countersunk pilot holes through the rail and into the stile. Fasten the rail to the stile with four 1¼" deck screws. Repeat the clamping, squaring, fastening process at each corner to complete the frame. Assemble the other frame in the same manner.

Cut the four feet to length at 12" each, using the cutoffs from the stiles. At one end of each foot piece, mark the center of the board's width (about 1¾" from the side edges). Then, mark each side edge at 2" from the same end of the foot. Draw a line between the side marks and center mark. Cut along these lines to create the pointed end for each foot.

Install each foot at the bottom corner of a frame so its top (square) end is flush with the top edge of the rail and its side edge is flush with the end of the rail. Fasten the foot to the rail and stile with two or three 2" screws; make sure these are offset from the original screws fastening the rails to the stiles.

Mark the hole locations for the webbing twine, 1" from the inside edge of each frame member. Mark the outer holes on each piece about 1" from the adjacent rails/stiles, then space the remaining holes at about 6½" intervals in between. Drill holes that are slightly larger than the thickness of the twine.

Attach a hinge to the top rail on each frame. Position one hinge 5" from each side edge on one of the frames. Drill pilot holes and fasten the hinge with the provided screws. Fasten the other half of each hinge to the other frame, making sure the gap between the rails is even.

Run the horizontal webbing strings: Cut 22 lengths of twine at about 60". Feed one end of each string through the front of a stile hole and knot it in back. Pull the string straight across to the other stile, down through the corresponding hole, and tie it with a double knot so the string is taut.

Tie off each vertical string at the top rail, using a knot behind, as before (you'll need 14 strings at about 96" each). Pull each string taut and hold or clamp it in place over the corresponding hole in the bottom rail, then mark each horizontal string at the point where it intersects with the vertical string, using a marker. The marks will help you keep the grid in line as you install the vertical strings.

Run the vertical strings from top to bottom, wrapping once around each horizontal string at the marked intersection. Keep the string taut as you work, and tie off the string at the bottom rail with a double knot, as before. Complete the webbing for the other frame, following the same process.

Trellis Planter

The decorative trellis and the cedar planter are two staples found in many yards and gardens. By integrating the appealing shape and pattern of the trellis with the rustic, functional design of the cedar planter, this project showcases the best qualities of both furnishings.

Because the 2 × 2 lattice trellis is attached to the planter, not permanently fastened to a wall or railing, the trellis planter can be moved easily to follow changing sunlight patterns or to occupy featured areas of your yard. It is also easy to move into storage during the winter. You may even want to consider installing wheels or casters on the base for greater mobility.

Building the trellis planter is a very simple job. The trellis portion is made entirely of strips of 2 × 2 cedar, fashioned together in a crosshatch pattern. The planter bin is a basic wood box, with panel sides and a two-board bottom with drainage holes that rests on a scalloped base. The trellis is screwed permanently to the back of the planter bin.

Stocking the trellis planter is a matter of personal taste and growing conditions. In most areas, ivy, clematis and grapevines are good examples of climbing plants that can be trained up the trellis. Ask at your local gardening center for advice on plantings. You can set containers of plants in the bin or fill the bin with potting soil and then add plants.

Tools & Materials ▸

(1) 2 × 6" × 8' cedar
(1) 2 × 4" × 6' cedar
(4) 2 × 2" × 8' cedar
(3) 1 × 6" × 8' cedar
(1) 1 × 2" × 6' cedar
Tape measure
Drill
Counterbore bit
Jigsaw
Compass

Square
Moisture-resistant
  glue
2" deck screws
1⅝" and 2½"
  deck screws
Finishing materials
Eye and ear
  protection
Work gloves

Trellis Planter

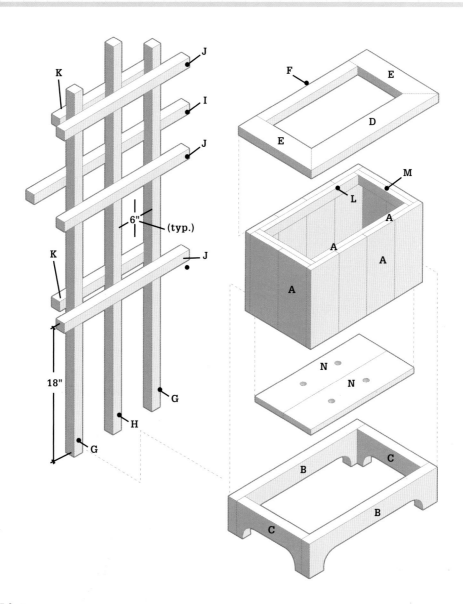

OVERALL SIZE:
69" HIGH
17¼" DEEP
30" LONG

6" (typ.)

18"

Cutting List

KEY	NO.	PART	DIMENSION	MATERIAL
A	12	Box slats	⅞ × 5½ × 13"	Cedar
B	2	Base front and back	1½ × 5½ × 25"	Cedar
C	2	Base ends	1½ × 5½ × 12¾"	Cedar
D	1	Cap front	1½ × 3½ × 25"	Cedar
E	2	Cap ends	1½ × 3½ × 14¼"	Cedar
F	1	Cap back	1½ × 1½ × 18"	Cedar
G	2	End posts	1½ × 1½ × 59½"	Cedar
H	1	Center post	1½ × 1½ × 63½"	Cedar

KEY	NO.	PART	DIMENSION	MATERIAL
I	1	Long rail	1½ × 1½ × 30"	Cedar
J	3	Medium rails	1½ × 1½ × 24"	Cedar
K	2	Short rails	1½ × 1½ × 18"	Cedar
L	2	Long cleats	⅞ × 1½ × 18½"	Cedar
M	2	Short cleats	⅞ × 1½ × 11"	Cedar
N	2	Bottom boards	⅞ × 5½ × 20¼"	Cedar

Note: Measurements reflect the actual size of dimension lumber.

How to Build a Trellis Planter

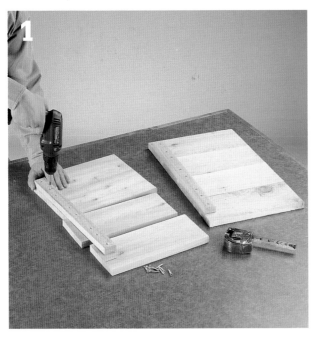

Attach the side cleats flush with the tops of the side boards.

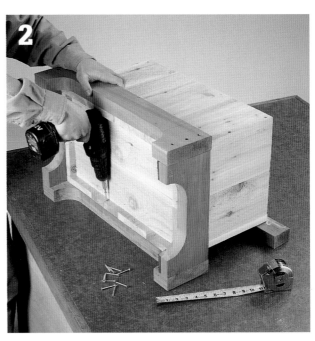

The recess beneath the bottom boards in the planter bin provides access for driving screws.

Before attaching the cap ends, drill pilot holes through the mitered ends of the cap-front ends.

Temporary spacers hold the posts in position while the rails are attached.

STEP 1: BUILD THE PLANTER BIN

1. Cut the box slats (A) and cleats (L, M) to length. Arrange the slats edge-to-edge in two groups of four and two groups of two, with tops and bottoms flush.

2. Center a long cleat (L) at the top of each set of four slats, so the distance from each end of the cleat to the end of the panel is the same. Attach the cleats to the four-slat panels by driving 1⅝" deck screws (photo 1) through the cleats and into the slats.

3. Lay the short cleats (M) at the tops of the two-slat panels. Attach them to the slats the same way.

4. Arrange all four panels into a box shape and apply moisture-resistant wood glue to the joints. Attach the panels by driving 1⅝" deck screws through the four-slat panels and into the ends of the two-slat panels.

STEP 2: INSTALL THE BIN BOTTOM

1. Cut the bottom boards (N) to length. Set the bin upside down on your work surface, and mark reference lines on the inside faces of the panels, ⅞" in from the bottom of the bin. Insert the bottom boards into the bin, aligned with the reference lines to create a ⅞" recess. Scraps of 1× cedar can be put beneath the bottom boards as spacers.

2. Drill ⅛" pilot holes through the panels. Counterbore the holes slightly with a counterbore bit. Fasten the bottom boards by driving 1⅝" deck screws through the panels and into the edges and ends of the bottom boards.

STEP 3: BUILD THE PLANTER BASE

1. The planter base is scalloped to create feet at the corners.

2. Cut the base front and back (B) and the base ends (C) to length. To draw the contours for the scallops on the front and back boards, set the point of a compass at the bottom edge of the base front, 5" in from one end. Set the compass to a 2½" radius and draw a curve to mark the curved end of the cutout. Draw a straight line to connect the tops of the curves, 2½" up from the bottom of the board, to complete the scalloped cutout.

3. Make the cutout with a jigsaw, then sand any rough spots. Use the board as a template for marking a matching cutout on the base back.

4. Draw a similar cutout on one base end, except with the point of the compass 3½" in from the ends. Cut out both end pieces with a jigsaw.

5. Draw reference lines for wood screws ¾" from the ends of the base front and back. Drill three evenly spaced pilot holes through the lines. Counter-bore the holes. Fasten the base ends between the base front and back by driving three evenly spaced deck screws at each joint.

STEP 4: ATTACH THE BIN TO THE BASE

1. Set the base frame and planter bin on their backs. Position the planter bin inside the base so it extends ⅞" past the top of the base.

2. Drive 1⅝" deck screws through the planter bin and into the base to secure the parts (photo 2).

STEP 5: MAKE THE CAP FRAME

1. Cut the cap front (D), cap ends (E), and cap back (F) to length. Cut 45° miters at one end of each cap end and at both ends of the cap front.

2. Join the mitered corners by drilling pilot holes through the joints (photo 3). Counterbore the holes. Fasten the pieces with glue and 2½" deck screws. Clamp the cap front and cap ends to the front of your worktable to hold them while you drive the screws.

3. Fasten the cap back between the cap ends with deck screws, making sure the back edges are flush. Set the cap frame on the planter bin so the back edges are flush. Drill pilot holes and counterbore them. Drive 2½" deck screws through the cap frame and into the side and end cleats.

STEP 6: MAKE THE TRELLIS

1. The trellis is made from pieces in a crosshatch pattern. The exact number and placement of the pieces is up to you—use the same spacing we used (see Drawing) or create your own.

2. Cut the end posts (G), center post (H) and rails (I, J, K) to length. Lay the end posts and center post together side by side with their bottom edges flush so you can gang-mark the rail positions.

3. Use a square as a guide for drawing lines across all three posts, 18" up from the bottom. Draw the next line 7½" up from the first. Draw additional lines across the posts, spaced 7½" apart.

4. Cut two 7"-wide scrap blocks and use them to separate the posts as you assemble the trellis. Attach the rails to the posts in the sequence shown in the Diagram, using 2½" screws (photo 4). Alternate from the fronts to the backs of the posts when installing the rails.

STEP 7: APPLY FINISHING TOUCHES

1. Fasten the trellis to the back of the planter bin so the bottoms of the posts rest on the top edge of the base. Drill pilot holes in the posts. Counterbore the holes. Drive 2½" deck screws through the posts and into the cap frame. With a 1"-dia. spade bit, drill a pair of drainage holes in each bottom board. Stain the project with an exterior wood stain.

Planter With Hanging Trellis

You don't need a large yard—or any yard at all for that matter—to have a garden. Planting in containers makes it possible to cultivate a garden just about anywhere. A container garden can be as simple as a small flowering annual planted in a single 4" pot or as elaborate as a variety of shrubs, flowering plants, and ornamental grasses planted in a large stationary planter.

This planter project combines a couple of different container options to create a larger garden in a relatively small space. The base is an 18 × 30" planter box that is large enough to hold several small plants, a couple of medium-sized plants, or one large plant. It features a trellis back that can be covered by climbing plants.

In addition to the planter and trellis, this project features two plant hangers that extend out from the back posts. Adding a couple of hanging plant baskets further extends the garden display without increasing the space taken up by the planter.

This project is easiest to build with a table saw, miter saw, jigsaw, and drill/driver. If you don't have access to a table saw, use a circular saw or jigsaw and

straightedge to rip the 1 × 6 siding boards. An even easier option is to replace the 2¾"-wide siding boards with 3½"-wide 1 × 4s. This modification makes the planter 4½" taller, so you also have to make the front posts 24½" long instead of 20" long and add 4½" to the front posts trim.

Tools & Materials ▸

(3) 1 × 2" × 8 ft. cedar	Tape measure
(3) 1 × 6" × 8 ft. cedar	Brad nails
(1) 2 × 4" × 10 ft. cedar	or finish nails
(2) 4 × 4" × 8 ft. cedar	Circular saw
(1) 2 × 2" × 6 ft. cedar	or table saw
(2) ⅜" locknuts	Jigsaw
(1) ¾ × 4" × 4 ft.	Drill
ext. plywood	Handsaw
Deck screws (2", 3")	Eye and ear protection
(2) ⅜ × 2-½" eyebolts	Work gloves
(4) ⅜" flat washers	

This efficient planter combines a box for container gardening with a climbing trellis and a pair of profiled arms for hanging potted plants.

Trellis Planter

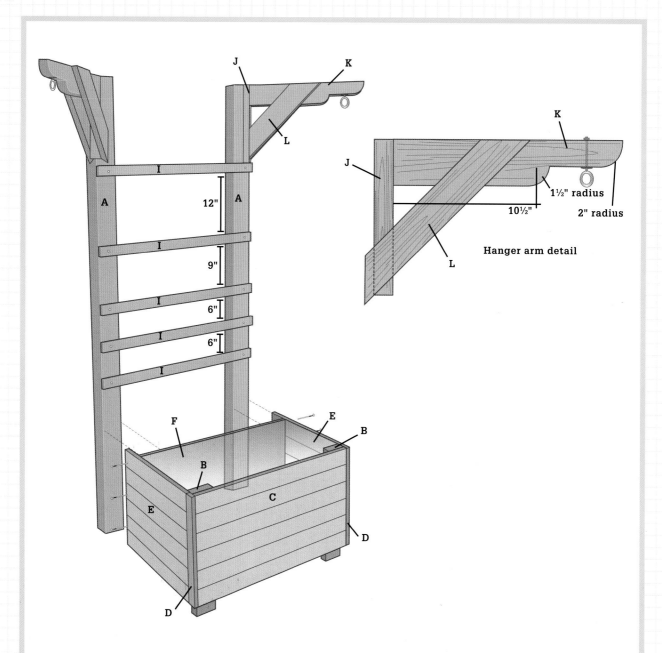

12"

9"

6"

6"

Hanger arm detail

1½" radius

2" radius

10½"

Cutting List

KEY	PART	DIMENSION	PCS.	MATERIAL
A	Back posts	3½ × 3½ × 72"	2	Cedar
B	Front posts	1½ × 3½ × 20"	2	Cedar
C	Front siding	¾ × 2¾ × 30"	6	Cedar
D	Front post trim	¾ × 1½ × 18"	2	Cedar
E	Side siding	¾ × 2¾ × 21½"	12	Cedar
F	Back panel	¾ × 18 × 30"	1	Ext. plywood
G	Bottom supports*	¾ × 1½ × 22¼"	2	Cedar

KEY	PART	DIMENSION	PCS.	MATERIAL
H	Bottom panel*	¾ × 22¼ × 30"	1	Ext. plywood
I	Climbing rails	¾ × 1½ × 30"	5	Cedar
J	Hanger backs	1½ × 1½ × 12"	2	Cedar
K	Hanger arms	1½ × 3½ × 18"	2	Cedar
L	Hanger braces	1½ × 3½ × 18"	4	Cedar

*Not shown

Trellis Planter

CUT THE BASE PARTS

Cutting the front posts (2 × 4) and back posts (4 × 4) to length is easy. Cutting the hanger parts is a bit trickier, primarily because the plant hangers splay out from the corners of the posts at a 45° angle. The top, outside post corners must be beveled to create flat mounting surfaces for the hangers. Mark the bevel cut lines on the outside and front faces of the posts (photo 1). Tilt the shoe of a jigsaw to 45° and bevel-cut along the layout lines (photo 2). Use a handsaw to make a stop cut that meets the bottom of the bevel cut in each back post, forming a shoulder (photo 3). Rip-cut some 1 × 6 stock to 2¾" wide (photo 4) using a table saw or a circular saw and a straightedge cutting guide. Cut six 30" long pieces and twelve 21½" long pieces to make the siding strips.

Also use a circular saw or table saw to cut the bottom and back panels to length and width. Cut 1½" long × 3½" wide notches out of the front corners of the bottom panel. Cut the front post trim, bottom supports, and back climbing rails to length from 1 × 2 boards.

ASSEMBLE THE BASE PLANTER

Attach the front siding strips to the front posts with 2" deck screws. Align the ends of the siding pieces flush with the sides of the front legs. Leave a ¼" space between the siding boards. Drive one screw through each end of each siding board and into the front legs. Drill a countersunk pilot hole for each screw. Attach the front post trim pieces to the front posts with three or four 2" brad nails or finish nails.

Mark the post bevel cuts. The lines at the top of each back post should be drawn 1" out from the corner and should run down the post for 12".

Cut the bevels. Tilt the foot of a jigsaw at a 45° angle so it will ride smoothly on the post face and follow the bevel cutting line. Make a bevel cut along the layout line.

Align the front edge of the trim pieces flush with the front face of the front siding. Attach the back panel to the back posts with six 2" screws. Drive three screws into each post.

Attach the back lattice rails to the back posts. Drive one screw through each end of each climbing rail (photo 5). Refer to the construction drawing on page 173 for lattice spacing. Place the front and back assemblies on their sides and install siding on the side that's facing up. The siding boards should be positioned against the front post trim board and flush with the back edge of the back post, spaced ¼" apart. Attach the siding with 2" screws (photo 6). Flip the project over and repeat the process to attach siding to the other side.

Attach the bottom supports to the front and back legs. The bottom of the front end of the bottom support should be flush with the bottom of the siding.

The bottom of the back end of the bottom support should be positioned 2" up from the bottom of the back post. Drive one screw through the front end of the support and into the front leg and two screws into the back legs. Attach the bottom to the bottom supports with four 2" screws—two into each support.

BUILD THE PLANT HANGERS

Cut the hanger backs, hanger arms, and hanger braces to length. Draw the hanger arm profile onto the side of each hanger arm, and use a compass to draw the radius profiles. Profile details are shown on the construction drawings (page 173). Use a jigsaw to cut along the profile layout lines on the hanger arms. Both ends of the hanger brace are mitered at 45°, but the back or bottom end is a compound miter cut, meaning that it has both a miter and a bevel component. Cut the top end 45° miters on all four braces. Then, make

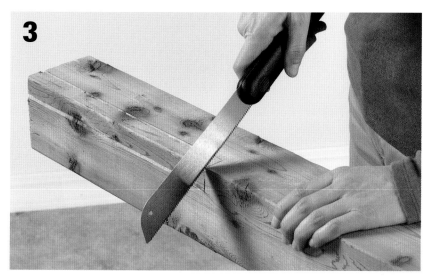

Make the shoulder cut. Use a handsaw to cut into the corner of the post to meet the bevel cut, creating a shoulder for the beveled corner.

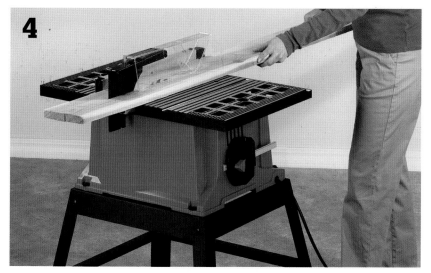

Rip 1 × 6 stock for siding. Using a table saw or a circular saw and cutting guide, rip enough material for the sides and the front to 2¾".

(continued)

Add the latticework. Attach the horizontal climbing rails to the back posts with 2" screws. Use one screw at each lattice connection to the posts.

Install siding. Attach the siding to the front and back posts with 2" screws. After completing one side, flip the project and complete the other side. Then, install siding strips on the front.

Cut the hanger brace angles. After cutting a flat 45° miter in the top end of the hanger brace, make a compound bevel/miter cut in the bottom end so it will fit flat against the bevel cut in the post.

compound cuts at the bottom ends of the hanger braces (photo 7). Make the cuts so the beveled end faces the post when it is attached.

Drill a ⅜"-dia. hole through the top of each hanger arm. Locate the hole 3" in from the end of the hanger arm. Fasten one eyebolt, two flat washers, and a locknut through each hanger arm. Attach the hanger back to the back end of the hanger arm with two 3" screws. Position a 2 × 2 hanger back and a 2 × 4 hanger arm against the beveled corner of each back post. Drive two 3" screws through the hanger back and into the back posts. Attach the hanger braces to the hanger back and hanger arm with 2" screws (photo 8). Make sure the hanger arms remain perpendicular to the posts when you attach the braces.

Line the container. Attach 4-mil black plastic liner with ⅜" stainless steel staples. Overlap the plastic in the corners and leave a small gap along the back bottom edge for drainage.

FILL PLANTER

The planter itself is lined with heavy (at least 4-mil thick) black plastic sheeting. Cut the sheeting pieces that cover the sides, front, and bottom several inches oversized so they overlap in the corners. Cut the back sheeting the same size as the back panel. Attach the plastic to the inside faces of the planter with staples (photo 9). Start with the bottom sheet, overlap the sides on the bottom, and then overlap the front over the sides and bottom. Finally overlap the back over the sides, leaving a small gap between the bottom of the back sheet and the bottom sheet to allow water to drain out. Fill the planter with potting soil and add your plants. *Tip: Adding a few inches of gravel to the bottom of the planting compartment allows for better drainage.*

Install the hanger braces. Clamp the hanger braces to the hanger arms and hanger backs. Attach the hanger braces with 2" screws driven into the hanger back and into the hanger arm. Drive two screws at each connection.

Diamond Trellis

The primary purpose of a trellis is to support climbing plants such as clematis or morning glory. But a trellis also serves as a visually pleasing vertical design element that offers additional benefits, including blocking sun and wind. Paired with a pergola overhead structure, a trellis can provide a living screen to create an intimate nook in the landscape. Or, placed against a home or wall, a trellis adds a cottage feel to a landscape design, allowing plantlife to scale its wooden rungs and add green character to any space.

To be sure, a trellis is eye candy for a landscape. But it also must be functional, and it should accommodate the space where you want to place it and the plants it will support. So before you dig in to this project, think first: What is the purpose for this trellis? What are the growing habits of the vines that will climb the structure? Fast growers, for example, require either a taller trellis or constant pruning. Also consider what, if anything, you are trying to cover up with a trellis. Perhaps it is a utility area with garbage cans or recycling bins; maybe it is a compost area; or, it might even be an unsightly view that is not part of your property.

You can experiment with the trellis motif—how cedar pieces are arranged in patterns to form the wall. You may try diamonds, or mimic existing themes in your garden. Trellises can be polished off with a bright coat of white paint. If they are built with exterior-rated lumber or even nonwood materials, they can be left unfinished to weather naturally. Because you can buy standard trellis material in lattice form and in a few simple shapes at garden centers, strive for something a little more unique if you are building the trellis yourself. At the very least, use good sturdy stock and exterior-rated screws to create a trellis that will last for many growing seasons.

Tools & Materials ▸

Drill	1¼" deck screws (ss)
Power miter saw	½ × 4½" (3)galvanized
Tape measure	lag bolts w/nuts
Framing square	and washers
1 × 2 × 8 ft. cedar (10)	Eye and ear protection
2 × 4 × 8 ft. cedar (1)	Work gloves

A well-designed trellis supports climbing plants during the growing season, and it also contributes to the appearance of the yard during the offseason when the plants die back.

Diamond Trellis

Cutting List

KEY	PART	PIECES	DIMENSION
A	Base Rail	2	¾ × 1½ × 40"
B	Upright-outer	2	¾ × 1½ × 91"
C	Upright-inner	2	¾ × 1½ × 93"
D	Upright-center	1	¾ × 1½ × 89"
E	Rail	6	¾ × 1½ × 38"
F	Filler-long	2	¾ × 1½ × 24"
G	Filler-short	2	¾ × 1½ × 21"
H	Diamond	4	¾ × 1½ × 12"
I	Base	2	1½ × 3½ × 48"

(all parts cedar)

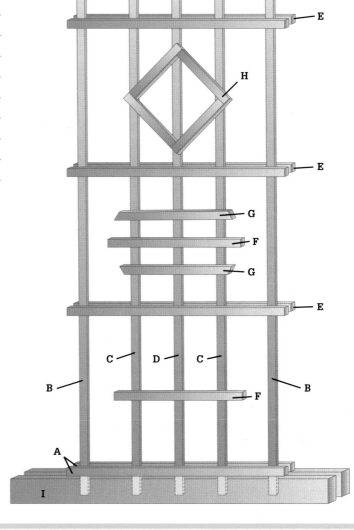

Trellis Design ▶

Sketch your trellis to scale and make a complete list of parts and sizes before you start any cutting. Choose an exterior-rated wood, such as cedar or pressure-treated pine. If you will be painting the trellis you can use dimensional construction lumber such as No. 2 or better pine. While treated lumber withstands the elements better, it is also more prone to twisting and, despite the recent switch to non-arsenic base treating chemicals, many homeowners are not comfortable working with treated lumber or using it around gardens. Choose lumber that is proportional to the scale of the project so it does not look too flimsy or clunky. Make sure, though, that the lumber is beefy enough to hold metal fasteners. For the design shown here, we used 1 × 2 cedar furring. The overall dimensions of the trellis (40 × 90") are large enough that 2 × 2 could also have been used.

How to Build a Diamond Trellis

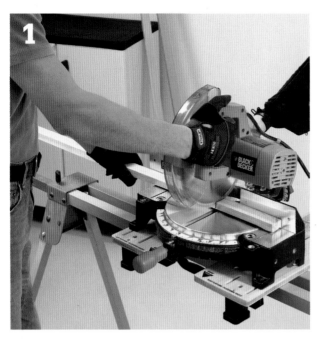

Cut the uprights and rails to length from 1 × 2 stock using a power miter saw. If your cedar stock has one rough face and one smooth, arrange the cut pieces so the faces all match.

Lay the uprights on a flat surface with their bottoms ends flush against a stop block and their edges touching. Draw reference lines across all five uprights to mark the bottom of each rail. Measuring from the bottoms, rail marks should be at the following distances: 3", 33", 57", 82½".

Spread the uprights apart with the bottoms remaining flush against the stop block. The gaps between the outer rails and the inner rail should be 8"; the gaps between the inner rails and the center rail should be 6¼". Lay rails across the uprights at the reference lines with equal overhangs at the ends. Drill a ³⁄₃₂" pilot hole through each rail where it crosses each upright.

Drive a 1¼" exterior screw at each pilot hole, taking care to keep the uprights and rails in alignment. *Tip: Stainless steel screws will not rust, corrode, or cause the wood to discolor. Overdrive the screw slightly so the screwhead is recessed.*

Flip the assembly over once you have driven a screw at each joint on the front face. Position the second set of rails so their tops are flush with the first rails and their ends align. Drill pilot holes at each joint. Offset the pilot hole by ½" so the screws do not run into the screws driven from the other side. Drive screws to attach all four rails.

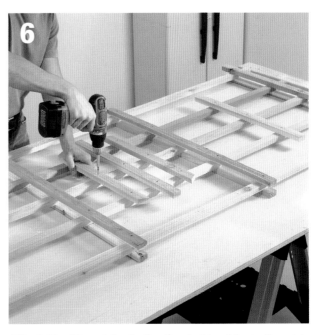

Attach the filler strips to the front side of the trellis according to the spacing on the diagram (page 179). Drill pilot holes so the filler strips don't split. The angled ends of the short filler strips should be cut at 30° with a power miter saw or miter box.

Make the decorative diamond appliqué. Cut four pieces of 1 × 2 to 12" long. Then, arrange the sticks into a diamond shape, with the end of each stick flush with the outer edge of the adjoining one. Drill a pilot hole and drive a screw at each joint. Attach the diamond shape to the top section of uprights, centered from side to side. Take care to avoid screw collisions in the diamond legs.

Install the base parts. The two-part 2 × 4 base seen here allows the trellis to be semi-freestanding. If it is located next to a structure you probably won't need to anchor the base to the ground, although you can use landscape spikes or pieces of rebar to anchor it if you wish. Cut the base parts to length and bolt them together, sandwiching the bottom 3" of the uprights. You can apply a UV-resistant deck finish to the wood, paint it, or let it weather.

Versailles Planter

Possibly the most famous gardens in the world, the gardens at King Louis XIV's Versailles palace are the birthplace of this famous rolling planter style. Reportedly created by landscape architect Andre Le Notre, the Versailles Planter was originally designed to accommodate the many orange trees that were moved in and out of the orange groves on the grounds. The planter seen here differs in several ways from the classic Versailles model, but anyone who has a historical sense of gardening will recognize the archetypal form immediately.

The classic Versailles planter is constructed from oak slats and is bound together with cast iron straps. Cast iron ball or acorn finials atop the corner posts are also present on virtually every version of the planter. Most of the planters that existed (and still exist) on the Versailles grounds today are considerably larger than the one seen here, with sides as wide as 5 feet, as tall as 7 feet. These larger models typically have hinged corners so the sides can be removed easily to plant the tree or shrub, as well as to provide care and maintenance. The X-shaped infill on the design seen here is present in some of the Versailles models, but many others consist of unadorned vertical slats.

At 24 × 24", this historical planter can be home to small- to medium-sized ornamental or specimen trees. The trees can be planted directly into the planter or in containers that are set inside the planter. If you wish to move the plants to follow sunlight or for seasonal protection, install the casters as they are shown. Otherwise, the casters can be left out.

Not a gardener? Try building a slatted top for the planter to create a rolling storage bin that, conveniently, is roughly the same height as a patio table. Or even make a few to serve multiple purposes around your yard while maintaining a consistent design theme.

Based on a classic design originated by the landscape architect for Louis XIV's Gardens at Versailles, this rolling planter can hold small fruit trees (its original purpose) or be put to use in any number of creative ways in your garden or yard.

Tools & Materials ▸

(1) 4 × 4" × 10 ft. cedar	Table saw
(1) 4 × 4" × 4 ft. cedar	Router
(1) 2 × 4" × 8 ft. cedar	Drill
(1) 2 × 6" × 8 ft. cedar	Exterior adhesive
(1) 1 × 6" × 8 ft. cedar	Caulk gun
(4) 3" casters	Clamps
(1) ¾ × 4" × 8 ft.	Jigsaw
ext. plywood	Straightedge
(4) 2 × 2" × 8 ft.	1" brass brads
treated pine	Eye and ear
Deck screws	protection
Tape measure	Work gloves

Versailles Planter

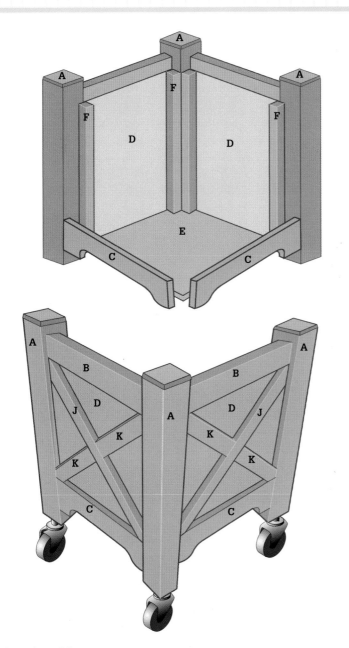

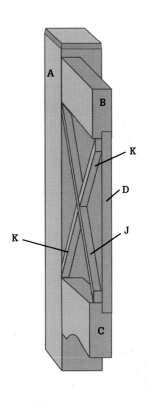

Cutting List

KEY	PART	DIMENSION	PCS.	MATERIAL
A	Corner post	3½ × 3½ × 30"	4	Cedar (4 × 4)
B	Top rail	1½ × 3½ × 17"	4	Cedar (2 × 4)
C	Bottom rail	1½ × 5½ × 17"	4	Cedar (2 × 6)
D	Side panel	¾ × 17 × 18½"	4	Ext. Plywood
E	Bottom panel	¾ × 17 ×17"	1	Ext. Plywood
F	Corner nailer	1½ × 1½ × 23"	8	PT pine (2 × 2)
G	Bottom brace*	1½ × 1½ × 17⅛"	2	PT pine (2 × 2)

KEY	PART	DIMENSION	PCS.	MATERIAL
H	Bottom brace*	1½ × 1½ × 14¼"	4	PT pine (2 × 2)
I	Blocking*	1½ × 1½ × 7"	3	PT pine (2 × 2)
J	X Leg — full	¾ × 2 × 24"	4	Cedar
K	X Leg — half	¾ × 2 × 11"	8	Cedar

*Not shown (see step 4, page 185)

Versailles Planter

MAKE THE BOX

Building the box for the Versailles Planter constitutes most of the work for this project. Start by cutting four 30"-long 4 × 4 cedar posts. Install a ¼" piloted chamfering bit in your router and chamfer all four sides of each post top to create 45° bevels (photo1). You may find that this is easier if you gang all four posts together edge-to-edge and then spin them each 90° after each cut.

Cut the 2 × 2 pressure-treated corner nailers to length and attach them to the inside faces of the posts so the nailers meet at the inside corners. The bottoms of the nailers should be 4" above the post bottoms and the tops should be 3" down from the post tops. Use exterior adhesive and 3" deck screws to attach the nailers.

Prepare a 2 × 4 for the top rails and a 2 × 6 for the bottom rails by cutting a rabbet into each work piece (photo 2). Located on the bottom inside edge of the 2 × 4 and the top inside edge of the 2 × 6, the rabbets should be ¾" wide × ¾" deep. You can cut it with a table saw or a router. After cutting the rabbet, cut the rails to length. Lay out the profile on the bottom rails and cut with a jigsaw. Sand smooth.

Cut the side panels from ¾" exterior plywood. Create four side assemblies by attaching the panels in the rabbets on pairs of mating top and bottom rails. Use adhesive and 1¼" deck screws driven through the plywood and into the rails.

Attach the side assemblies to the 2 × 2 nailers on the inside faces of the posts. The top rails should all align 1" down from the post tops. Use adhesive and 3" deck screws driven through the nailers and into the rails. Also drive a few 1¼" deck screws through the panels and into the nailers, making sure to countersink the screwheads slightly so they can be concealed with wood putty (photo 3).

Flip the box so it is top-down on your work surface and then install the 2 × 2 bottom braces and blocking. It will work best if you first create the brace grid by end-screwing through the four outer braces and into the inner braces and blocking. Then, attach the four outer braces to the bottom rails with adhesive and 3" deck screws driven every 4" or so (photo 4). Then, cut the bottom panel to size. Drill a 1" drain hole every 6" (resulting in nine drain holes). Cut 1½" notches at the corners of the bottom panel using a jigsaw. Set the box with the top up and attach the bottom panel to the braces with adhesive and 1¼" deck screws.

Make the posts. After cutting them to length from 4 × 4 cedar, make a ½" chamfer cut around all the tops. Gang the posts together for profiling if you like.

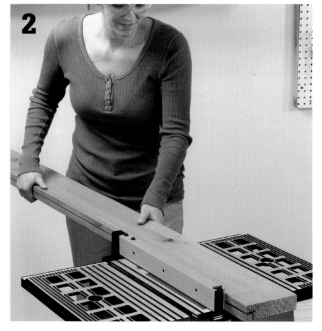

Cut panel rabbets. Make the ¾ × ¾" rabbet cuts in the rail stock using a table saw or router. The rabbets will accept the plywood side panels.

ADD DECORATIVE TOUCHES

Rip-cut an 8-ft.-long cedar 1 × 6 into two 2"-wide strips using a tablesaw or circular saw and straightedge guide. Cut the legs of the X's to length. Cut off the corners of the full-length legs on a miter saw to create arrow shapes. Install the legs between opposite corners of the side panel on the outside faces using adhesive and a few 1" brass brads. Cut the half-length X legs with a square end and a pointed end and attach them to the side panels, completing the X shapes (photo 5).

Turn the box back upside down and install 3" exterior-rated casters at the corners of the bottom panel. Flip it onto the casters and attach cedar post cap finials (acorn-shape or round) to the tops of the posts if you wish. Or, leave the tops unadorned. Apply two or three coats of exterior trim paint to the outside of the planter and to the inside at least 6" down from the top. If you will be placing dirt directly into the planter, line it with sheet plastic first. A better idea is to plant your tree or shrub in a square pot and set the pot into the planter. *Tip: If you wish to use the planter form as a patio table, attach some cedar 1× 4 slats to a pair of 17"-long 2 × 4 stretchers and set the top (called a duckboard) onto the planter.*

Attach the side assemblies. First, drive 3" deck screws through the corner nailers and into the rails. Then, drive 1¼" deck screws through the side panels and into the nailers. Reinforce the joints with adhesive.

Attach the bottom braces. Assemble the braces into a square grid using adhesive and screws and then attach the whole assembly to the base rails by screwing through the four outer braces that meet the rails.

Make the X shape. The distinctive X shape on the outer surfaces of the side panels is made with 2" wide strips of cedar that are fastened with adhesive and 1" brass brads.

Planter Boxes

Decorating a garden is much like decorating a room in your home—it's nice to have pieces that are adaptable enough that you can move them around occasionally and create a completely new look. After all, most of us can't buy new furniture every time we get tired of the way our living rooms look. And we can't build or buy new garden furnishings every time we want to rearrange the garden.

That's one of the reasons this trio of planter boxes works so well. In addition to being handsome —especially when flowers are bursting out of them— they're incredibly adaptable. You can follow these plans to build a terrific trio of planter boxes that will go well with each other and will complement most gardens, patios, and decks. Or you can tailor the plans to suit your needs. For instance, you may want three boxes that are exactly the same size.

Or you might want to build several more and use them as a border that encloses a patio or frames a terraced area.

Whatever the dimensions of the boxes, the basic construction steps are the same. If you decide to alter the designs, take a little time to figure out the new dimensions and sketch plans. Then devise a new cutting list and do some planning so you can make efficient use of materials. To save cutting time, clamp together parts that are the same size and shape and cut them as a group (called gang cutting).

When your planter boxes have worn out their welcome in one spot, you can easily move them to another, perhaps with a fresh coat of stain and add new plantings. You can even use the taller boxes to showcase outdoor relief sculptures—a kind of alfresco sculpture gallery.

Whether you build only one or all three, these handy cedar planters are small enough to move around your gardens and inside your greenhouse or garden shed.

Building Planter Boxes

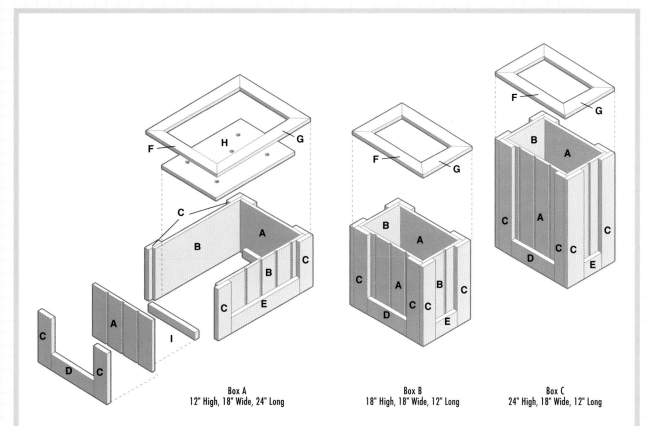

Box A
12" High, 18" Wide, 24" Long

Box B
18" High, 18" Wide, 12" Long

Box C
24" High, 18" Wide, 12" Long

Tools & Materials

Tape measure
Circular saw
Straightedge
Drill
Finishing sander
Miter box and backsaw

(3) 8-ft. cedar 1 × 2s
(6) 8-ft. cedar 1 × 4s
4 × 8-ft. sheet of ⅝" T1-11 siding
2 × 4-ft. piece ¾" CDX plywood
Deck screws (1¼", 1½")

6d galvanized finish nails
Exterior wood stain
Paintbrush
Eye and ear protection
Work gloves

Cutting List

KEY	NO.	PART	BOX A DIMENSION	BOX B DIMENSION	BOX C DIMENSION	MATERIAL
A	2	End panel	⅝ × 15 × 11⅛"	⅝ × 15 × 17⅛"	⅝ × 15 × 23⅛"	Siding
B	2	Side panel	⅝ × 22¼ × 11⅛"	⅝ × 10¼ × 17⅛"	⅝ × 10¼ × 23⅛"	Siding
C	8	Corner trim	⅞ × 3½ × 11⅛"	⅞ × 3½ × 17⅛"	⅞ × 3½ × 23⅛"	Cedar
D	2	Bottom trim	⅞ × 3½ × 9¼"	⅞ × 3½ × 9¼"	⅞ × 3½ × 9¼"	Cedar
E	2	Bottom trim	⅞ × 3½ × 17"	⅞ × 3½ × 5"	⅞ × 3½ × 5"	Cedar
F	2	Top cap	⅞ × 1½ × 18"	⅞ × 1½ × 18"	⅞ × 1½ × 18"	Cedar
G	2	Top cap	⅞ × 1½ × 24"	⅞ × 1½ × 12"	⅞ × 1½ × 12"	Cedar
H	1	Bottom panel	¾ × 14½ × 19½"	¾ × 14½ × 8½"	¾ × 14½ × 8½"	Plywood
I	2	Cleat	⅞ × 1½ × 12"	⅞ × 1½ × 12"	⅞ × 1½ × 12"	Cedar

Note: Measurements reflect the actual size of dimension lumber.

How to Build Planter Boxes

Cut all the wood parts to size according to the Cutting List on page 187. Use a circular saw and a straightedge cutting guide to rip siding panels (if you have access to a tablesaw, use that instead).

Assemble the box frame. Place the end panel face down and butt it against a side panel. Mark the locations of several fasteners on the side panel. Drill counterbored ³⁄₃₂" pilot holes in the side panel at the marked locations and fasten the side panel to the end panel with 1½" deck screws. Fasten the opposite side panel the same way. Attach the other end panel with deck screws.

Attach the corner trim. Position one piece of corner trim flush to the corner edge and fasten to the panels with 1½" galvanized deck screws driven into the trim from the inside of the box. Place the second piece of trim flush to the edge of the first piece, creating a square butt joint. Attach to the panel with 1½" galvanized deck screws. For extra support, endnail the two trim pieces together at the corner with galvanized finish nails.

Attach the bottom trim. Fasten the bottom trim to the end and side panels, between the corner trim pieces and flush with the bottom of the box. Drive 1½" deck screws through the panels from the inside to fasten the trim pieces to the box.

Attach the cap pieces. Cut 45° miters at both ends of one cap piece using a miter box and backsaw or a power miter saw. Tack this piece to the top end of the box, with the outside edges flush with the outer edges of the corner trim. Miter both ends of each piece and tack to the box to make a square corner with the previously installed piece. Once all caps are tacked in position and the miters are closed cleanly, attach the cap pieces using 6d galvanized finish nails.

Install the cleats to hold the box bottom in place. Screw to the inside of the end panels with 1½" deck screws. If your planter is extremely tall, fasten the cleats higher on the panels so you won't need as much soil to fill the box. If doing so, add cleats on the side panels as well for extra support.

Finish and install the bottom. Cut the bottom panel to size from ¾"-thick exterior-rated plywood. Drill several 1"-dia. drainage holes in the panel and set it onto the cleats. The bottom panel does not need to be fastened in place, but for extra strength, nail it to the cleats and box sides with galvanized finish nails.

Finish the box or boxes with wood sealer-preservative. When the finish has dried, line the planter box with landscape fabric, stapling it at the top of the box. Trim off fabric at least a couple of inches below the top of the box. Add a 2" layer of gravel or stones, then fill with a 50/50 mix of potting soil and compost. *Tip: Add wheels or casters to your planter boxes before filling them with soil. Be sure to use locking wheels or casters with brass or plastic housings.*

Hypertufa Planter

Gardening magazines and catalogs often feature stone or concrete troughs brimming with flowers or planted as alpine gardens. Many of the pieces pictured in magazines are antiques, but others are reproductions that merely look weathered and worn. With all the interest in them, antique versions have become hard to find, and even reproductions are expensive.

With hypertufa, you can create inexpensive, long-lasting planters that resemble aged stone sinks or troughs. Or, if your taste runs more toward contemporary shapes, you can easily create more streamlined pieces. Hypertufa is a versatile material, and the simple construction methods are fun to use.

You have to plan ahead for this project. It takes several weeks for hypertufa to cure and several more to wash out the alkaline residue enough to use the planter.

Tools & Materials & Cutting List ▸

Tape measure
Jigsaw
Straightedge
Drill
Hacksaw
Wheelbarrow or
   mixing trough
Hammer
Chisel or paint scraper
Wire brush
Propane torch
12-quart bucket
2"-thick polystyrene
   insulation board
3½" deck screws (40)

Duct tape
Scrap of 4"-dia.
   PVC pipe
Dust mask
Gloves
Portland cement
Peat moss
Perlite
Fiberglass fibers
Concrete dye
   (optional)
Plastic tarp
Scrap 2 × 4
Eye and ear
   protection

OUTER FORM	INNER FORM
22" × 32" (1, for floor)	7" × 24" (2, for sides)
11" × 32" (2, for sides)	7" × 10" (3, for ends
11" × 18" (2, for ends)	and center support)

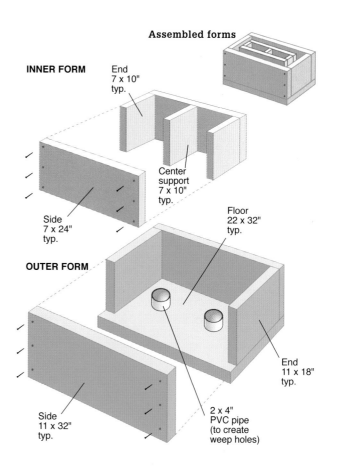

Assembled forms

INNER FORM
End 7 x 10" typ.
Center support 7 x 10" typ.
Side 7 x 24" typ.

OUTER FORM
Floor 22 x 32" typ.
End 11 x 18" typ.
Side 11 x 32" typ.
2 x 4" PVC pipe (to create weep holes)

How to Build a Hypertufa Planter

BUILD THE FORMS

1. Measure, mark, and cut pieces of 2"-thick polystyrene insulation board to the dimensions in the cutting list above, using a jigsaw.
2. To construct the outer form, fit an end piece between the two side pieces and fasten each joint, using three 3½" deck screws. Repeat to fasten the other end. Wrap duct tape entirely around the form. Place one loop of tape near the top and another near the bottom of the form. Set the bottom squarely on top of the resulting rectangle, and then screw and tape it securely in place.
3. Construct the inner form, following the same method.
4. Cut two 2" pieces of 4"-dia. PVC pipe, using a hacksaw, and set them aside.

FORM THE FLOOR

1. Center the pieces of PVC pipe in the floor of the outer form and press them into the foam; these pipes establish the planter's weep holes.

To construct the forms, fasten the joints with 3½" deck screws; then reinforce them with duct tape.

(continued)

2. Mix the hypertufa, following the directions on the next page. Be sure to wear a dust mask and gloves when handling dry cement mix; also wear gloves when working with wet cement.

3. Pack hypertufa onto the floor of the form, pressing it down firmly and packing it tightly around the pieces of PVC. Continue to add hypertufa until you've created a solid, level, 2"-thick floor.

BUILD THE WALLS

Place the inner form within the outer form, centering it carefully. Add hypertufa between the outer and inner forms, using a scrap 2 × 4 to tamp it down as you go. Try to be consistent in the amount of pressure

you use while tamping the hypertufa—the walls of the planter need to be strong enough to withstand the weight and pressure of soil, moisture, and growing plants. Continue adding and tamping the hypertufa until it reaches the top of the forms.

ALLOW TO DRY & REMOVE THE FORMS

1. Cover the planter with a plastic tarp, and let it dry for at least 48 hours. If the weather is exceptionally warm, remove the tarp and mist the planter with water occasionally during the curing process.

2. Remove the tape and screws from the outer form, working carefully so the form can be reused, if desired. If the walls appear to be dry enough to handle without damaging the planter, remove the inner forms. If not, let the planter cure for another 24 hours, then remove the inner form.

You may notice that the planter's surface looks almost hairy, an effect created by the fiberglass in the hypertufa mixture. Don't be concerned about it at this point—the hairy fringe will be removed later.

COMPLETE THE CURING PROCESS

1. Many of the stone planters on the market have a somewhat rustic appearance. If you like that look, this is the time to create it. Working slowly and carefully, use a hammer to round the corners and rough up the edges of the planter.

2. To add texture, gouge grooves on the sides and ends of the planter, using a chisel or paint scraper.

Pack hypertufa onto the floor of the form; press it down firmly to create a level, 2"-thick floor.

Center the inner form within the outer form, and then tamp hypertufa between the two, forming the walls.

After the planter has dried for 48 hours, remove the screws and carefully disassemble the forms.

Complete the aging process by brushing the entire planter with a wire brush. Be bold with these aging techniques—the more texture you create, the more time-worn the planter will appear to be.

3. Cover the planter with plastic, and let it cure for about a month. Uncover it at least once a week, and mist it with water to slow down the curing process. Although it's natural to be impatient, don't rush this step. The more slowly the hypertufa cures, the stronger and more durable the planter will be.

4. Unwrap the planter and let it cure outside, uncovered, for several weeks. Periodically wash it down with water to remove some of the alkaline residue of the concrete (which would otherwise endanger the plants grown in the planter). Adding vinegar to the water speeds this process somewhat, but it still takes several weeks. Again, this step is important, so don't rush it.

After the planter has cured outside for several weeks, put it inside, away from any sources of moisture, to cure for several more weeks.

5. When the planter is completely dry, use a propane torch to burn off the hairy fringe on the surface. Move the torch quickly, holding it in each spot no more than a second or two. If pockets of moisture remain, they can get so hot that they explode, leaving pot holes in the planter. To avoid that problem, make sure the planter is dry before you begin, and work quickly with the torch so no significant amount of heat builds up.

Round the edges and corners of the planter with a hammer, and gouge it with a chisel or paint scraper. Brush the entire planter with a wire brush, and then set it outside to cure.

Working with Hypertufa ▶

Hypertufa is wonderfully suited to building garden ornaments. There are many recipes available, and some are more reliable than others. Below are two of the best options. Recipe #1, which contains fiberglass fibers, is ideal for producing lightweight, durable, medium-to-large planting containers. Recipe #2, which contains sand, is especially appropriate for smaller items and those that must hold water.

The ingredients for both recipes are widely available at home and garden centers. Use portland cement rather than a prepared cement mix that contains gravel (which contributes unnecessary weight and gives the finished container a coarse texture). In Recipe #1, perlite, a soil lightener, takes the place of the aggregate typically found in concrete. For Recipe #2, use fine-textured mason's sand—it produces a stronger container than coarser grades of sand.

Peat moss naturally includes a range of textures, some of which are too coarse for hypertufa. Sifting the peat moss through hardware cloth takes care of that problem. If you plan to make several hypertufa pieces, it's most efficient to buy a large bale of peat moss, sift the entire bale, then store the sifted material for use over time.

The fiberglass fibers in Recipe #1 contribute strength to the mixture. This product is available at most building centers, but if you have trouble locating it, try a concrete or masonry supply center.

Hypertufa dries to the color of concrete. If you prefer another color, simply add a powdered concrete dye during the mixing process. Tinting products are very effective, so start with a small amount and add more if necessary.

RECIPE #1
2 buckets portland cement
3 buckets sifted peat moss
3 buckets perlite
1 handful of fiberglass fibers
Powdered cement dye (optional)

RECIPE #2
3 buckets portland cement
3 buckets sand
3 buckets sifted peat moss

Hypertufa Birdbath

Birds add color, movement, and music to a garden. As if that's not enough to make them welcome guests, some species eat their weight in mosquitoes, grubs, and insects daily. The single most important thing you can do to attract birds is to provide a source of water, a fact that puts a birdbath near the top of any list of appealing garden ornaments.

This birdbath is sturdy, inexpensive, and easy to build. Best of all, its classic lines only improve with age. If you place it in a shady spot and encourage patches of moss to develop, it will blend into the landscape as if it's been part of your garden for decades.

It's made from hypertufa—a mixture of portland cement, peat moss, and sand or perlite. Working with hypertufa is like making mud pies, except that it dries into an attractive substance that holds its shape and stands up to years of use. For general instructions on working with hypertufa, see page 193. For this birdbath, use Recipe #2, which creates a watertight formula.

Since birdbaths need to be cleaned frequently, this one is designed in sections that are easy to take apart. When it's assembled, the sections are held in place by interlocking pieces of PVC pipe that keep it from being toppled by strong winds or aggressive creatures.

To help attract birds to your birdbath, keep it clean, refill it with fresh water regularly, and place stones or branches in it to provide footing for your guests.

Tools & Materials & Cutting List ▶

Tape measure
Straightedge
Jigsaw
Drill
Hacksaw
Hoe
Trowel
2" polystyrene
   insulation board
Duct tape
3" deck screws

Gloves
Scrap of 2" PVC pipe,
   at least 6"
2" PVC pipe caps (4)
Portland cement
Peat moss
Sand
Scrap 2 × 4
Shallow plastic bowl
Vegetable oil
Eye and ear protection

PEDESTAL FORM	BASIN & BASE FORMS
7¾" × 22" (2)	15" × 5½" (4)
11¾" × 22" (2)	19" × 5½" (4)
11¾" × 11¾" (1)	15" × 15" (2)

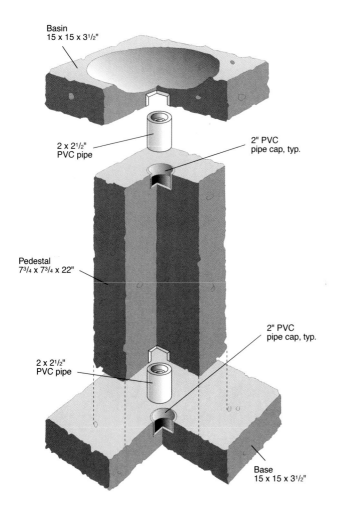

Basin
15 x 15 x 3½"

2 x 2½"
PVC pipe

2" PVC
pipe cap, typ.

Pedestal
7¾ x 7¾ x 22"

2" PVC
pipe cap, typ.

2 x 2½"
PVC pipe

Base
15 x 15 x 3½"

How to Build a Hypertufa Birdbath

BUILD THE FORMS

1. Following the cutting list (below, left) measure and mark dimensions for the forms onto polystyrene insulation. Cut out the pieces, using a jigsaw.
2. Construct the forms, supporting the joints with duct tape (see page 191), then securing them with deck screws. The goal is to create forms for a 15" × 15" × 3½" base, a 15" × 15" × 3½" basin, and a 7¾" × 7¾" × 22" pedestal.

The mass of the pedestal piece creates quite a bit of pressure against the walls of the form when the hypertufa is wet, so you may want to screw together a 1 × 2 collar to support the form, as shown in Photo 3. Or, you could use strap clamps to reinforce the forms, if necessary.

POUR THE BASE

1. Mix the hypertufa, using Recipe #2 (see page 193 for recipe and instructions).
2. Mark the center of the form, and then center a pipe cap exactly over the mark, open side down.

Build forms, using polystyrene insulation board, duct tape, and deck screws.

(continued)

Pack hypertufa into the form, and tamp it down, using a short piece of 2 × 4. Continue packing and tamping until the hypertufa is level with the top of the form.

3. Rap the surface with the 2 × 4 to eliminate air bubbles. Smooth the surface, using a trowel. Cover the piece with plastic and allow it to cure.

POUR THE PEDESTAL

1. Mark the exact center of the bottom of the pedestal form, and then place the open end of a PVC pipe cap on the form, centered over the mark.

2. Pack hypertufa into the form until it's nearly level with the top. Insert a PVC pipe cap at the center of the form, open side up, so its top edge is flush with the top of the form. Tamp and smooth as directed in #3 of Step 2. Cover the piece with plastic and allow it to cure.

POUR THE BASIN

1. Mark the center on the bottom of the form, and press the open end of a PVC pipe cap into the form, centered over that mark.

2. Pack the hypertufa into the form in a layer about 2" thick.

3. Coat a shallow, gently sloped plastic bowl with vegetable oil, and then press it into the hypertufa, forming the depression of the basin. Continue packing and tamping the hypertufa around the bowl until you've created a smooth, even surface that's level with the top of the form. When the hypertufa is set, remove the bowl, cover the basin with plastic, and let it cure.

CONSTRUCT THE BIRDBATH

1. After the pieces have dried for 48 hours, disassemble the forms and remove the pieces of the birdbath. If you like a weathered look, now's the time to distress the pieces. Using a hammer and chisel, knock off corners and remove any sharp edges.

2. Set the pieces outside, cover them with a tarp, and let them cure for several weeks. Every few days, rinse the pieces with water to remove some of the alkaline residue from the hypertufa.

3. After several weeks, move the pieces back indoors and protect them from moisture. When you're

Place the open end of a PVC pipe cap over the exact center of the base form. Pack and tamp hypertufa into the form, making sure the end cap stays in place. Add hypertufa until it reaches the top of the form.

Place a PVC pipe cap over the center of the bottom of the pedestal form, and then pack hypertufa into the form. Embed a PVC pipe cap at the top of the pedestal, centered within the form.

sure the hypertufa is completely dry, paint a coat of good quality masonry sealer onto the depression of the basin.

4. Cut two 2½" pieces of 2" PVC pipe, using a hacksaw. Make sure the cuts are square.

5. Position the base, and then insert one 2½" piece of pipe into the pipe cap at the center of the base. Align the pieces and connect the PVC pipe to the cap embedded in the pedestal.

6. Insert the other 2½" piece of pipe in the cap at the bottom of the basin. Align this pipe with the cap on the top of the pedestal, joining the pieces.

Place a PVC pipe cap at the exact center of the basin form, and then pack a layer of hypertufa into the form. Use an oiled plastic bowl to create a depression in the basin.

Insert a 2½" piece of PVC pipe into the cap at the center of the base and connect it to the pipe cap in the bottom of the pedestal. Insert another 2½" piece of PVC pipe into the cap in the basin and connect it to the cap in the pedestal.

Tip: Attracting Birds to Your Garden ▶

If you want to attract birds to your garden, remember that they have much the same physical needs as humans: water, shelter, and food. Include garden features that will satisfy these needs—a birdbath, water garden, or fountain for water; trees, shrubs, and birdhouses for shelter; feeders or edible plants for food.

You can encourage birds to make a home in your garden by choosing plants that appeal to them. Hummingbirds are drawn to bright flowers, especially red and violet annuals. Other birds are attracted by sunflowers, marigolds, asters, and other flowers that produce lots of seeds, especially if you let the plants go to seed rather than deadheading them.

Birds are attracted to water at ground level, but that puts them in a vulnerable position when predators approach. Place water basins two to three feet above ground and close enough to shrubs or trees that birds have a place to flee if necessary—but not so close that predators can hide in them.

Clean your birdbath thoroughly every few days: Remove algae and bird droppings, and wash the basin with a solution of vinegar and water.

Copper/Bamboo Border

A touch of copper wire adds interest and whimsy to bamboo garden edging.

Want to call attention to your favorite flowers or set aside a section of your garden for herbs or exotic tropicals? Adding a support structure is one dramatic way to define a garden space. This project combines the natural beauty and structure of bamboo with the flowing accent of copper. As a three-part folding form, it can be shaped in a variety of ways: as a triangle, as a zigzag or as a straight edge border. Whichever form you choose, the beauty of bamboo and the rich color of copper will create a design reward in your garden.

You can create any design you wish, but we have used a large, spiral cee-shaped scroll hooked over itself, and a small loop-the-loop to help hold it in place.

Heights for edging can vary depending on the height of featured plants. An herb garden edging would be a smaller height than an edging for taller perennial plants. Our example is for middle range plants.

Tools & Materials ▸

Tubing cutter	Tape measure	9 bamboo hoops, 3 separate forms	14-gauge copper wire (12 ft.)
Wire cutter	Pliers	16-gauge copper wire (12 ft.)	22-gauge copper wire (7 ft.)

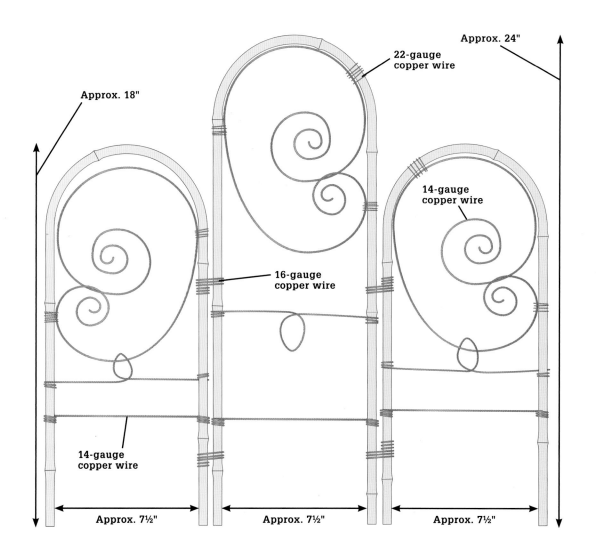

Approx. 18"

Approx. 24"

22-gauge copper wire

14-gauge copper wire

16-gauge copper wire

14-gauge copper wire

Approx. 7½"   Approx. 7½"   Approx. 7½"

How to Make a Copper/Bamboo Border

CUT THE BAMBOO SUPPORTS

Divide the bamboo supports (sold at most garden centers) into three groups of three. Work one section of three supports at one time to form three separate panels. Measure 23" from the top of the center hoop and mark both sides of the hoop with a marker. Mark the other two hoops at 18". Use the tubing cutter to cut the bamboo to the desired height. (Using a tubing cutter instead of a saw will prevent the bamboo from splintering during the cutting process).

WRAP THE LEGS

To hold the legs of the hoops parallel, cut a length of 14-gauge wire about 8" longer than the width of the hoop. Wrap one end of the wire tightly around one hoop leg, about 5" from the bottom of the leg. Pull the hoop legs parallel, if necessary, and wrap the other end of the wire around the second leg. Repeat for the other hoops.

Cut the bamboo hoops to the desired length using your tubing cutter.

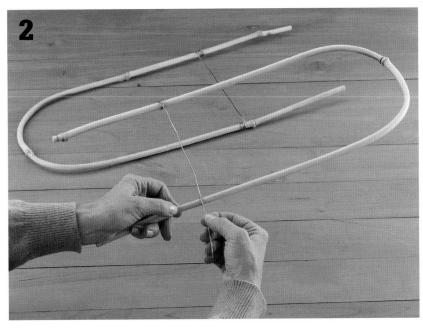

Hold the legs of the hoops parallel by wrapping wire around each side.

(continued)

FORM THE HINGES

On a flat surface line up the three hoops with the tallest hoop in the middle. Cut four pieces of 16-gauge wire to 14". Make the hinges to join each section by wrapping the wire around one hoop leg twice, then around both of the legs. Use a pliers to flatten the wire ends against the bamboo. Repeat to form two hinges on each side.

MAKE THE SCROLL SPIRALS

To make the cee-shaped scroll spiral, cut a length of 14-gauge wire that is six times the length of the space between the hoop legs. Mark it to divide it into ⅔ and ⅓ sections. Wrap the ⅔ section around a 1½" dowel or pipe. Remove from the form. Wrap the ⅓ section around the same form, but in the opposite direction to create a C scroll. Use a pliers to twist the wire ends into slightly smaller circles. Gently expand the remaining circles to form a C scroll that fits inside the hoop. Create matching or slightly different scrolls for the remaining two hoops. Loop the smaller side of the scroll over the larger side so they interlock. Position the scrolls within the hoops and attach to the hoops by wrapping with 12" of 22-gauge wire.

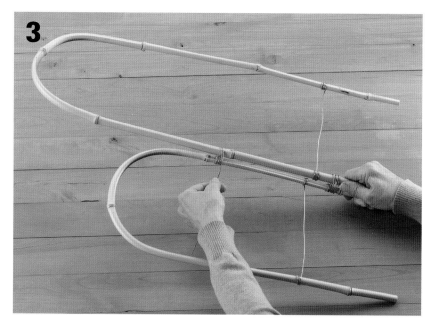

Create the hinges between the smaller side hoops and the middle hoop by wrapping wire around one leg to secure them, then around both legs to create the joint.

Make the large cee-shaped scrolls by first wrapping both ends of the wire around a round form, then gradually expanding the circles to create the scroll.

ADD DECORATIVE PIECES

Cut a length of 16-gauge wire that is about twice as long as the space between the hoop legs. Wrap the middle of the wire around a 2" dowel or pipe. Remove from the pipe and crimp the circle to give it a peaked top. Loop this circle around the lower edge of the cee-scroll. Wrap the wire ends around the hoop legs. Cut off excess wire if necessary.

Construct the next two bamboo sections as the first section. Join the three panels together with hinges if desired. Install in the garden and enjoy.

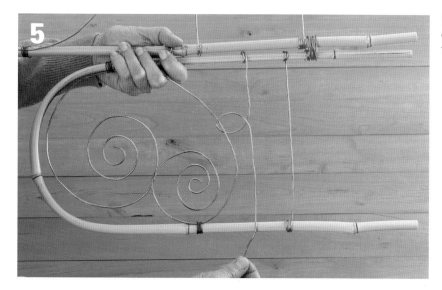

Make the decorative loop, then slide it over the bottom of the C scroll and wrap the ends around the hoop legs.

Make several pieces to create a border around a larger garden.

Copper Lantern

Night or day, this lantern and stand will delight visitors to your garden.

Candles instantly create a romantic atmosphere, perhaps because they cast a soft, warm glow that's flattering to both people and places. Low-voltage lights illuminate many gardens, but even the most sophisticated lighting systems can't duplicate the mood that candles create. Some occasions and circumstances call for candlelight, even in the garden.

By combining a handful of copper plumbing supplies and a few other inexpensive materials, you can create a garden lantern that enhances your garden by day as well as by night. Reshaped copper pipe straps form a support system for the top and bottom of the lantern; a ring of silicone caulk provides a buffer to keep the glass hurricane globe from tipping or rattling; a brass machine screw secures the candle to the frame; a threaded brass rod connects the frame to the hanging arch.

Before you go shopping for a candle or hurricane globe, check the dimensions in the diagram on the next page. Be sure the globe you select is proportional to the lantern and leaves enough clearance for you to light the candle with a long match. *Note: Although the sturdy framework and hurricane globe of this lantern shelter the candle, as with any open flame, it should not be left unattended while burning.*

How to Build a Copper Lantern

CUT & FIT COPPER PIPE

Measure and mark the copper pipe, following the cutting list. Cut the copper pipe, using a tubing cutter.

Dry-fit the pieces of the frame, top, and base, following the diagram on page 203. If you have trouble getting the pieces to stay in place as you work, tape down each tee, which will hold the base steady. When all the connections fit properly, disassemble the frame and rebuild it, soldering the joints as you go (see sidebar, page 205).

ATTACH THE PIPES

Center one ½" copper pipe strap along each side of the top and each side of the bottom of the frame. Wrap one side of each strap around the pipe and extend the other end toward the center of the frame. Later, these extensions will support the base and top.

Connect copper pipes, elbows, and tees to form the base of the frame, and then add the legs and top.

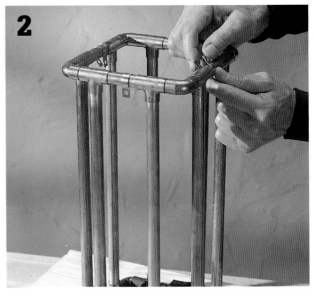

Bend pipe straps around the sides of the frame, positioning them to support the covers on the base and top of the lantern.

Copper Lantern

Tools & Materials

Tape measure
Tubing cutter
Propane torch
Flux brush
Aviation snips
Drill
½" copper pipe (10 ft.)
½" copper 90° elbows (8)
½" copper tees (16)
Sheet of thin copper, at least 16" square
½" copper pipe straps (8)
#6-32 × ⅜" brass machine screws (8)
#6-32 brass machine screw nuts (9)
#6-32 × 2½" machine screw
⅛" threaded brass rod, 11" long
Nuts to fit threaded rod (3)
Acorn nut to fit threaded rod
⅝" flexible copper tubing, 100" long
Plywood, 20" × 20"
#4 rebar, 30" long (2)
Candle
Hurricane globe
Flux
Emery cloth
Silicone caulk
Petroleum jelly
Duct tape
Eye and ear protection
Work gloves

Cutting List

½" COPPER QUANTITY	PIPE LENGTH
8	14"
8	2½"
16	1"

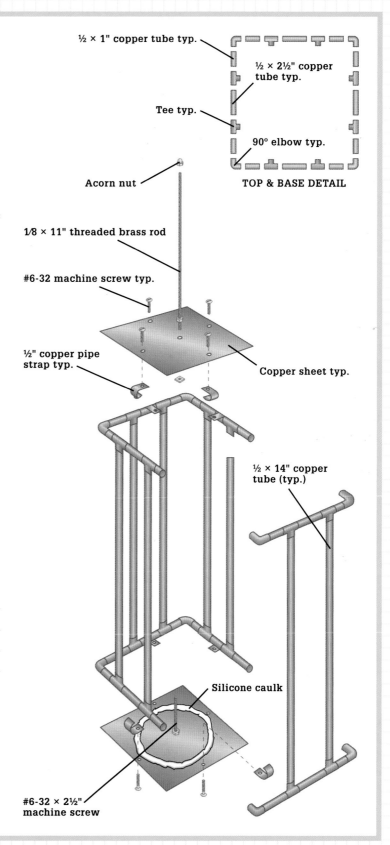

½ × 1" copper tube typ.

½ × 2½" copper tube typ.

Tee typ.

90° elbow typ.

TOP & BASE DETAIL

Acorn nut

1/8 × 11" threaded brass rod

#6-32 machine screw typ.

½" copper pipe strap typ.

Copper sheet typ.

½ × 14" copper tube (typ.)

Silicone caulk

#6-32 × 2½" machine screw

MAKE THE BASE

Measure the inside dimensions of the base of the frame, and then mark and cut a sheet of copper to match, using aviation snips. Position the base so the straps support the edges, and mark the locations of the pipe strap holes. Drill a hole through the cover at each of these marks, as well as at the exact center of the cover.

Center the globe over the hole in the middle of the base, draw a pencil line just outside the lip, then remove the globe. To form a buffer for the globe, run a bead of silicone caulk around this circle, just inside the line. While the caulk sets up, apply petroleum jelly to the lip of the globe and use it to make an impression in the bead of caulk.

Working up from the bottom, attach the base cover to the frame, threading #6-32 × ⅜" machine screws through the pipe straps and the sheet of copper and securing them with machine screw nuts.

ADD THE CANDLE

Run a #6-32 × 2½" machine screw through the hole in the center of the base cover and secure it with a nut. Thread the candle onto the screw, and then position the hurricane globe over the candle.

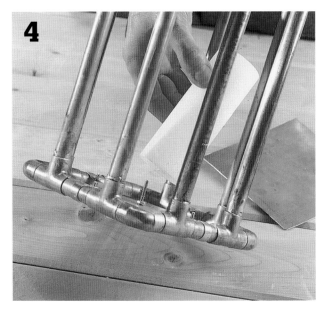

4

Run a 2½" machine screw through the center of the base cover and secure it with a nut. Thread a candle onto the screw, and then settle the hurricane globe into place.

3

Cut a piece of sheet copper for the base cover and secure it to the pipe straps, using machine screws and nuts. Add a circle of silicone caulk to buffer the lantern's globe.

5

Run a piece of threaded brass rod through the center of the top and secure it with one nut above and one below the sheet of copper.

MAKE THE COVER

Measure the inside dimensions of the top of the frame, and then mark a sheet of copper to match. Cut the sheet, using aviation snips. Position the top cover and mark the locations of the pipe strap holes. Drill a hole at each mark as well as at the exact center of the cover.

Working from the top down, secure the top cover to the frame, again using #6-32 × ⅜" machine screws and machine screw nuts.

Insert the threaded rod through the hole in the center of the top, and secure it with one nut below and one above.

ADD THE HANGING ROD

Cut a 100" long piece of ⅝" flexible copper tubing. Mark the center, and drill a ⅛" hole all the way through the tubing.

Cut a plywood circle 20" in diameter and bend the sides of the tubing down around the circle, forming a smooth arch.

Press the legs of the arch into the ground to mark the leg positions. At each mark, drive a 30" piece of #4 rebar about 18" into the ground. Slide the legs of the arch over the rebar and press down to seat the copper firmly into the ground. Screw a nut onto the hanging rod, and then insert the rod into the hole at the center of the arch. Thread an acorn nut onto the rod and tighten it.

Add a nut to the top of the hanging rod; slide it through the hole in the supporting arch. Secure the rod with an acorn nut.

Variation: Shepherd's Hook ▸

Tools & Materials

½" flexible copper tubing	½" copper coupler	Fine sand	Votive candle
½" copper pipe	½" copper elbow	6-strand twisted copper	Chandelier globe
½" copper end cap (1)	16-gauge copper wire	wire (2 ft.)	

Cut an 18" piece of ½" flexible copper tubing and a 6-foot piece of ½" rigid copper pipe. Form the flexible copper into a curlicue as shown; solder an end cap onto one end and a coupler onto the other. Solder the coupler to the copper pipe, using an elbow, to form a hook. Plant the completed hook in the soil of a large potted plant.

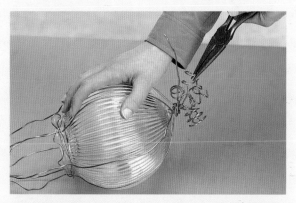

Untwist the first 10" of a 24" piece of twisted copper wire. Shape the individual strands around a round 6" chandelier globe; use one strand to band a pigtail at the bottom of the globe. Curl the tails around a dowel, then bend them into a pleasing arrangement. Wrap a piece of 16-gauge copper wire around the lip of the globe to cradle it within the wires. Form a loop at the opposite end of the twisted wire; untwist and shape the first 4 or 5" of each strand. Add sand and a votive candle, then hang the lantern from the hook.

Cedar Garden Bench

Casual seating is a welcome addition to any outdoor setting. This lovely garden bench sits comfortably around the borders of any porch, patio, or deck. With a compact footprint, it creates a pleasant resting spot for up to three adults without taking up a lot of space. Station it near your home's rear entry for a convenient place to remove shoes or set down grocery bags while you unlock the door.

The straightforward, slatted design of this bench lends itself to accessorizing. Station a rustic cedar planter next to the bench for a lovely effect. Or, add a framed lattice trellis to one side of the bench to cut down on wind and direct sun. You can apply exterior stain or a clear wood sealer with UV protectant to keep the bench looking fresh and new. Or, leave it unfinished and let it weather naturally to a silvery hue.

Tools & Materials ▸

(1) 2 × 8" × 6 ft. cedar
(4) 2 × 2" × 10 ft. cedar
(1) 2 × 4" × 6 ft. cedar
(1) 2 × 6" × 10 ft. cedar
(1) 2 × 2" × 6 ft. cedar

(1) 1 × 4" × 12 ft. cedar
Deck screws (1½", 2½")
Moisture-resistant glue
Wood sealer or stain
Drill

Tape measure
Hammer
Saw
Flexible ruler
Jigsaw

Sandpaper
Mineral spirits
Eye and ear protection
Work gloves

Graceful lines and trestle construction make this bench a charming furnishing for any garden as well as porches, patios, and decks.

Cedar Garden Bench

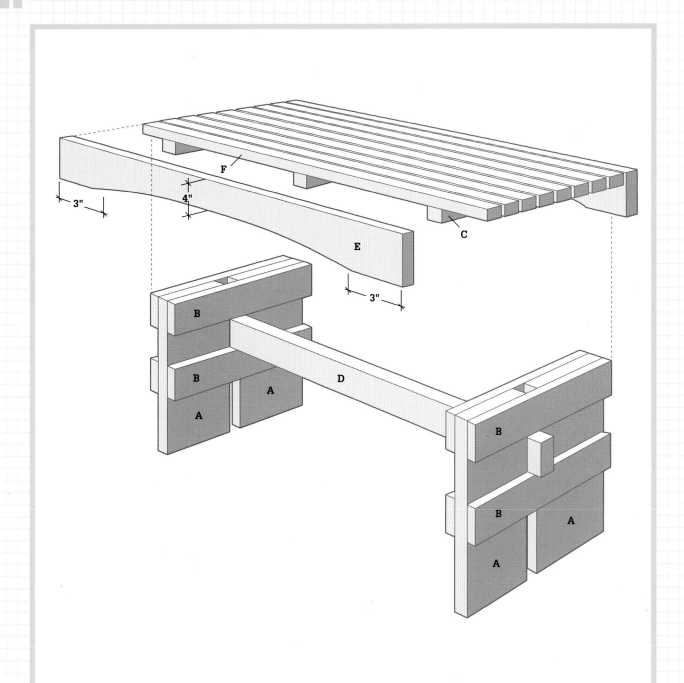

Cutting List

KEY	PART	DIMENSION	PCS.	MATERIAL
A	Leg half	1½ × 7¼ × 14½"	4	Cedar
B	Cleat	¾ × 3½ × 16"	8	Cedar
C	Brace	1½ × 1½ × 16"	3	Cedar
D	Trestle	1½ × 3½ × 60"	1	Cedar
E	Apron	1½ × 5½ × 60"	2	Cedar
F	Slat	1½ × 1½ × 60"	8	Cedar

Cedar Garden Bench

BUILD THE BASE

Cut the leg halves, cleats, and trestle to length. Sandwich one leg half between two cleats so the cleats are flush with the top and the outside edge of the leg half. Then, join the parts by driving four 1½" deck screws through each cleat and into the leg half. Assemble two more cleats with a leg half in the same fashion.

Stand the two assemblies on their sides, with the open ends of the cleats pointing upward. Arrange the assemblies so they are roughly 4 feet apart. Set the trestle onto the inner edges of the leg halves, pressed flush against the bottoms of the cleats. Adjust the position of the assemblies so the trestle overhangs the leg half by 1½" at each end. Fasten the trestle to each leg half with glue and 2½" deck screws (photo 1).

Attach another pair of cleats to each leg half directly below the first pair, positioned so each cleat is snug against the bottom of the trestle. Slide the other leg half between the cleats, keeping the top edge flush with the upper cleats. Join the leg halves with the cleats using glue and 2½" deck screws (photo 2). Cut the braces to length. Fasten one brace to the inner top cleat on each leg assembly, so the tops are flush (photo 3).

MAKE THE APRONS

Cut the aprons to length. Lay out the arc profile onto one apron, starting 3" from each end. The peak of the arch, located over the midpoint of the apron, should be 1½" up from the bottom edge. Draw a smooth, even arc by driving a casing nail at the peak of the arc and at each of the starting points. Slip a flexible ruler or strip of thin plywood or hardboard behind the nails at the starting points and in front of the nail at the peak to create a smooth arc. Then, trace along the inside of the ruler to make a cutting line (photo 4). Cut along the line with a jigsaw and sand the cut smooth. Trace the profile of the arc onto the other apron and make the cut. Sand the cuts smooth.

Cut the slats to length. Attach a slat to the top inside edge of each apron with glue and deck screws (photo 5).

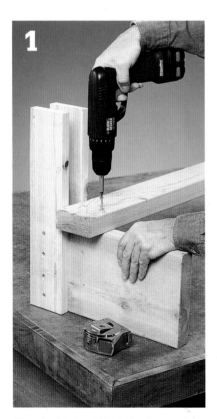

Attach the trestle to the legs, making sure it is positioned correctly against the top cleat bottoms.

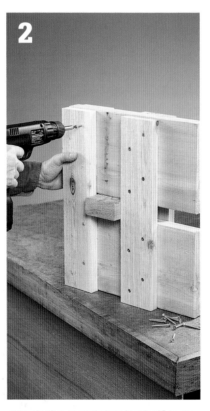

Attach the remaining leg half to the cleats on both ends, sandwiching the trestle on all sides.

Attach the outer brace for the seat slats directly to the inside faces of the cleats.

Mark the profile cuts on the aprons. Use a flexible ruler pinned between casing nails to trace a smooth arc.

Attach a 2 × 2 slat to the top inside edge of each apron using 2½" deck screws and glue.

INSTALL THE APRONS & SLATS

Apply glue at each end on the bottom sides of the attached slats. Flip the leg and trestle assembly and position it flush with the aprons so that it rests on the glue of the two slatted bottoms. The aprons should extend 1½" beyond the legs at each end of the bench. Drive 2½" deck screws through the braces and into both slats.

Position the middle brace between the aprons, centered end-to-end on the project. Fasten it to the two side slats with deck screws. Position the six remaining slats on the braces using ½"-thick spacers to create equal gaps between them. Attach the slats with glue and drive 2½" deck screws up through the braces and into each slat (photo 6).

APPLY FINISHING TOUCHES

Sand the slats smooth with progressively finer sandpaper, up to 150-grit. Wipe away the sanding residue with a rag dipped in mineral spirits. Let the bench dry. Apply a finish of your choice—a clear wood sealer protects the cedar without altering the color.

Attach the seat slats with glue and 2½" deck screws. Insert ½"-thick spacers to set gaps between the slats.

Tiled Garden Bench

Unique materials make for unique outdoor carpentry projects. On this creative garden bench, an assortment of ceramic tiles and accent tiles are set onto the bench top and produce quite an impact. In fact, those accents and a few dozen 4 × 4" tiles transform a plain cedar bench into a special garden ornament. And you can easily accomplish the whole project over one weekend.

In addition to the standard carpentry tools, you need some specialized but inexpensive tile setting tools. A notched trowel, grout float, and sponge are necessary for setting the tiles. Snap-style tile cutters are fairly inexpensive but don't do a very good job cutting floor tiles like the ones used in this project. You'll have much better luck with a wet saw. Wet saws are more expensive than snap cutters, though they have become more affordable in recent years. They are readily available from rental centers and tile retailers. Because you will be charged an hourly rate (or by half-days in some cases), have all of your tiles premarked for cutting so you can get right to work once you get the wet saw home. If you have never set tile before or feel at all unsure of your skills, many home centers and tile retailers offer free classes on tiling techniques.

Tools & Materials ▸

(2) 2 × 4" × 10 ft. cedar	Plastic sheeting	Grout	Masking tape
(1) 2 × 6" × 8 ft. cedar	Deck screws (2", 3")	Grout sealer	Notched trowel
(1) 4 × 4" × 8 ft. cedar	1¼" cementboard screws	Circular saw	Grout float
(1) ¾ × 4" × 4 ft. exterior plywood	Clear wood sealer	Tape measure	Sponge
	Field and accent tiles	Drill	Eye and ear protection
(1) ½ × 3" × 5 ft. cement board	Thinset mortar	Sandpaper	Work gloves
	Tile spacers	Wood sealer	

A ceramic tile arrangement creates a decorative bench top that stands up well to the elements.

Tiled Garden Bench

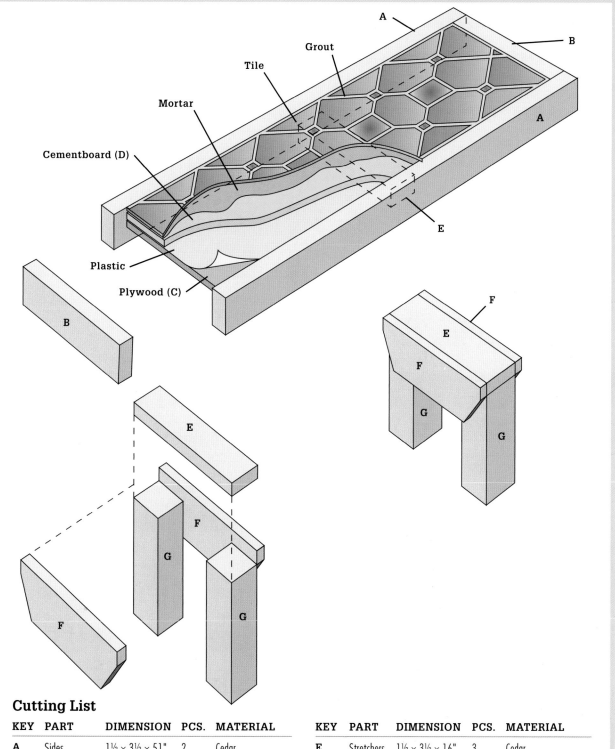

Grout

Tile

A

B

A

Mortar

Cementboard (D)

E

Plastic

Plywood (C)

B

F

E

F

G

G

E

F

G

G

F

Cutting List

KEY	PART	DIMENSION	PCS.	MATERIAL
A	Sides	1½ × 3½ × 51"	2	Cedar
B	Ends	1½ × 3½ × 16"	2	Cedar
C	Subbase	¾ × 15 × 48"	1	Ext. plywood
D	Underlayment	½ × 15 × 48"	1	Cementboard

KEY	PART	DIMENSION	PCS.	MATERIAL
E	Stretchers	1½ × 3½ × 16"	3	Cedar
F	Braces	1½ × 5½ × 16"	4	Cedar
G	Legs	3½ × 3½ × 13"	4	Cedar

▌Tiled Garden Bench

BUILD THE FRAME

Cut two sides and two ends, then position the ends between the sides so the edges are flush. Make sure the frame is square. Drill ⅛"-dia. pilot holes through the sides and into the ends and then drive 3" screws through the pilot holes.

Cut three stretchers. Mark the sides 4½" from the inside of each end. Using 1½" blocks as spacers beneath the stretchers, position each stretcher and make sure they're all level. Drill pilot holes and fasten the stretchers to the sides with 3" screws (photo 1).

MAKE THE TILE BASE

Cut the subbase from ¾" exterior-grade plywood. Cut the tile underlayment from cementboard. Staple plastic sheeting over the plywood, draping it over the edges. Lay the cementboard rough-side up on the plywood and attach it with 1¼" cementboard screws driven every 6". Make sure the screw heads are flush with or slightly below the surface. Position the bench

frame upside down on the underside of the subbase and attach it with 2" deck screws driven through the stretchers and into the plywood (photo 2).

BUILD THE LEGS

The braces are angled to be more aesthetically pleasing. Cut four braces from a cedar 2 × 6. Mark the angle on each end of each brace by measuring down 1½" from the top edge and 1½" along the bottom edge. Draw a line between the two points and cut along that line using a circular saw.

On each brace, measure down ¾" from the top edge and draw a reference line across the stretcher for the screw positions. Drill ⅛"-dia. pilot holes along the reference line. Position a brace on each side of the end stretchers and fasten with 3" deck screws driven through the braces and into the stretchers.

Cut four 13" legs from a 4 × 4. Position each leg between a set of braces and against the sides of the bench frame. Drill pilot holes through each

Assemble the frame. Use 1½" blocks to support the stretchers. Drill pilot holes and fasten the stretchers to the sides with 3" deck screws.

Position the frame over the subbase and fasten it by driving 2" deck screws through the stretchers and into the plywood. Also drive some screws down through the cementboard underlayment and plywood and into the stretchers.

Position each leg between a set of braces and against the sides of the bench frame. Drill pilot holes through each brace and attach the leg to the braces.

Dry-fit the field tiles using tile spacers to set consistent gaps. Set the accent tiles in place and mark the field tiles for cutting.

brace and attach the leg to the braces by driving 3"
screws through the braces and into the leg (photo 3).
Repeat the process for each leg. Sand all surfaces with
150-grit sandpaper, then seal all wood surfaces with
clear wood sealer.

SET THE TILE

Field tiles are the main tiles in any given design. In
this project, square field tiles are cut to fit around four
decorative picture tiles and bright blue accent tiles.
Snap perpendicular reference lines to mark the center
of the length and width of the bench. Beginning at
the center of the bench, dry-fit the field tiles using
tile spacers to set consistent gaps. Set the accent tiles
in place and mark the field tile for cutting (photo 4).
Cut the tiles as necessary and continue dry-fitting the
bench top, including the accent and border tiles.

Mix the thinset mortar, starting with the dry
powder and gradually adding water. Stir the mixture to
achieve a creamy consistency. The mortar should be
wet enough to stick to the tiles and the cementboard,
but stiff enough to hold the ridges made when applied
with the notched trowel. Remove the tiles from the
bench and apply thinset mortar over the cementboard
using a notched trowel (photo 5). Apply only as much
mortar as you can use in ten minutes.

Set the tile into the thinset mortar using a slight
twisting motion as you press down. Do not press too
hard—the goal is to seat the tile, not to displace the
mortar. Continue adding thinset and setting the tiles
until the bench top is covered (photo 6). Remove the
tile spacers using a needlenose pliers, and allow the
mortar to set up and dry.

GROUT THE TILE

Grout fills the gaps between the tiles. Apply masking
tape around the wood frame to prevent the grout
from staining the wood. Mix the grout and latex grout
additive according to package instructions. Use a grout
float to force the grout into the joints surrounding the
tile, holding the float at an angle (photo 7). Do not apply
grout to the joint between the tile and the wood frame.

Wipe the excess grout from the tiles with a damp
sponge. Rinse the sponge between each wipe. When the
grout has dried slightly, polish the tiles with a clean, dry
cloth to remove the slight haze of grout. Seal the grout.

Apply a setting bed of thinset mortar onto the cementboard
using a notched trowel.

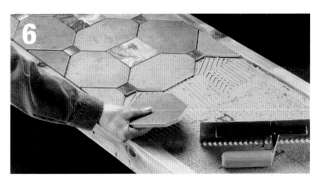

Set the tiles into the thinset mortar using a slight twisting
motion as you press down.

Mix a batch of grout and use a grout
float to force it into the joints between
tiles. Buff off the excess once the grout
sets up.

Mini Garden Shed

Whether you are working in a garden or on a construction site, getting the job done is always more efficient when your tools are close at hand. Offering just the right amount of on-demand storage, this mini garden shed can handle all of your gardening hand tools but with a footprint that keeps costs and labor low.

The mini shed base is built on two 2 × 8 front and back rails that raise the shed off the ground. The rails can also act as runners, making it possible to drag the shed like a sled after it is built. The exterior is clad with vertical-board-style fiber-cement siding. This type of siding not only stands up well to the weather, but it is also very stable and resists rotting and warping. It also comes preprimed and ready for painting. Fiber-cement siding is not intended to be in constant contact with moisture, so the manufacturer recommends installing it at least 6" above the ground. You can paint the trim and siding any color you like. You might choose to coordinate the colors to match your house, or you might prefer a unique color scheme so that the shed stands out as a garden feature.

The roof is made with corrugated fiberglass roof panels. These panels are easy to install and are available in a variety of colors, including clear, which will let more light into the shed. An alternative to the panels is to attach plywood sheathing and then attach any roofing material you like over the sheathing. These plans show how to build the basic shed, but you can customize the interior with hanging hooks and shelves to suit your needs.

Working with Fiber-cement Siding ▶

Fiber-cement siding is sold in ¼"-thick, 4 × 8-ft. sheets at many home centers. There are specially designed shearing tools that contractors use to cut this material, but you can also cut it by scoring it with a utility knife and snapping it—just like cement tile backer board or drywall board. You can also cut cementboard with a circular saw, but you must take special precautions. Cementboard contains silica. Silica dust is a respiratory hazard. If you choose to cut it with a power saw, then minimize your dust exposure by using a manufacturer-designated saw blade designed to create less fine dust and by wearing a NIOSH/MSHA-approved respirator with a rating of N95 or better.

This scaled-down garden shed is just small enough to be transportable. Locate it near gardens or remote areas of your yard where on-demand tool storage is useful.

Tools, Materials & Cutting List

(2) 24"-wide × 8 ft. roof panels
Large utility or gate handle
Exterior-rated screws (1½", 2½")
1½" siding nails

2" galvanized finish nails
16d common nails
1" neoprene gasket screws
Excavation tools
Compactable gravel
Level
Circular saw

10d common nails
Power miter saw
Hammer
Clamps
Drill with bits
Utility knife
Straightedge

Framing square
Jigsaw with fine tooth blade
Finishing tools
Exterior-grade latex paint
(4) Door hinges
Eye and ear protection
Work gloves

KEY	PART	DIMENSION	PCS.	MAT.
Lumber				
A	Front/back base rails	1½ × 7¼ × 55"	2	Treated pine
B	Base crosspieces	1½ × 3½ × 27"	4	Treated pine
C	Base platform	¾ × 30 × 55"	1	Ext. plywood
D	Front/back plates	1½ × 3½ × 48"	2	SPF
E	Front studs	1½ × 3½ × 81"	4	SPF
F	Door header	1½ × 3½ × 30"	1	SPF
G	Back studs	1½ × 3½ × 75"	4	SPF
H	Side bottom plate	1½ × 3½ × 30"	2	SPF
I	Top plate	1½ × 3½ × 55"	2	SPF
J	Side front stud	1½ × 3½ × 81"	2	SPF
K	Side middle stud	1½ × 3½ × 71"	2	SPF
L	Side back stud*	1½ × 3½ × 75¼"	2	SPF
M	Side crosspiece	1½ × 3½ × 27"	2	SPF
N	Door rail (narrow)	¾ × 3½ × 29¾"	1	SPF
O	Door rail (wide)	¾ × 5½ × 23"	2	SPF
P	Door stiles	¾ × 3½ × 71"	2	SPF
Q	Rafters	1½ × 3½ × 44"	4	SPF
R	Outside rafter blocking*	1½ × 3½ × 15¼"	4	SPF
S	Inside rafter blocking*	1½ × 3½ × 18¾"	2	SPF
Siding & Trim				
T	Front left panel	¼ × 20 × 85"	1	Siding
U	Front top panel	¼ × 7½ × 30"	1	Siding
V	Front right panel	¼ × 5 × 85"	1	Siding

KEY	PART	DIMENSION	PCS.	MAT.
W	Side panels	¼ × 30½ × 74½"	2	Siding
X	Back panel	¼ × 48 × 79"	1	Siding
Y	Door panel	¾ × 29¾ × 74"	1	Ext. plywood
Z	Front corner trim	¾ × 3½ × 85"	2	SPF
AA	Front top trim	¾ × 3½ × 50½"	1	SPF
BB	Side casing	¾ × 1½ × 81½"	2	SPF
CC	Top casing	¾ × 1½ × 30"	1	SPF
DD	Bottom casing	¾ × 2½ × 30"	1	SPF
EE	Trim rail (narrow)	¾ × 1½ × 16½"	3	SPF
FF	Trim rail (wide)	¾ × 3½ × 16½"	1	SPF
GG	Side trim	¾ × 2½ × 27"	2	SPF
HH	Side trim	¾ × 2½ × 27¾"	2	SPF
II	Side corner trim (long)	¾ × 1¾ × 85¼"	2	SPF
JJ	Side corner trim (short)	¾ × 1¾ × 79½"	2	SPF
KK	Side trim (wide)	¾ × 3½ × 27"	2	SPF
LL	Side trim (narrow)	¾ × 1½ × 69"	2	SPF
MM	Back corner trim	¾ × 3½ × 79"	2	SPF
NN	Back trim (wide)	¾ × 3½ × 50½"	2	SPF
OO	Back trim (narrow)	¾ × 1½ × 72"	2	SPF
PP	Side windows	¼ × 10 × 28"	2	Acrylic
Roof				
QQ	Purlins	1½ × 1½ × 61½"	5	
RR	Corrugated closure strips	61½" L	5	
SS	Corrugated roof panels	24 × 46"	3	

Not shown

Mini Garden Shed

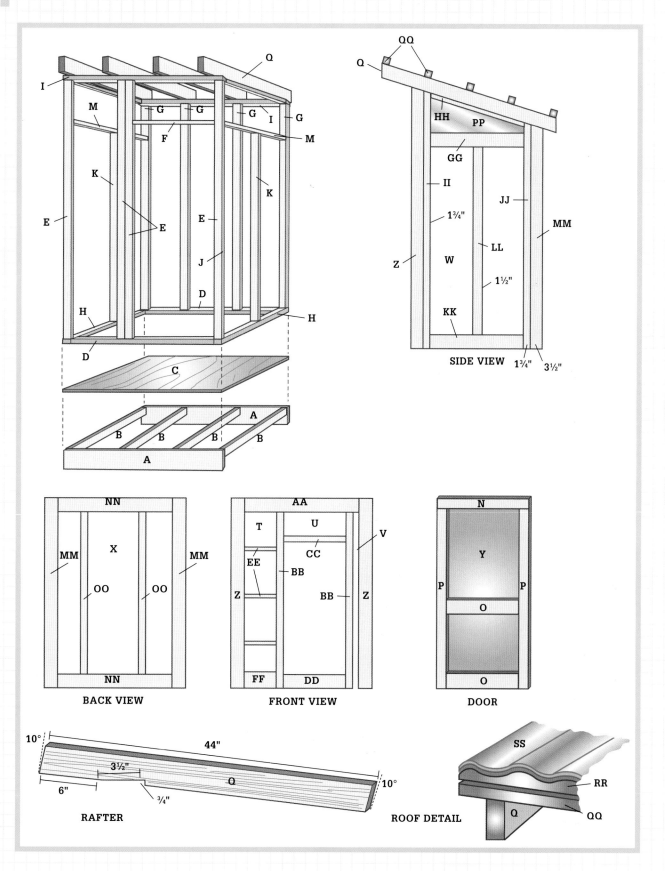

Q

QQ

I

M   G   G   G   G

F   I

M

K

E

E   E

K

J

E

D

H   D   H

C

A   A

B   B   B   B

A

SIDE VIEW   1¾"   3½"

QQ

Q

HH   PP

GG

II

JJ

MM

1¾"

Z   W   LL

1½"

KK

NN

MM   X   MM

OO   OO

NN

BACK VIEW

AA

T   U

CC

EE   BB

Z   BB   Z

FF   DD

FRONT VIEW

N

Y

P   P

O

O

DOOR

SS

RR

10°   44"

3½"

Q   10°

6"   ¾"

RAFTER

ROOF DETAIL   Q   QQ

How to Build a Mini Garden Shed

BUILD THE BASE

Even though moving it is possible, this shed is rather heavy and will require several people or a vehicle to drag it if you build it in your workshop or garage. When possible, determine where you want the shed located and build it in place. Level a 3 × 5-ft area of ground. The shed base is made of treated lumber, so you can place it directly on the ground. If you desire a harder, more solid foundation, dig down 6" and fill the area with tamped compactable gravel.

Cut the front and back base rails and base crosspieces to length. Place the base parts upside-down on a flat surface and attach the crosspieces to the rails with 2½" deck screws. Working with the parts upside-down makes it easy to align the top edges flush. Cut the base platform to size. Flip the base frame over and attach the base platform (functionally, the floor) with 1½" screws. Set and level the base in position where the shed will be built.

FRAME THE SHED

Cut the front wall framing members to size, including the top and bottom plates, the front studs, and the door header. Lay out the front wall on a flat section of ground, such as a driveway or garage floor. Join the wall framing components with 16d common nails (photo 1). Then, cut the back-wall top and bottom plates and studs to length. Lay out the back wall on flat ground and assemble the back wall frame.

Cut both sidewall top and bottom plates to length, and then cut the studs and crosspiece. Miter-cut the ends of the top plate to 10°. Miter-cut the top of the front and back studs at 10° as well. Lay out and assemble the side walls on the ground. Place one of the side walls on the base platform. Align the outside edge of the wall so it is flush with the outside edge of the base platform. Get a helper to hold the wall plumb while you position the back wall. If you're working alone, attach a brace to the side of the wall and the platform to hold the wall plumb (photo 2).

Place the back wall on the platform and attach it to the side wall with 2½" deck screws (photo 3). Align the outside edge of the back wall with the edge of the platform. Place the front wall on the platform and attach it to the side wall with 2½" screws. Place the

Build the wall frames. For the front wall, attach the plates to the outside studs first and then attach the inside studs using the door header as a spacer to position the inside studs.

Raise the walls. Use a scrap of wood as a brace to keep the wall plumb. Attach the brace to the side-wall frame and to the base platform once you have established that the wall is plumb.

Fasten the wall frames. Attach the shed walls to one another and to the base platform with 2½" screws. Use a square and level to check that the walls are plumb and square.

Make the rafters. Cut the workpieces to length, then lay out and cut a birdsmouth notch in the bottom of the two inside rafters. These notches will keep the tops of the inside rafters in line with the outside rafters. The ends should be plumb-cut at 10°.

Install rafter blocking. Some of the rafter blocking must be attached to the rafters by toe-screwing (driving screws at an angle). If you own a pocket screw jig you can use it to drill angled clearance holes for the deck screw heads.

Install the roofing. Attach the corrugated roof panels with 1" neoprene gasket screws (sometimes called pole barn screws) driven through the panels at closure strip locations. Drill slightly oversized pilot holes for each screw and do not overdrive screws—it will compress the closure strips or even cause the panels to crack.

second side wall on the platform and attach it to the front and back walls with 2½" screws.

Cut the rafters to length, then miter-cut each end to 10° for making a plumb cut (this way the rafter ends will be perpendicular to the ground). A notch, referred to as a "birdsmouth," must be cut into the bottom edge of the inside rafters so the tops of these rafters align with the outside rafter tops while resting solidly on the wall top plates. Mark the birdsmouth on the inside rafters (see Diagram, page 217) and cut them out with a jigsaw (photo 4). Cut the rafter blocking to length; these parts fit between the rafters at the front and back of the shed to close off the area above the top plates. Attach the rafters to the rafter blocking and to the top plates. Use the blocking as spacers to position the rafters and then drive 2½" screws up through the top plates and into the rafters. Then, drive 2½" screws through the rafters and into the blocking (photo 5). Toe-screw any rafter blocking that you can't access to fasten through a rafter. Finally, cut the door rails and stiles to length. Attach the rails to the stiles with 2½" screws.

INSTALL THE ROOFING

This shed features 24"-wide corrugated roofing panels. The panels are installed over wood or foam closure strips that are attached to the tops of 2 × 2 purlins running perpendicular to the rafters. Position the purlins so the end ones are flush with the ends of the rafters and the inner ones are evenly spaced. The overhang beyond the rafters should be equal on the purlin ends.

Cut five 61½"-long closure strips. If the closure strips are wood, drill countersunk pilot holes through the closure strips and attach them to the purlins with 1½" screws. Some closure strips are made of foam with a self-adhesive backing. Simply peel off the paper backing and press them in place. If you are installing foam strips that do not have adhesive backing, tack them down with a few pieces of double-sided carpet tape so they don't shift around.

Cut three 44"-long pieces of corrugated roofing panel. Use a jigsaw with a fine-tooth blade or a circular saw with a fine-tooth plywood blade to cut fiberglass or plastic panels. Clamp the panels

(continued)

Cut the wall panels. Use a utility knife to score the fiber-cement panel along a straightedge. Place a board under the scored line and then press down on the panel to break the panel as you would with drywall.

Attach siding panels. Attach the fiber-cement siding with 1½" siding nails driven through pilot holes. Space the nails 8 to 12" apart. Drive the nails a minimum ⅜" away from the panel edges and 2" from the corners.

Cut the acrylic window material to size. One way to accomplish this is to sandwich the acrylic between two sheets of scrap plywood and cut all three layers at once with a circular saw (straight cuts) or jigsaw.

together between scrap boards to minimize vibration while they're being cut (but don't clamp down so hard that you damage the panels). Position the panels over the closure strips, overlapping roughly 4" of each panel and leaving a 1" overhang in the front and back.

Drill pilot holes 12" apart in the field of panels and along the overlapping panel seams. Fasten only in the valleys of the corrugation. The pilot hole diameter should be slightly larger than the diameter of the screw shanks. Fasten the panels to the closure strips and rafters with hex-head screws that are pre-fitted with neoprene gaskets (photo 6, page 219).

ATTACH THE SIDING

Cut the siding panels to size by scoring them with a utility knife blade designated for scoring concrete and then snapping them along the scored line (photo 7). Or, use a rented cementboard saw (see page 214). Drill pilot holes in the siding and attach the siding to

the framing with 1½" siding nails spaced at 8 to 12" intervals (photo 8). (You can rent a cementboard coil nailer instead, see page 214.) Cut the plywood door panel to size. Paint the siding and door before you install the windows and attach the wall and door trim. Apply two coats of exterior latex paint.

INSTALL THE WINDOWS

The windows are fabricated from ¼"-thick sheets of clear plastic or acrylic. To cut the individual windows to size, first mark the cut lines on the sheet. To cut acrylic with a circular saw, secure the sheet so that it can't vibrate during cutting. The best way to secure it is to sandwich it between a couple of pieces of scrap plywood and cut through all three sheets (photo 9). Drill ¼"-dia. pilot holes around the perimeter of the window pieces. Position the holes ½" from the edges and 6" apart. Attach the windows to the side wall framing on the exterior side using 1½" screws (photo 10).

ATTACH THE TRIM

Cut the wall and door trim pieces to length. Miter-cut the top end of the side front and back trim pieces to 10°. Attach the trim to the shed with 2" galvanized finish nails (photo 11). The horizontal side trim overlaps the window and the side siding panel. Be careful not to drive any nails through the plastic window panels. Attach the door trim to the door with 1¼" exterior screws.

HANG THE DOOR

Make the door and fasten a utility handle or gate handle to it. Fasten three door hinges to the door and then fasten the hinges to a stud on the edge of the door opening (photo 12). Use a scrap piece of siding as a spacer under the door to determine the proper door height in the opening. Add hooks and hangers inside the shed as needed to accommodate the items you'll be storing. If you have security concerns, install a hasp and padlock on the mini shed door.

Attach the window panels. Drill a ¼"-dia. pilot hole for each screw that fastens the window panels. These oversized holes give the plastic panel room to expand and contract. The edges of the windows (and the fasteners) will be covered by trim.

Attach the trim boards with 2" galvanized finish nails. In the areas around windows, predrill for the nails so you don't crack the acrylic.

Door

Hang the door using three exterior-rated door hinges. Slip a scrap of ¼"-thick siding underneath the door to raise it off the bottom plate while you install it.

Cast Concrete Ornaments

Casting decorative objects for the home and yard is an entertaining and creative exercise in handling concrete. Locating and making forms is a challenge itself, and the specific nature of the objects you eventually cast is often dictated by the potential you see in everyday objects that you encounter.

The best forms for casting are rigid or semirigid with a slick surface and the ability to contain water. Plastic and rubber objects are ideal, but you can really use just about any material, especially if you use it for a single casting and are not concerned about breaking it when you release the cast object. Some examples of useful "found" forms include five-gallon plastic buckets (insert a smaller bucket or a tube to cast a large concrete pot); trash can lids (pavers); nesting plastic bowls (pots and planters); or any sphere shapes, such as a basketball, that can be split in two (decorative orbs, bowls).

Making your owns forms is another fun exercise in creativity. Melamine-coated particleboard is a great material for this job because it holds its shape and the concrete will not stick to the surface. When combined with other materials such as the metal flashing used to form the patio tabletop in this chapter, your casting options are practically unlimited.

For more complex and sophisticated castings, you can buy reusable forms in a very wide array of shapes and sizes. Garden benches, birdbaths, landscape edging, pavers, and statuary are just some of the objects you can cast with a couple bags of concrete and a purchased form. The best source for concrete casting forms is the Internet (see Resources section).

One of the best reasons to cast your own decorative and functional objects from concrete is that you can customize the finished look by coloring the concrete or using creative surface treatments such as the footsteps in the pavers seen below.

Casting concrete is a DIY-friendly way to gain experience with handling concrete. No matter your masonry skills, there is a casting project that will challenge and reward you. Projects can be made using purchased molds or everyday objects.

Introduction to Casting

Many objects can be used as forms for casting concrete. Semirigid items work best because they require no special preparation, often include embossed shapes or designs, and are usually easy to strip from the cast object.

Once you try casting, you'll begin to think of every inanimate object as a potential "form" for a concrete structure. Start with simple, easy-to-cast forms such as plastic bowls or buckets. Choose forms that have interesting textures. Consider how you will use the cast concrete when the project is complete: Will it be functional or decorative? You may decide to create a form to suit your needs.

Constructed forms can cast items of practically any size or shape. For flat items, such as tabletops and stepping stones, melamine-coated particleboard is a good choice because the melamine side does not require a release agent. Wood should be treated with a release agent like nonstick cooking spray.

You'll need to reinforce large concrete objects with metal rods and mesh. Be sure to keep metal away from the edges. Mix in synthetic reinforcing fibers if not included in your mix. You can purchased bagged concrete with fiber reinforcement blended in at the plant. These products are ideal for large castings that will undergo stress, such as stepping stones or tabletops. For small items, use sand mix. In both cases, add acrylic fortifier to make the mixture more slippery without decreasing strength. Add a coloring agent (liquid or dry) to the mixture to enhance the finished piece.

Sample Casting Projects

A deck bowl is cast using two nesting mixing bowls. This technique can be used with plastic bowls and buckets and planters of all sizes. Larger containers should be split in half and taped back together so you can extract the cast object more easily. We used sand mix with acrylic fortifier and black concrete pigment for this deck bowl.

Sand casting is a great way to use up the leftovers from a larger poured concrete project. To make this birdbath, you simply pile up some coarse wet sand and pour the leftover concrete onto the pile. Birds love the rough texture of the concrete surface.

Garden Column

Prefabricated concrete casting forms give you the ability to make objects for your yard and garden that rival the best (and very expensive) artwork pieces sold at garden centers. Garden benches and birdbaths are among the most popular, but you can locate an array of forms for just about any objects you can imagine.

Because most of the objects cast with readymade forms feature grooves, flutes, or complex patterns, you'll have the best luck if you use a relatively wet mixture of concrete with small or sand-only aggregate. Adding latex bonding agent or acrylic fortifier also makes the concrete more slippery so it can conform to odd shapes more readily, but these agents do not reduce concrete strength, as adding more water does.

If your cast project will be placed outdoors, apply a penetrating concrete sealer about a week after the casting.

Tools & Materials ▸

Shovel
Mortar box
Concrete forms
Bagged concrete mix
   (fiber reinforced)
Acrylic fortifier
Nonstick cooking spray
Duct tape
Exterior landscape
   adhesive

Prefabricated casting forms typically are made from rugged PVC so they may be reused many times. You can mix and match the forms to create different objects. The forms above include a column form with grapevine or fluted insert, two different pedestal shapes, and an optional birdbath top.

This classical concrete column is cast using a simple plastic form purchased from an Internet supplier (see Resources). It can be used to support many garden items, including a display pedestal, a birdbath, or a sundial.

How to Cast a Garden Column

Choose a column form insert (optional) and slide it into the column form as a liner so the edges meet neatly. Tape the column together at the seam. Coat the insides of all form parts with a very light mist of nonstick cooking spray as a release agent.

Choose a sturdy, level work surface. Set the column form upright on a small piece of scrap plywood. Tape down the form with duct tape, keeping the tape clear of the form top. Mix a batch of fiber-reinforced concrete with an acrylic fortifier and shovel it into the forms. Rap the forms with a stick to settle the concrete and strike off the excess with a screed. Run additional tape 'hold-downs" over the top of the column form to secure it to the plywood scrap tightly enough that the concrete will not run out from the bottom.

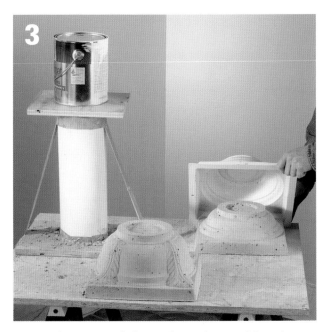

Set another scrap of plywood onto the top of the column form and weight it down. Let the parts dry for two days and then release them from the forms. Wash and rinse the parts to remove dusty residue.

Apply exterior landscape adhesive to the top of the base pedestal and set the column end into the adhesive so the column is centered. Bond the top pedestal in the same manner. Apply penetrating sealant. If it is not nearby, transport the column and pedestals to the location before bonding the parts.

Stepping Stones

In some gardens, stepping stone paths beckon, virtually begging to be followed. Handmade stones add a unique, personal touch to a garden—you can even inscribe them to commemorate special days, such as birthdays or anniversaries.

This is a great project to share with children—there's almost no way to go wrong and you can use a nearly infinite variety of materials, depending on the ages and interests of the children. There are many stepping-stone kits on the market, but you don't need one—the materials are readily available.

To form stepping stones, use quick-setting concrete mix—about one 40-lb. bag of mix for each 18"-square stone. This mix is caustic: Wear a dust mask and gloves when using it.

Experiment with textures, patterns, and shapes. If you don't like a pattern, smooth the surface and start again. Remember, though, that you must work fairly quickly—quick-setting concrete sets up within 30 minutes. To slow the process, you can lightly mist the surface with water after "erasing" a pattern.

In addition to the decorative techniques described on the next page, you can make gorgeous accent stones from pieces of broken china or pottery. You can buy broken bits of china at craft stores, but it's less expensive to buy old dishes at garage sales or flea markets and break them yourself. Place the dishes in a heavy paper bag and then tap the bag with a rubber mallet. Wear safety goggles and heavy gloves when handling broken pieces, and file any sharp edges with a masonry file.

How to Build Stepping Stones

Tools & Materials ▸

Shovel
Hand tamp
Containers to be
    used as molds
Petroleum jelly
Gloves
Dust mask

Quick-setting
    concrete mix
Bucket
Mason's trowel
Embellishments,
    as desired
Compactible gravel

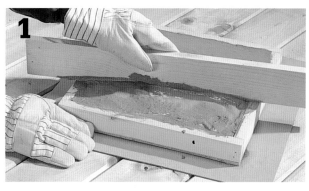

Select molds; coat them with petroleum jelly. Mix quick-setting concrete and fill the molds. Skim off excess water.

PREPARE THE MOLDS & POUR THE CONCRETE

1. Select molds for the stepping stones. Use aluminum pie plates, plastic plant saucers or large plastic lids, plywood forms or shallow boxes. Select molds deep enough (1½" to 2") and large enough (12" to 18") to make stones that can bear weight and comfortably accommodate an adult's foot.
2. Fill the molds with dry concrete mix to estimate the amount necessary. Following manufacturer's instructions, mix water, concrete dye if desired, and the concrete mix. Check a handful—it should hold its shape when squeezed, something like cookie dough. If necessary, add water and mix again.
3. Coat the molds with petroleum jelly, covering all the corners and edges.
4. Fill the forms with concrete. Smooth the surface with a mason's trowel, and then use a scrap 2 × 4 to skim off any excess water.

EMBELLISH THE SURFACE

1. Decorate the stones as desired.
    Stamping Technique: Let the concrete dry for 10 to 15 minutes. While it's still damp, press ornaments firmly onto the surface, and then remove them. You can use a variety of natural ornaments such as leaves, twigs, small evergreen branches, shells, or stones. Or, you can use rubber stamps, available at craft stores.
    Embedding Technique: Let the concrete dry for 10 minutes. Press ornaments into the surface, partially submerging them. Make sure the ornaments are firmly settled into the cement.
2. Let the stones cure several hours or overnight. Remove them from the molds.

Decorate the stones with stamped designs or embedded ornaments. Let the stepping stones harden thoroughly.

Cut out the turf and remove 3½" to 4" of soil. Add a layer of compactible gravel, and then set each stone in place. Adjust until each stone is level and stable.

INSTALL THE STEPPING STONES

1. Cut out the turf and dig out 3½" to 4" of soil, following the shape of the stones.
2. Add a 2" layer of compactible gravel and tamp it thoroughly. Test-fit each stone, adjusting the gravel layer until the stone is level and stable.

Concrete Landscape & Garden Borders

Decorative and durable edging can have any number of uses in an outdoor home. It makes great garden borders, turf edges, driveway and parking curbs, decorative tree surrounds, and barriers for loose ground covers—just to list its most popular applications. You can buy factory-made edging in masonry and other materials, but few prefab products can match the stability and longevity of poured concrete, and none can have the personal touch of a custom casting.

In this project, you'll learn how to cast your own border sections with poured concrete and a reusable wood mold. The process is so simple and the materials so inexpensive that you'll feel free to experiment with different shapes and surface treatments; see page 231 for ideas on customizing borders using trim moldings and other materials. Coloring the concrete is an even easier option for a personal decorative effect (see tip, below).

The best all-around concrete to use for small casting projects like this is crack-resistant concrete, which contains small fibers to add strength to the finished product without the use of metal reinforcement. However, for any casting that's less than 2" thick, use sand mix. This special concrete mix has no large aggregates, allowing it to form easily into smaller areas. Either type of concrete must cure for 48 hours before you can remove the mold; to speed your productivity, you may want to build more than one mold.

Tools & Materials ▸

Saw
Drill
Tape measure
Concrete
  mixing tools
Concrete trowel
¾" exterior-grade
  plywood or
  melamine-covered
  particleboard

2" coarse-thread
  drywall screws
Silicone caulk
Vegetable oil or other
  release agent
Crack-resistant
  concrete
Plastic sheeting
Rubber mallet

Coloring Concrete ▸

For a personal touch, add liquid cement color to your concrete mix before pouring it into the mold. One 10 oz. bottle can color two 60-lb. or 80-lb. bags of concrete mix. Experiment with different proportions to find the right amount of color for your project.

Building a Mold for Cast Concrete

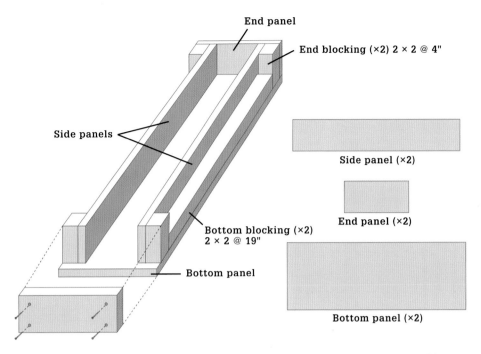

End panel

End blocking (×2) 2 × 2 @ 4"

Side panels

Bottom blocking (×2)
2 × 2 @ 19"

Bottom panel

Side panel (×2)

End panel (×2)

Bottom panel (×2)

Casting size = 4 × 4 × 22"

Mold construction: Build your mold with ¾" plywood or ¾" melamine-coated particleboard and 2 × 2 lumber. The melamine creates an exceptionally smooth finish and doesn't need oil or a release agent to prevent the concrete from sticking. Follow the basic construction shown here; you can use the dimensions given or change the height, length, or width of the mold as desired.

How to Build Cast Concrete Borders

Cut the pieces for the mold. Fasten the end blocking pieces flush with the ends of the side panels using pairs of 2" drywall screws driven through pilot holes. Fasten the bottom blocking to the side panels, flush along the bottom edges.

Fasten the end panels to the end blocking with 2" screws. Install the bottom panel with screws driven through the panel and into the bottom blocking. Make sure all panels and blocking are flush along the top and bottom edges. *Note: You may need to leave one end open in order to work, as we have done here.*

Add trim or other elements as desired for custom shaping effects (see page 231). Here, we used crown molding, which we fastened to the blocking with finish nails using a nail set. Cover the screw heads on the inside of the mold with silicone caulk; then flatten to create a smooth, flat surface.

(continued)

4

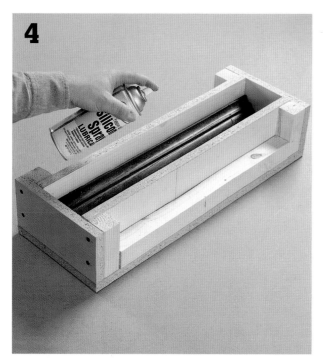

Coat the inside of the mold (all nonmelamine parts) with clean vegetable oil or another release agent. Mix a batch of concrete following the product directions. An 80-lb. bag of crack-resistant concrete will fill two of the molds.

5

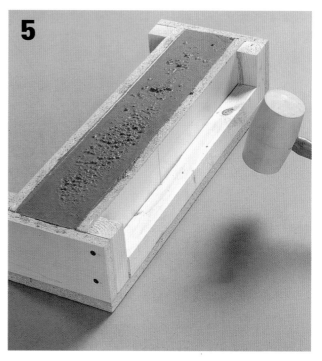

Fill the mold with concrete. Settle the pour into the mold by pounding the work surface with a mallet or lifting the corners of the mold and tapping it onto the work surface.

6

Screed or trowel the concrete so it is flat and flush with the top of the mold. Cover the mold with plastic sheeting and let it cure undisturbed for 48 hours.

7

Carefully disassemble the mold by unscrewing the ends and bottom from the sides, as needed. Scrape, file, or grind any ragged edges for clean detailing in the finished piece. For maximum strength, set the casting in a shaded area and moist-cure it for three to five days, keeping it damp under plastic sheeting.

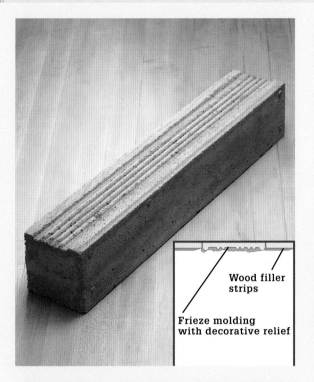

Wood filler
strips

Frieze molding
with decorative relief

⅞" cove molding

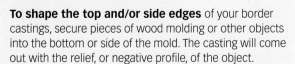

Inlaid tiles

Crown molding

To shape the top and/or side edges of your border castings, secure pieces of wood molding or other objects into the bottom or side of the mold. The casting will come out with the relief, or negative profile, of the object.

When fastening the object to the mold, think about how you'll take the mold apart. For wood trim, fasten the pieces with finish nails, and fill the nail holes with caulk. For tile and other inlay materials, secure the tiles to the mold bottom with adhesive shelf paper; peel off the paper after removing the casting from the mold.

How to Make a Poured-in-Place Border

Lay out the project. Using a garden hose or rope, lay out the border design contour. The border width should be a minimum of 5".

Excavate the border layout to an 8" width and 4" depth. Compact the soil to create a solid base for the concrete border.

Stake the contours. Drive 1 × 1 × 12" wood stakes at 18" intervals along the contours of the curved border.

Attach curved forms. Use ¼ × 4 × 8" flexible hardboard or plywood to the wood stakes using 1" wood screws.

Anchor the forms. Cut 1 × 1" boards in lengths equal to the width of the border for use as spacers. Set 1 × 1 × 12" wood stakes along the outside contour of the border layout in 3-ft. intervals. Use 1 × 1" spacers placed along the bottom edge of the hardboard form to maintain consistent border width.

Pour the concrete. Mix concrete to a firm workable consistency and pour into the border form. Use a margin trowel to spread and consolidate the mix.

Tool the concrete. Once the bleed water has disappeared, smooth the surface with a wood float. Using a margin trowel, cut control joints a minimum of 1" deep into the concrete at 3-ft. intervals. Consolidate and smooth the border edges using a concrete edging tool.

Seal the concrete. Apply acrylic concrete sealer to the concrete and let it cure for three to five days before removing the forms. Backfill against the lawn border with sod or dirt.

Conversions

Metric Conversions

TO CONVERT:	TO:	MULTIPLY BY:
Inches	Millimeters	25.4
Inches	Centimeters	2.54
Feet	Meters	0.305
Yards	Meters	0.914
Square inches	Square centimeters	6.45
Square feet	Square meters	0.093
Square yards	Square meters	0.836
Ounces	Milliliters	30.0
Pints (U.S.)	Liters	0.473 (Imp. 0.568)
Quarts (U.S.)	Liters	0.946 (Imp. 1.136)
Gallons (U.S.)	Liters	3.785 (Imp. 4.546)
Ounces	Grams	28.4
Pounds	Kilograms	0.454

TO CONVERT:	TO:	MULTIPLY BY:
Millimeters	Inches	0.039
Centimeters	Inches	0.394
Meters	Feet	3.28
Meters	Yards	1.09
Square centimeters	Square inches	0.155
Square meters	Square feet	10.8
Square meters	Square yards	1.2
Milliliters	Ounces	.033
Liters	Pints (U.S.)	2.114 (Imp. 1.76)
Liters	Quarts (U.S.)	1.057 (Imp. 0.88)
Liters	Gallons (U.S.)	0.264 (Imp. 0.22)
Grams	Ounces	0.035
Kilograms	Pounds	2.2

Converting Temperatures

Convert degrees Fahrenheit (F) to degrees Celsius (C) by following this simple formula: Subtract 32 from the Fahrenheit temperature reading. Then, multiply that number by $5/9$. For example, 77°F - 32 = 45. 45 $\times$ $5/9$ = 25°C.

To convert degrees Celsius to degrees Fahrenheit, multiply the Celsius temperature reading by $9/5$. Then, add 32. For example, 25°C $\times$ $9/5$ = 45. 45 + 32 = 77°F.

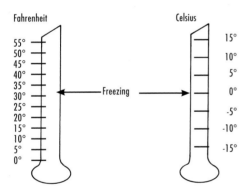

Metric Plywood Panels

Metric plywood panels are commonly available in two sizes: 1,200 mm × 2,400 mm and 1,220 mm × 2,400 mm, which is roughly equivalent to a 4 × 8-ft. sheet. Standard and Select sheathing panels come in standard thicknesses, while Sanded grade panels are available in special thicknesses.

STANDARD SHEATHING GRADE		SANDED GRADE	
7.5 mm	($5/16$ in.)	6 mm	($4/17$ in.)
9.5 mm	($3/8$ in.)	8 mm	($5/16$ in.)
12.5 mm	($1/2$ in.)	11 mm	($7/16$ in.)
15.5 mm	($5/8$ in.)	14 mm	($9/16$ in.)
18.5 mm	($3/4$ in.)	17 mm	($2/3$ in.)
20.5 mm	($13/16$ in.)	19 mm	($3/4$ in.)
22.5 mm	($7/8$ in.)	21 mm	($13/16$ in.)
25.5 mm	(1 in.)	24 mm	($15/16$ in.)

Lumber Dimensions

NOMINAL - U.S.	ACTUAL - U.S. (IN INCHES)	METRIC
1 × 2	$3/4$ × $1 1/2$	19 × 38 mm
1 × 3	$3/4$ × $2 1/2$	19 × 64 mm
1 × 4	$3/4$ × $3 1/2$	19 × 89 mm
1 × 5	$3/4$ × $4 1/2$	19 × 114 mm
1 × 6	$3/4$ × $5 1/2$	19 × 140 mm
1 × 7	$3/4$ × $6 1/4$	19 × 159 mm
1 × 8	$3/4$ × $7 1/4$	19 × 184 mm
1 × 10	$3/4$ × $9 1/4$	19 × 235 mm
1 × 12	$3/4$ × $11 1/4$	19 × 286 mm
$1 1/4$ × 4	1 × $3 1/2$	25 × 89 mm
$1 1/4$ × 6	1 × $5 1/2$	25 × 140 mm
$1 1/4$ × 8	1 × $7 1/4$	25 × 184 mm
$1 1/4$ × 10	1 × $9 1/4$	25 × 235 mm
$1 1/4$ × 12	1 × $11 1/4$	25 × 286 mm
$1 1/2$ × 4	$1 1/4$ × $3 1/2$	32 × 89 mm
$1 1/2$ × 6	$1 1/4$ × $5 1/2$	32 × 140 mm
$1 1/2$ × 8	$1 1/4$ × $7 1/4$	32 × 184 mm
$1 1/2$ × 10	$1 1/4$ × $9 1/4$	32 × 235 mm
$1 1/2$ × 12	$1 1/4$ × $11 1/4$	32 × 286 mm
2 × 4	$1 1/2$ × $3 1/2$	38 × 89 mm
2 × 6	$1 1/2$ × $5 1/2$	38 × 140 mm
2 × 8	$1 1/2$ × $7 1/4$	38 × 184 mm
2 × 10	$1 1/2$ × $9 1/4$	38 × 235 mm
2 × 12	$1 1/2$ × $11 1/4$	38 × 286 mm
3 × 6	$2 1/2$ × $5 1/2$	64 × 140 mm
4 × 4	$3 1/2$ × $3 1/2$	89 × 89 mm
4 × 6	$3 1/2$ × $5 1/2$	89 × 140 mm

Liquid Measurement Equivalents

1 Pint	= 16 Fluid Ounces	= 2 Cups
1 Quart	= 32 Fluid Ounces	= 2 Pints
1 Gallon	= 128 Fluid Ounces	= 4 Quarts

Drill Bit Guide

Twist Bit	Self-piloting	Spade Bit	Adjustable Counterbore	Hole Saw

  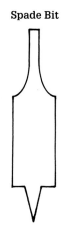 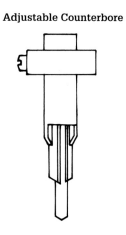 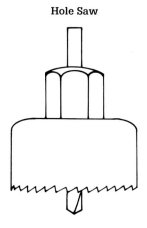

Counterbore, Shank & Pilot Hole Diameters

Screw Size	Counterbore Diameter for Screw Head	Clearance Hole for Screw Shank	Pilot Hole Diameter	
			Hard Wood	Soft Wood
#1	.146 9/64	5/64	3/64	1/32
#2	1/4	3/32	3/64	1/32
#3	1/4	7/64	1/16	3/64
#4	1/4	1/8	1/16	3/64
#5	1/4	9/64	5/64	1/16
#6	5/16	5/32	3/32	5/64
#7	5/16	5/32	3/32	5/64
#8	3/8	11/64	1/8	3/32
#9	3/8	11/64	1/8	3/32
#10	3/8	3/16	1/8	7/64
#11	1/2	3/16	5/32	9/64
#12	1/2	7/32	9/64	1/8

Abrasive Paper Grits - (Aluminum Oxide)

Very Coarse	Coarse	Medium	Fine	Very Fine
12 - 36	40 - 60	80 - 120	150 - 180	220 - 600

Resources

ACF Greenhouses
888 888 9050
email: help@LittleGreenhouse.com
www.littlegreenhouse.com

Black & Decker
Portable Power Tools & More
www.blackanddecker.com

Greenhouses.com
800 681 3302
www.greenhouses.com

GreenhouseKit.com
877 718 2865
www.greenhousekit.com

History Stones
Decorative Concrete Forms (page 224)
360 834 7021
www.historystones.com

Hoop House Greenhouse Kits
800 760 5192
email: hoop@cape.com
www.househouse.com

Juliana Greenhouses
Vanlet ® Gravity Feed Watering System (page 36)
www.julianagreenhouses.com

North Florida REC (NFREC)
Suwannee Valley
386 362 1725
http://nfrec-sv.ifas.ufl.edu

Palram Americas
Palsun ® and Suntuf® Polycarbonate Panels (page 52)
800 999 9459
www.palramamericas.com

Red Wing Shoes Co.
Work shoes and boots shown throughout book
800 733 9464
www.redwingshoes.com

Sturdi-built Greenhouses
Redwood greenhouse kits
800 334 4115
www.sturdi-built.com

Photo Credits

p.6, Clive Nichols/www.clivenichols.com
p.11, Rodolphe Foucher/www.rodolphefoucher.com
p.15, David Markson/ Elizabeth Whiting & Associates/ www.ewastock.com
p.26, David Markson/Elazabeth Whiting & Associates/ www.ewastock.com
p.27, Courtesy of Renaissance Conservatories/ www. Renaissanceconservatories.com
p.28, Michael Harris/Elizabeth Whiting & Associates/ www.ewastock.com
p.36, Courtesy Juliana America, www.greenhouses.com
p.37, Dreamstime.com
p.38, Magnus Persson/Getty Images
p.39 (top) Courtesy of Solar Innovations; (Bottom) Courtesy of Sturdi-built
p.40, Courtesy of Sturdi-built
p.46, Courtesy of Solar Innovations
p. 47 (top), Courtesy of Solar Innovations
p.48, Peter Anderson/Getty Images
p.49, Courtesy of Sturdi-built
p.50, Rick Lew/Photolibrary
p.51, Courtesy of NFREC: (top, right) Robert Hochmuth, Multi County Extension Agent, UF/IFAS North Florida Research and Education Center, Suwannee Valley, Live Oak, FL
p.106-107, Friedrich Strauss/age footstock

Index